IN THE EVENT OF WOMEN

IN THE
EVENT
OF
WOMEN

TANI BARLOW

DUKE UNIVERSITY PRESS · DURHAM AND LONDON · 2021

Designed by MaᴛᴛHew Tauch
Typeset in Arno Pro Regular and Barlow by Westchester
Publishing Services

Library of Congress Cataloging-in-Publication Data
Names: Barlow, Tani E., author.
Title: In the event of women / Tani Barlow.
Description: Durham : Duke University Press, 2021. | Includes biblio-
graphical references and index.
Identifiers: ʟᴄᴄɴ 2020052856 (print)
ʟᴄᴄɴ 2020052857 (ebook)
ɪsʙɴ 9781478013518 (hardcover)
ɪsʙɴ 9781478014447 (paperback)
ɪsʙɴ 9781478021742 (ebook)
Subjects: ʟᴄsH: Women—China—History—20th century.| Women
in advertising—China. | Feminism and mass media—China. | Mass
media—Political aspects—China. | Advertising—Social aspects—
China. | Events (Philosophy) | ʙɪsᴀᴄ: HɪsᴛᴏʀY / Asia / China |
sᴏᴄɪᴀʟ sᴄɪᴇɴᴄᴇ / Women's Studies
Classification: ʟᴄᴄ HQ1767 .B3627 2021 (print) | ʟᴄᴄ HQ1767 (ebook)
| ᴅᴅᴄ 305.4095109/04—dc23
ʟᴄ recordavailableathᴛᴛps:// lccn.loc.gov/2020052856
ʟᴄ ebook recordavailableathᴛᴛps:// lccn.loc.gov/2020052857

Duke University Press gratefully acknowledges the support of
the Rice University Dean of Humanities, Chao Center for
Asian Studies, and the Department of History, which provided
funds toward the publication of this book.

Cover art: General Electric bulb girl at advertising desk, ᴅFᴢᴢ
19, no. 1 (January 10, 1922).

To Ruri

Contents

Acknowledgments

There are so many friends and colleagues I want to recognize and thank. On archival issues and questions of detail: Bridie Anderson, Richard Carkeek, Chen Jing, Chen Zu'en, Sherman Cochran, Christian dePee, Antonia Finnane, Grace Fong, John Foster, Lara Friedenfelds, Bryna Goodman, Michael Griffey, Chris Hamm, Yukiko Hanawa, Hao Xiaowen, He Qiliang, Robert Hegel, Hsiang Jieh, Max K'o-wu Huang, Ruri Ito, Nick Knight, Ellen Laing, Fabio Lanza, Li Hsiao-t'i, Miho Matsumura, Christopher Massie, Barbara Mittler and Kaja Meuller-Wang (who allowed me access to their online HEIDENC, Institute of Chinese Studies, Heidelberg version of the *New Erya* while I was in China), the late Andrea Noble, Thy Phu, Martin Powers, Qian Nanxiu, Yuanzhu Bamboo Ren, Leon Rocha, Alessandro Russo, Sakamoto Hiroko, Andrew Satori, Haun Saussy, Laurie Sears, Zhijia Shen, Nicola Spakowski, Christine Tan, Ta Trinh, Kathy Tsiang, Suzanne Vromen, Ann Waltner, Wang Hui, Wang Xiaoming, Diana Xu, Yu Chien ming, Zang Jian, Peter Zarrow, Judith T. Zeitlin, Madeline Zelin, and Jennifer Ning Zhang. I am grateful to the following for translation support: Yizhong Gu, Robert Hegel, Nicole Huang, Liang Xia, Miho Matsumura, Haun Saussey, Yukiko Shigeto, and Judith Zeitlin.

To the following, I remain awed at my good fortune to have enjoyed your scholarly hospitality: Chen Jing, Chen Yungfa, Chua Beng Huat, Ruri Ito, Helena Kolenda, Liu Kang, Naoko Miyaji, Navaneetha Mokkil, Alessandro Russo, Yu Chien ming, Zhou Xian, and Kathy Woodward. I am indebted to their institutions: the Simpson Center for the Humanities, University of Washington; Asia Research Institute, Singapore; the Chao Center for Asian Studies, Rice University; the Program in Global Sociology, Hitotsubashi University; the Institute for Gender Studies, Ochanomizu Women's University; Academia Sinica, Taiwan; the Institute of Advanced Study, University of Bologna; the Institute for Arts and Humanities, Shanghai Jiao Tong University; the Institute for Arts and the Humanities and the Institute for Advanced Study at Nanjing University; Jawaharlal Nehru University, Women's Studies, GIAN; and the Luce Foundation.

Scholar comrades sustain me in ways difficult to put into words. Fabio Lanza read this manuscript twice, each time with exceptional critical patience and insight. Jing "CJ" Chen, Rebecca Karl, Anna Krylova, Tom Lamarre, Alida Metcalf, Rosalind Morris, and Kerry Ward graciously read parts. So many students have handled the data, and the collection project has gone on for so long, that at least two are tenured professors themselves. Special thanks to Professors Helen Schneider and Teresa Mares as well as certified public accountant Mengliang "Rosy" Zhang. While the following were never my students, I also thank Professors Kristy Leisle and Riki Thompson, and Brandy Parris, PhD, for advice, editorial support, and image handling.

Over the years, research librarians, bibliographers, and library curators have played an enormous positive role in my life. My deepest debts are to Michael Zhenhua Meng, curator of the Asian Library at Yale University, who has worked on this project for decades. I have also benefited from the attention of University of Washington Asia librarian Shen Zhijia; Valentina de Monte of the Bibliothèque municipal de Lyon; Lin He, director of information processing, Shanghai Library; Anna Shparberg, Fondren Library at Rice University; archivists at the Club Cosmetics Archive in Osaka; and kind librarians at Duke Archives, National University of Singapore, Toyo Bunko, and Stanford University. I gratefully acknowledge the kindness of Nancy Hearst, Fairbank Center librarian at Harvard University, and Michael Meng in securing a copy of the rare *Liushi fufu milan de shenghuo chou'e de linghun.*

In the years it has taken me to shape these ideas, family members have died. I remember them here: my mother, Alice Voorsanger Barlow; my husband, Donald Ming-dah Lowe; and my sister-in-law, Adrienne Jampolis Lowe, one of Los Angeles's first female advertising executives. The marriage of my parents-in-law, C. H. Ch'uan-hua Gershom Lowe and Hsien-en Sharon Lowe, née Nieh, allowed me intimate insight into modern Chinese life in Shanghai before the Japanese occupation.

Ruri Ito, Carol Roland-Nawi, and Angela Zito have heard a lot about this book. So has James Paskowitz, M.D. Professor Chen Jing of Nanjing University, who came to Rice University as a Luce Foundation postdoctoral fellow at the Chao Center for Asian Studies, has taken my old-fashioned image collecting into a whole new dimension. The digital archive that she imagined, the Chinese Commercial Advertising Archive (https://ccaa .nju.edu.cn/html/index.html), is open to scholars, teachers, and readers. In Houston, Yasmine Ballantyne, Jane DiPaolo, Mary Kesterson,

Jan Duncan, Morgan Moody, and Sergey Vasiliev have added spice and fun to my life. In Tokyo, Adachi Mariko, Vera Mackie, Sakamoto Hiroko, Barbara Sato, and the late Takemura Kazuko became valued associates. Friends at the University of Washington—Andrea Gurvitz Arai, Davinder Bhowmik, Vince Rafael, Laurie Sears, and John Treat—helped me make the introduction to this book less bewildering. In New York City, the endlessly creative Angela Zito is a source of intellectual pleasure. East Coast comrades Rebecca Karl, Suzy Kim, Yukiko Koga, Tom Lamarre, and Aminda Smith are beloved fellow travelers. Listeners and respondents at universities where I have given the talks that preceded this book have helped me in ways that did not always seem apparent at the time but that helped me grow in unanticipated directions.

This book has a rich prehistory. In 2004 Professor Ruri Ito and I cohosted the memorable "Modern Girl, Asia and Beyond: Global Capital, Colonial Modernities and Media Representations" (http://www .igs.ocha.ac.jp/moga/index.html), a meeting of U.S.- and Asia-located modern-girl scholars. At the University of Washington, I had cofounded the Modern Girl around the World Research Group (Madeline Dong, Uta Poiger, Priti Ramamurthy, Lynn Thomas, Elys Weinbaum), and in 2000–2001, when I met Ito at the Institute of Gender Studies, Ochanomizu Women's University, she and I cofounded a sister collective (Adachi Mariko, Ruri Ito, Kim Eunshil, Ko Ikujo, Muta Kazue, Sakamoto Hiroko, Barbara Sato, and Tachi Kaoru). *The Modern Girl around the World: Consumption, Modernity, and Globalization* (Duke University Press, 2008) focused on globalization, and *Modan garu to shokuminchi taki kindai higashijia ni okeru teikoku shihon jenda* (*The Modern Girl, Colonial Modernity, and East Asia*) (Iwanami shoten, 2010) raised questions of colonialism and imperialism. Under a Program in Global Sociology fellowship at Hitotsubashi University in 2010, Ito introduced me to Miho Matsumura, who supported my work on Club Cosmetics and the Morishita Jintan Corporation. Also, Ruri Ito helped me place 1,600 photo images of Tokyo, Kamakura, and Awa Kominato everyday life that my father, Claude A. Barlow, took in 1962–1963.

Ken Wissoker's editorial direction and encouragement improved the book. Reviewer 1 gave helpful directions after reading a remarkably nebulous first draft. Tracy Stober made sense out of the notes, Dr. Yizhong Gu checked translations and citations, Kimberly Miller gave me the best copyedit ever, and Professor Ping Zhu provided a second pair of eyes reading proofs. Editor Anita Grisales provided development advice, including pointing out places where readers with no background in Chinese history needed more information. I hope that together we have made this a more accessible read.

━━━━━━

Parts of the following essays appear in altered form in this book. My grateful thanks to the copyright owners for allowing alteration and republication.

"Advertising Ephemera and the Angel of History," *positions: asia critique* 20, no. 1 (Winter 2012).

"Buying In: Advertising and the Sexy Modern Girl Icon in Shanghai in the 1920s and 1930s," in *The Modern Girl around the World: Consumption, Modernity, and Globalization*, edited by the Modern Girl around the World Research Group (Durham, NC: Duke University Press, 2008).

"Commercial Advertising Art in 1840s–1940s 'China,'" in *A Companion to Chinese Art*, edited by Martin J. Powers and Katherine R. Tsiang (Chichester, UK: Wiley Blackwell, 2016).

"Event, Abyss, Excess: The Event of Women in Chinese Commercial Advertisement, 1910s–1930s," *differences: a journal of feminist cultural studies* 24, no. 2 (2013).

"Gender," in *The Making of the Human Sciences in China: Historical and Conceptual Foundations*, edited by Howard Chiang (Leiden: Brill, 2020).

"History and Border," *Journal of Women's History* 18, no. 2 (2006).

Review of *The Birth of Chinese Feminism: Essential Texts in Transnational Theory*, edited by Lydia H. Liu, Rebecca E. Karl, and Dorothy Ko, MCLC online, 2013. https://u.osu.edu/mclc/book-reviews/chinese-feminism-barlow/.

"Wanting Some: Natural Science, Social Science and Consumerism," in *Women in China: The Republican Period in Historical Perspective*, edited by Mechthild Leutner and Nikola Spakowski (Berlin: LIT, 2005).

"'What Is a Poem?': The Event of Women and the Modern Girl as Problems in Global or World History," in *Immanuel Wallerstein and the Problem of the World: System, Scale, Culture*, edited by David Palumbo-Liu, Bruce Robbins, and Nirvana Tanoukhi (Durham, NC: Duke University Press, 2011).

Introduction to the Event

On April 10, 1967, the Red Guard Jinggangshan Regiment at Qinghua University staged a series of struggle sessions against Wang Guangmei (1921–2006), a high-ranking Communist Party member and Chinese premier Liu Shaoqi's wife. The trial sounded core themes in the Great Proletarian Cultural Revolution (aka the Cultural Revolution), conventionally dated 1966 to 1976. In Wang's case, Jiang Qing (1914–1991), a leading member of the Gang of Four directing the Chinese Cultural Revolution, authorized a Red Guard undergraduate faction under chemical engineering student Kuai Dafu's (1945–) leadership to organize the trial against Wang.[1] In this book's final chapter, I describe and analyze the "line error," or crime charged, that Wang was pursuing a Khrushchevian, revisionist, anti-Communist diplomacy. But at immediate stake is Wang's singular offense, the characteristics that made her more than just another high-ranking official who had "taken the capitalist road."

According to the students' charge document, Wang had traveled to Indonesia on state business in 1963 and was photographed offering Sukarno a light for his cigarette. Also in the course of the trip, Wang had worn a hat made in Hong Kong, an allegedly provocative dress, a brooch, and a string of pearls that Jiang Qing, also ranked *nomenklatura* and Chairman Mao Zedong's wife, had ordered her *to not wear*.[2] At stake in the conflict, then, was whether Wang's performance of Chinese state femininity had been adequate: once her antagonists successfully criminalized this behavior, they set off what became a far-reaching crisis over the political truth of Chinese women. In the lopsided struggle between an ascendant Jiang Qing and an embattled Wang, the question facing revolutionary youth in the Mao political movement was how to install a *true* truth of women. Kuai prevailed in 1967. Wang gave a series of self-criticisms and spent twelve years in prison.[3] Jiang Qing was sentenced to death in 1981 for her criminal behavior, including the persecution of Wang. Throughout the 1980s and 1990s, significant cohorts of Chinese men and women convulsively repudiated the truth of women that Jiang Qing's group had sought to install politically. And eleven years into her commuted sentence Jiang hung herself.

Since an event is a politically inspired action to install a newly discovered truth, what is at stake in the political event of women? In the late seventeenth century, a cohort of friends in Holland and England concluded that life involved eggs. Egg theory dominated speculative European material philosophy for 150 years while at the same time no one knew for sure what eggs did. Ovists and spermists debated whether sperm were actually tiny little eggs and the ovum a mere culture or medium or, contrarily, whether sperm's vapors were stimulating latencies in eggs. Since no one (including Baruch Spinoza, active in this debate) knew how eggs created new individuals, egg discoveries were a nonevent. Mathematician Pierre Louis Maupertuis (1698–1759), entomologist Renè Antoine Ferchault de Reaumur (1683–1757), and precursor geneticist Gregor Mendel (1822–1884) each added building blocks; Matthias Jakob Schleiden (1804–1881) and Theodor Schwann (1810–1882) demonstrated that life existed at the cellular level; and, finally, Oscar Hertwig (1849–1922) became the first person to see an egg and a sperm create a zygote and to definitively show that the conceptus was alive. And still this did not constitute a political event.

The event of women is the political determination that in human social existence women are men's equivalent because physiological sexual reproduction is true. Rather than being always absent or latent or forgotten participants in historical events, political voluntarism has and continues to transform physiological truth about women into its own historical event: this is part of "in the event of women." Another is that even today the biology of reproduction, human or chicken, is not fully understood; investigations always find more data to adjust what can be considered truth.[4] But we know that out of the laboratory science of Darwin's time, which enfolded seventeenth- and eighteenth-century egg and sperm theory and practical experiments in nineteenth-century industrial cattle breeding, the truth of sex surged into philosophical circles. Charles Darwin had correctly argued that huge numbers of life-forms reproduce by fusing bits of spermatic material to egg material: activists made his insight politically potent. So-called social Darwinian sociologists and general philosophers acted on this truth. Even as we move toward extrauterine reproduction and the cyberneticization of humanity, altering nineteenth and twentieth-century understanding, the truth of women's contribution to human sexual reproduction cannot be rescinded or denied.

Significant implications follow. First, there is nothing Chinese or European about human physiology or for that matter the physiological truth that women are humans: political actions taken on the basis of eighteenth- to nineteenth-century reproductive science *are* historically singular and contingent, obviously. Second, events are not discoveries; they are prolonged efforts to demonstrate a truth, in this case that women are, just like men, procreative human beings, mammals with natural rights, and that women are different because in species life, organic vital elements originating in different organs, the testes and ovaries, are sine qua non for regenerative life. It turns out that Wang Guangmei and Jiang Qing's 1967 conflict over women's feminine performance is only one episode in a longer, unresolved political and historical event of women.[5]

NATURAL AND SOCIAL FACTS

Establishing how women are the reproductive equivalent of men transformed truth. All over the educated world, women abruptly appeared at the center of national history. News about our mammal origins accompanied the commodity form, too, and tangible domestic commodities materialized the event of women under conditions of late nineteenth-century corporate imperialism. Branded soap and insecticide ads, rolled tobacco, neomedical elixirs, affordable automobiles, chemical and bean effluvia fertilizer, birth control and venereal disease potions, hormonal treatments, Kotex pads, chemical masculinity enhancers, romance-inducing body improvements, and so on all conveyed the new procreation story. So, while the truth of sexual reproduction is going to always be transitive, the event of women is a lavishly documentable, never fully completed political struggle to establish truth and social justice.

Historians often define woman in relation to man. They draw on measures like sexual difference, psychic difference, sex-coded labor, or role theory. For instance, a now-everyday argument explains individual variety in terms of "gender difference." The gender debate has bravely struggled to fuse the natural science of physiological difference to the social science of behavior and in so doing to capture the differences among women, including disparities like ethnicity, racial coding, class, sexual orientation, and desire. Gender is also, historically speaking, a way of reconfiguring colonial discourses, what economic imperialism revealed about human diversity, and this includes the distinctions—women, men, and others—drawn everywhere differently. Understanding women not as latent participants in events but an event as such focuses us on women's recent origin story and helps peel away gender theory's wobbly efforts to reconcile the natural and the social.

Installing evolutionary truth demanded attention and flexibility. This is easier to see analogically: if you get an infection in your toe and you soak it, cauterize it, keep it clean, and invite a shaman to pray over it, your toe usually heals. You do not need to know the etiology of infectious agents. Since 1890 modernists have developed germ theory to explain what is going on in your toe. By the 1920s antibiotics often cured the infection without the shaman. We still use shamans, but science has altered our worldly understanding of why shamans are helpful. What happens when we examine how transitive and profoundly disturbing discoveries change thinking and living? How does medicine, your toe healing because you have eaten a known active agent, transform your perception of your body? We know not only that antibiotics have cured tuberculosis but also that there are now antibiotic-resistant forms of tuberculosis. But the scientific imprimatur, even when the science becomes outdated or is proven untrue, changes historical subjects and our perception of our humanity.

Imagine believing that according to the best and most scientific theories available in the whole world, women *naturally* choose to mate with the best available males, just like other mammals? That only culture or tradition stands in the way of natural female sexual desire and racial improvement? And what about the alleged truth that in their natural state women have created the male to aid in human species evolution? *In the Event of Women* reconstructs moments when these novel modern concepts of sexuality and difference rose to the status of a truth. But the book's argument considers a realization about historical universals in a place where truth claims are not usually sought. Knowledge, the indisputable truth of women in this case, concerns the world. In this book, that world is China. Arguments and evidence are located in Chinese modern treaty ports, and at the end of this book, these resolve in a paroxysm of Chinese revolutionary evental struggle over the truth of women.

China is a place where people live and think and act. It need not always be a place where historians compare things because difference is not always the most urgent question. Nonetheless, a historian must conjecture what is singular about this world—not in relation to somewhere else, but, rather, asking, "What is singular about the event of women *in China*?" Singularities arise explicitly and implicitly throughout this book. First is the role that revolutionary politics has played in the historical struggle over women in China. Marxist philosophy and critical sociology not only played a distinctive role in struggles for power but prevailed after the People's Republic of China became a sovereign state. In simple chronological terms, 1920 through 2020 is an entire century of violent bloody insurrections; the violence lasts a century and a half and is even more catastrophic if one begins with women soldiers in the mid-nineteenth-century Taiping Revolution, a civil war costing approximately forty million people their lives. There may be similarities to the Chinese case elsewhere in the world, but the role played by women in China's revolutionary history is substantial.

A second singularity is likely the language revolution. Literate Chinese elites played a significant role in the event of women. Not only did a great late-dynastic language revolution upend conventional literary expression, but in the crushing effort to establish mass literature, a language revolution disrupted elite monopoly over high literacy. When the imperial examination system was abolished in 1905, modernist conceptual problems and scientific and social scientific theories flooded into mass circulation. Literati educated under the old system argued that hybridization of literary expression had to occur or too many "untranslatables" would thwart Chinese efforts to understand physical science. Particularly objective social sciences would remain out of reach because sophisticated Chinese writing always referred back to itself. This perception lies behind the well-known flow of nouns or neologisms into modern Chinese, particularly out of Japanese. In the process, generic forms, including those associated with conventional (i.e., nonmodernist) female writers and poets, got savaged and kicked aside.[6] As this book's chapters on sociology and mimeses argue, the language revolution anchored a belief that written texts in Chinese could represent reality, the real, of social life but only after the Chinese language adjusted the relation of written and spoken expressions. Scientific language reform and mobilization of the event of women into revolutionary goals are fundamental singularities characterizing Chinese conditions in the event of women.

National differences and singularities in everyday life aside, my approach to writing the event of women modifies what historians mean when using the term *context*. The prevailing method supposes people live inside a context. Texts, what people write or draw, fit into a context like puzzle pieces fit into a larger image. In this view, historians adjust for bias—a class bias or a national bias, for instance—but texts are read in order to illustrate real class relations or real empirical conditions. This book assumes, on the contrary, that people act under given conditions beyond which, in most circumstances, nothing else is thinkable. In mundane times, we establish a world where we can live and explain our existence. Every once in a while, however, a wager is thrown and a truth proposed that lies beyond these normative conditions. That is how an event is triggered. Those who see or appreciate the new truth will assert it and argue out its implications, even fight other people, to determine how the new truth will be established. *In the Event of Women* presumes that there is no privileged position where a text represents a context. Conditions are conditions. They remain inert. To explain how new things enter the world (the child in Europe, the event of a global proletariat, a steam engine, a colonial bourgeoisie, extermination camps, the science of homosexuality, society as the sine qua non of human life, etc.), historians amass evidence and clarify conditions where these new truths became actable. When woman is an event, not a representation or a performance, there is no comparative axis, no other, but rather a voluntarist action to confirm a new truth. In the event of women, this new truth is that every woman possesses natural rights and an innate knowledge about sexual selection. When freed to express those inborn rights and to choose to procreate with the best available mate, women perfect life itself and the social processes that accompany evolution.[7]

From the mid-nineteenth through the early twenty-first century, theorists, consumers, and readers in China decided that they lived, *as all humans do*, in a society and not in a cosmos or an empire. Society became the platform where they hammered out all the implications this new knowledge brought with it. Ontologies (what is Being) and epistemologies (the ways we know things) got tested. All problems became social problems. All behaviors became social roles. The claims natural sciences made about factual truth got hammered into theory and practice on the anvil of social science. Society gave access to what new intellectuals believed were previously unreachable yet universally incontestable truths underlying cultural differences. Social structures, social problems, social roles, social epistemology, and the various ontologies of social existence had the power to resituate educated Chinese people in New China, in the new world.

Why a string of pearls is worth fighting over and why, indeed, it has a role to play in a history written fifty-five years later are good questions. A social performance, a contest over what is real, unfolded on a social platform, on a planet accurately described in astrophysics, during the social evolutionary ascent of humanity, and in the larger struggle to figure out Chinese society's place in the universe. Blasting out of the river of time and explaining a struggle over the first lady's dress rests on far-flung conditions and human voluntarism, commitment, and someone's passionate willingness to act on women's social and natural truth. This book proposes that in the event of women, the female person—woman or women—became a pivot in modernist intellectual work. The shock of physiologically distinguished human sexual reality set off ingeniously creative theoretical projects. The book analyzes some of them. But it also argues that "women" is not a projection, an abstraction, a gender, a signifier, a flow, or a void. It is also not an effect of Western representation or cultural imperialism. Nor is it some great reveal or preexisting condition, since projecting physiologically defined women backward in time cannot explain female's or human's historical experience.

THE EVENT IN THE EVENT OF WOMEN

Focusing history on events has advantages. It highlights the fact that people do things. Whether people are acting in response to an apprehension that Christ has risen or in relation to having established that human ovaries contribute an egg to procreation, historiography of events presupposes action, or volition. Moreover, theories of event are neither structuralist nor poststructuralist, because they rest on the assumption of historical presence rather than the vortex of representation. In Alain Badiou's philosophy, the vortex supports naming, nomination, but the worlds' presence means that human subjects are acting inside their real conditions; they are not merely discursive subjects or subject to discourse. One need not embrace the ancient Greek theory that the universal is the real apprehended mathematically, or Badiou's idiosyncratic point that Paul Cohen's modern set theory explains how historical newness enters the world, to appreciate that history is material in the sense of leaving indelible marks. Events not only arise out of human acts but accrete. They even wait, as Walter Benjamin pointed out, for historians to wrench them up out of disremembered or buried materials.[8] Who acts, what temporality animates accretions, what the relation of politics is to history, are acutely difficult matters. In a post-Engelsian, post-Foucauldian historiography of the event, there is no teleology, no evidence of epistemic rupture or temporal termination, only subjective action, latent novelty, and discoveries that are universalizable.

Some theorists have argued that events should be understood using notions of emplotment or "discursive construction." According to Hayden White, literary narrative emplots or colors or emotionally characterizes the transmission of past events. Since we cannot write history without using narratives, history in its written form must consist of novelistic typologies of emplotment. Historian-philosopher Michel Foucault demonstrated why many historical things are in fact *non*events (prison reforms, for instance) because these nonevents do not change things (they actually extend the existing power of carceral disciplinary logic, for instance); modernity changes little except to provide even more punitive punishments such as the panopticon, surveillance society, and rationality. Like White, Foucault was relatively disinterested in *philosophizing* events, but unlike White he did not take the event for granted. *Eventalization* (a Foucauldian neologism) means the historian intervenes in a structuralist historical account to highlight or demonstrate a relative discontinuity, an "epistemic shift" or a rupture, in the otherwise expected. As Arianna Bove has noted, Foucault used Annales school historiography to anchor his own historico-philosophical concerns and to initiate ways of extracting singularities or in his language "eventalizing" topics like biopower, sexuality, and discipline. This gave him a way to claim that an epistemic shift had taken place even in the absence of structural change in the historical *longue durée*.[9]

Gilles Deleuze, Badiou's favorite antagonist, in contrast, held (contra Foucault) that events originate in speech or illocutionary acts. Rooted in the Greek Stoics' axiom of the power of propositions, as cited in Patton, Deleuze held that events "actualize particular events in the social field"; this is why "politics frequently takes the form of struggle over the appropriate description of events."[10] The notion that illocutionary acts are a foundation for historical truth is widespread. Deleuze's distinction between the ideal (illocutionary) event and an actualized event is the problem here. Once the claim shifts from philosophical questions to historical truth, Deleuze's idealist periodization of historical time is unhelpful and anyway not sustainable.[11] Nonetheless, given persistent low-key debates over historiography and historical method, it is not surprising that some China and India historians consider Foucauldian eventality to be a heuristic and argue, in one famous example, that modern Chinese historiography "dispersed" and denigrated the past and therefore denied the *real*. A good historian's job, this argument went, is to rescue real, that is native, history from something called the nation and to redeem events, developing a more sympathetic reading rooted in a traditional or *indigenous* cultural context.[12]

Badiou's key value to the event debate is political, and that is the primary reason I agonistically contest him, rather than engaging other theorists of the event. This study seeks to grasp how new things occur. In the event of women, the stakes are revolutionary: women's recently discovered biogenetic, hormonal body appears historically as a newly realized social temporality. One implication is that modern women from the outset have been a set of commands to recognize and authorize a subject's integral station and to evaluate her acts as different from yet (in the future) equal to those of men. Given these practical claims to modern standing, to be a co-modernist in a modern society, women categorically will be "victims of oppression" who "declare" and are "part of a tentative search for an autonomous politics of the oppressed."[13] In sociological rationality, women's natural rights will be violated *even as they are installed* since inherent rights are latent, not necessarily manifest: natural rights do not need to be manifest in order to exist. In this scheme newness arrives in the world because subjects laying claim, or *fidelity* in his philosophical language, to the new will, slightly adjusting Badiou's position, open a way of writing history, acknowledging that women and men who share the belief that women are full natural or physiological subjects will continue presenting themselves.

Technically, an event, in Badiou's philosophy, is something that happens within a set of possibilities, when a latency or so-called ultra-one is noticed; notation changes how that given set is understood. But events are not possible in the absence of a subject that recognizes and militates (i.e., sets into motion a generic procedure) for that newly configured, formerly latent entity. When significant things are recognized, and the thing gets acted on, it is possible that actors rupture an older order on the bases of new truths. Woman appears, a native to a situation, and the event's adherents recognize woman's claims to personhood. While a subject, the biological female human is an element arising out of unfathomably complex historical conditions, once it is discerned or declared or noticed, declaration makes the subject an immanently discovered truth.[14] The conditions underlying the event of women in China as laid out in this book's chapters are precisely that set of possibilities, just as the figures stepping forward to iterate over and over the qualities and capacities of women demonstrate the truth of the initial assertion.

There are, nonetheless, two hesitations about Badiou's philosophy of the event. The first is its ambiguous or even slippery relation to the world, to history not just of politics but of philosophical, artistic, affective, scientific thought and action. Many critics have remarked on this, but Alenka Zupančič said it best when she noted that in fact for Badiou, "there is [an implicit] fifth condition of philosophy" beyond art, mathematics, love, and politics, which is that philosophy has to pull itself away from the immediate grip of its own conditions, while nevertheless remaining under the effect of these conditions.[15] Zupančič is noting a useful paradox in Badiou, which is that to *be philosophical* (i.e., generic), philosophy must pull away from precisely the worldly conditions that it seeks to interpret, conditions that can be neither fully denied nor fully determined yet that announce philosophy's own arrival onto the scene. The other basic reservation concerns how Badiou restricts the relation of truth and worldly circumstance to what he calls *sequence*. This, as many critics note, impoverishes history and runs the risk that a great-man political history is reinstalled. In a sleight of hand, in other words, political sequence comes to substitute for history as such, which allows the Badiou scholar to engage in what historians would recognize to be history writing, while at the same time disavowing the relation of the political sequence to the conditions for thought that have played a role in revolutionary transformation. This definitively marks Badiou's distance from the Marxian tradition.[16]

In the Event of Women exploits these ambiguities in Badiou's philosophy of event.[17] It goes directly to what Zupančič calls the fifth condition of philosophy in order to divulge a past space of thinking and political action and to extend that past space into our contemporary moment. Technically this involves weighing not philosophy but *thinking*, that is, local debates in Chinese treaty-port scholarly communities, side by side with the physical conditions where these communities worked and the economic and political processes restructuring the social field of life. Reconstructing a century-old world of conditions for thinking and the content of thinking is an unapologetically historical task. So is archiving and analyzing vernacular expression of advanced modernism in modernity's actual physical environment, the "grip" or restrictions of philosophy's conditions.

Juxtaposing materials opens to visibility spaces where people were thinking and engaging in political action. An archive of Chinese commercial advertising images dating from the late nineteenth through the first half of the twentieth century, for instance, illuminates contemporaneous theoretical work aimed at strategizing advertising methods and selling science in those decades; lays out histories of corporations that extended finance capital into Chinese emergent commodity markets, along with their commodity-distribution plans; raises to the horizon of history the output of creative intellectuals, literary figures, translators, critics, social science theorists, commentators, and scholars who established the *thereness* of society and its facticity and who eventually institutionalized a logos of sociology and the core rationality of the social sciences.

In a consequently frenzied world, translating and interpreting calques or neologisms accompanied sociology's advance into a physical environment that would overnight become saturated with social logics and motivated by what Tong Lam calls a new "passion for facts."[18] In addition to advertising arts, industry, statist social surveys, and the dynamic world of imaginative vernacular sociology, *In the Event of Women* also considers the tense relation of what Asia historians consider an important economic regime, that of international finance capital, to the logos of social theory.[19] New conditions for thinking and the modernist philosophies that thinkers developed revolved around changing economic regimes; political contradictions; logical impasses; theories of society, femininity, humanity, and sexuality; the struggle to evaluate how scientific truths worked in liberated social relationships; and, most centrally, the appearance of a revolutionary subject, women, in society.

This study is thus neither philosophy nor a helpful subsidiary effort to provide Badiou's philosophy with a "ground." Zupančič's assertion, coming as it does from Badiou's own camp of psychoanalytic philosophers, suggests that Badiou's ahistorical theory of the event inhabits the double bind described in the following.[20] Zupančič declines Badiou's injunction against history in a way long familiar in Lacanian feminist positions, which, while psychoanalytic, parts ways from Badiou's and Lacan's austere, authoritarian politics and judgmental prescriptions against castrated subjects.[21] Demanding that the haughty Badiou "venture into the dense thickets of real history, into the social and historical determination of events," Daniel Bensaïd also relentlessly noted the contradictory or magical way that Badiou claims on the one hand that "there can be no transcendental truth, only truths in situation and in relation," while on the other hand adamantly refusing to consider that truths are in fact deduced from premises. "Detached from its historical conditions," Bensaïd wrote in apparent revulsion, the "pure diamond of truth, the event, just like the notion of the absolutely aleatory encounter in the late Althusser, is akin to a miracle. . . . [A] politics without politics is akin to a negative theology."[22] Bensaïd dislodged the event from Badiou's philosophical moorings in the name of history, as Zupančič had in a less manifest or gross fashion.

And yet Badiou remains a better theorist of event than disciplinary historians like Foucault or Joan Scott because Badiou insists that an event is never a piece of the banal flow of vegetative life. Unlike Foucault, who simply left sexual difference out of his theory of sexuality, Badiou cleanly admits into his schema the scandal of the impossibility of a psychoanalytic female subject. This separates him from Scott's psychodynamic fiction of a gender, in which she claims to recognize the female subject while at the same time disavowing it. The strength of the Badiou proposal, therefore, is that he restricts the notion to phenomena that are subjective, unprecedented, and broadly or irrevocably transformative. To the degree that philosophy can never fully extricate its mechanisms from the conditions that support their rationality, Badiou initiates a vision of event that can in fact accommodate the event of women, the revolutionary appearance of a female, libidinous, mammal, human subject on the historical horizon. A history of the event of women distinguishes *eventality* from *event* and, the most popular clichéd meme of all, the *epistemic event*. Finally, it may help establish what is possible "in the event of women" to reposition feminist critique historically, a sound strategic weapon with a cogent logos of its own.

Yan Fu, Kawakami Hajime, Shusui (Kotoku Denjiro), Qu Qiubai, Chen Han-seng, Li Da, Immanuel Kant, Karl Marx, Nicolai Bukharin,

Vladimir Lenin, Rudolf Hilferding, Charles Darwin, Herbert Spencer, Georg Simmel, Lester Frank Ward, and many other Chinese Enlightenment sources established definitive logics, authoritatively proclaiming that humans live in society and are social animals and that society is organized in developmental stages. In enclaves like Shanghai, they wrote about uneven social progress in capitalist development and about how to situate oneself in the world. Historically, then, how true are their "Chinese" theories; were these people right? Usually, confronted with such a question, historians respond that all ideas are divisible back into their contexts and that ideas make sense only contextually, which is to say that history cannot be true or untrue, because it is always a version of something alleged to be truer or even unknowably true. The cliché that truth is contextual does not resolve problems inherent in the question of whether Chinese social theory had truly diagnosed its own socioeconomic conditions. Early twentieth-century Chinese intellectuals worked at the edge of the discernible. Further, the truths established a century ago are still considered true, for the most part.

In the tradition of Walter Benjamin, Henri Lefebvre, and Michel de Certeau, this study finds correlations everywhere. One of the means by which credence is established or by which people show in their activities and their protestations that society exists, that women are subjects, and so on is by situating and recognizing how everyday life is defined sociologically. The conditions of thought are found in what Johanna Drucker insists is the material communication of ideas in graphic form.[23] "The task of making knowledge visible," she writes, "does not depend on an assumption that images represent things in the world. Graphics make and construct knowledge in a direct and primary way."[24] When I understand commercial ephemera as "arguments made in graphical form" and take these graphical arguments to be an underused archive, advertisement images suddenly become surprisingly philosophically and sociologically useful.

So historical visibility in the form, for instance, of a toothpaste advertising image is not a metaphor or a representation; it is a graph of the real. Cartoon images like the light-bulb woman are meaningful because they are, among other factors, a *pictorial* version of ideas. A reason to write the history of the Chinese advertising industry is that ads transformed the landscape; inside new media and outside, in the street, on the trolley, on the building tops, cartoon and photo images of social life surrounded and reconfirmed the newness of the new society. Graphesis raises questions about precedent and about how meaning changes, since graphic artists also draw on past and present to imagine the future, just as arguments based in literacy do. Coded into little commercial cartoons and large billboards, however much precedent is in play, are the same questions intellectual historians, militants, and engaged critics confronted: what is modern, how past is the past, what ghosts haunt colonial modernity that might undermine the revolutionary future, how is newness recognizable and what will it take to expand it, what guarantees the new?

Writing in the event of women peels away the gender dilemma and places women in the same modern historical framework as the proletariat, the White, the national. In the world of history, nothing is forever, but it is material, which is why the Chinese bourgeoisie or aspirational middle class struggled over the truth of women under specific conditions laid out here: imperialism, commercial capitalism, commodity culture, nationalism and anti-imperialism, natural rights claims, social science theory, and so on. In the historical event of women, the woman is a thing. That is why in the discussion of women's modern history, there is a beginning, an event, a history, and no going back. *In the Event of Women* predicates conditions of thought inextricable from thought's content, and willed actions taken in the moment of a perceived historical now. Conditions, thoughts, and actions are visible and open to discovery and analysis, no matter where on the globe historical action was taken. The question of the relation of the event of women to feminist struggles for justice remains open.

There are six tightly linked chapters in this argument. Chapter 1, "Conditions of Thinking," lays out the economic upheaval that ushered in circumstances making an event of women thinkable. Chinese modern social theory starting in the mid-nineteenth century repeatedly and with increasing urgency declared that woman is a finite, localized organism, a something, a living categorical, a someone specific. Pretty much everyone agreed on the alleged fact that women's eugenic contribution accelerated when they bought and used new industrially made commodities. Therefore, the chapter focuses on Andersen, Meyer & Company (AMCO); Morishita Jintan; British American Tobacco Company (BAT); Nanyang Brothers Tobacco Company; and Brunner Mond and Co. also known, after 1926, as Imperial Chemical Industries or ICI. It introduces the late nineteenth-century international firm, or limited liability company (LLC), and shows how the LLC's financialization of capital in Chinese treaty ports and its strategic, fantastic market-building strategies worked. As Wen-hsin Yeh pointed out years ago, becoming modern poses a historical problem.[25] One means of approaching the modernity question is to scrutinize industrially produced commodities, particularly branded ones. The conditions for desiring and acquiring industrially produced commodities are present in the financialized, large-scale, imperialist corporations, the technological revolution in printing, and the social science of advertising. All of these are visible in the lovely image of a Shanghai female advertising agent at the center of a large GE electric bulb (see figure 1.1). This image—a conventional, homely bit of ephemera—encodes corporate governance, "the firm," banking and investment strategies, colonial law in Chinese treaty ports (established through a system of unequal treaties), legal and corporate institutions, economic theories, and efforts to control property rights over corporate, branded commodities and electricity itself. Like most of the book's chapters, this one generalizes from massive publication projects including newspapers, journals of opinion, and corporate histories.

Chapter 2, "Foundational Chinese Sociology," analyzes how a leading sociological stream developed the truth of sexual difference in social life. Sociology founders Qu Qiubai and Li Da both took the truth of women to be a given. Major figures interpreting European philosophy and Bolshevik Marxism, these two sociologists fused modes of production, relations of production, and social evolution to the biology of human reproduction. Because they began from the assumption that social and biological evolution are inextricably entwined and that labor had to have evolved in a bodily or reproductive sense, they concurred that primitive society had been matriarchal. And in Li Da's case, that biological humanity originated in female form and only gradually, under conditions of natural selection, produced a male capable of inseminating a female partner. Recognizing that science and sexual sciences are truthful caused Qu Qiubai and his peers to reconsider how language itself communicates truth. Particularly Qu but also most May Fourth intellectuals and social scientists came to advocate a mimetic Chinese. Mimesis or representationalism is the epistemological problem lying at the bottom of arguments for vernacular language reform. The chapter opens vernacular language reform contextually in this regard: language had to support women's truth to be considered truthful accounting, a presentation of the real.

Chapter 3, "Vernacular Sociology," refers to an incompatible mix of natural science, social science, and theories of literary mimesis that constituted Chinese cosmopolitan opinion. Physiological women's prominent role in evolutionary theory has meant that natural and social science are difficult to disaggregate in modern thinking no matter where on the planet sociology and biology appear. Vernacular sociology fuses social evolution with commodity distribution. That is its first special characteristic. Chinese Marxist sociology proposes that procreation and labor power are tightly wound together, so that changes in evolutionary biology are intertwined with how labor power supports specific kinds of social relations like the primal horde, the matriarchy, feudal patriarchy, and so on. In vernacular sociological theory, the motor for change is usually instinct. In this set of beliefs, humans are animals, and animals have instincts, so social relations must be the effect of our instinctive needs and actions. The result is often eugenic history. A civilizational form of history, writing about the struggle of the fittest resolves in a triumphant announcement about eugenically superior stocks. Humanity can do this because, on the one hand, we are sexually differentiated, like all other mammals, and, on the other, we are wholly unlike other animals because as we evolve we change our habitat. Unlike bees or ants, we can humanly engineer prostheses to improve our social life.

Chapter 4, "The Social Life of Commercial Ephemera," delineates Chinese commercial ephemera generically and links them to how a local ad industry sponsored modern knowledge. The knowledge embedded in ephemera is real. It remains true and has not yet been surpassed or debunked. We are evolutionary biological animals. Acknowledging that some theories are incontestably true helps clarify why history cannot just be discourse or a narrative representation of differing opinions. But it also helps explain why wrenching out old ephemera clarifies historical norms and weakens Badiou's insupportable notion that decisive political sequences, rare and miraculous, are *historical*, while other given conditions for thinking philosophy (ephemera, waste, excrement, trivia, feminism) are historicist rubbish. It also collapses a gap separating historians and our modernist subjects. He-Yin Zhen, Qu Qiubai, Li Da, Yan Fu, Ariga Nagao, and Jiang Qing were not discursive subjects. Their declarative statements fortified truths that were and remain verifiable, that evolution explains human species-being, women are human, and so on. We continue to struggle with what our physiology means in relation to our collectivities and solidarities, even in highly philosophical projects like Lacanian psychoanalysis.

Chapter 5, "Nakedness and Interiority," shows psychodynamic theories marking out a modern interiority for new women. This chapter proposes that embedded, latent Freudian psychology and eugenic theory saturated mass culture and set the terms of a historical unconscious that was popularly expressed in commercial art and ad images. Vernacular sociology set a low bar and popularized instinct theory. Voiced explicitly in the speculative work of eugenic sociologist Pan Guangdan, developed over an ongoing struggle to distinguish art from pornographic advertising images, a consensus position arose that Chinese women were narcissistic. It is not completely clear why an oceanic tide of mirror-gazing girl icons swept Shanghai advertising campaigns in particular. But it certainly fortified arguments being made in contemporary social science circles about the ontological being of women. Freudian psychoanalysis emerged into Chinese translation around the same time that the European nude also made its public appearance. And while the advertising girl image is generic, its presence indicates anatomical and physiological models of female desire. Girl-centered commercial ephemera and theories of female centrality established the sticky, complex relation of advertising graphesis in commercial ephemera and vernacular sociology at elite and plebian levels.[26]

As chapters 2 and 4 suggest, the glamor of commodity advertising saturated the truth of women. Almost by default women became an "other other," not just of bioman but in advertising other scenes of use value, attached to the commodity form itself.

Chapter 6, "Wang Guangmei's *Qipao*," lays out in hyperbolic detail the political conflict between Wang Guangmei and Jiang Qing mentioned earlier in this chapter. While this struggle was an explicit political battle pitting one vision of the truth of women against another, it was not a disagreement over the sexed body. Rather, the brutal conflict involved a hideous symptomatic conflict over what social reality an evolutionary female subject ought to live to be true to itself, or herself. Second, it proposes that a struggle session among Wang and Jiang and Red Guard factions in Beijing in 1967 can help explain why it is not possible to write modern Chinese history without recognizing the event of women.

CHAPTER ONE

Conditions of Thinking

In the AMCO-General Electric (GE) advertisement in figure 1.1, a woman sits in a light bulb–shaped balloon. Here AMCO is the trade and brand name of Andersen, Meyer & Company, Limited, of China, a limited liability company (LLC) formed in 1906 to sell "packages" to treaty port–based corporations and Chinese power holders: provincial warlord juntas, nationalist parties, Chinese companies, city governments, and so on. The product line of AMCO included industrial machines and accounting technologies, commercial investment packages, banking services, big turbines, and industrial chemicals, as well as lifestyle products like bulbs, table fans, light fixtures, flashlights, and so on. An LLC is a legal fiction limiting individual liability to the amount invested and making the fictive firm responsible for the rest. The firm owns debt; the partners take the profits and pay tax only on what their investment yielded. Under the unequal treaty system, beginning in 1842 when China lost the First Opium War, LLCs like AMCO proliferated, suggesting that the LLC form may have been corporate imperialism's sine qua non. The girl in the GE bulb ad, a sophisticated, generic example of 1920s and 1930s Chinese commercial art, is drawing her own image in an endless mise en abyme. Trite, fragmentary, partial, ephemeral, and snatched out of oblivion, it encodes real conditions, just not in a totalizing or narrative account. Still, commercial ephemera alert historians to how advertising naturalized an infrastructural revolution underway in the colonial world.[1]

1.1 General Electric bulb girl at advertising desk. *Dongfang zazhi* 19, no. 1 (January 10, 1922).

Advertising, an industrial project, saturated treaty ports more effectively than commodified objects themselves. In this chapter and chapter 4, we see brokers and commercial advertising agencies subsidizing the mass media's production costs as they made profits. Decade after decade, the newspapers, mosquito press, high- and lowbrow journals, and even academic publications rented out ad space and, beginning in the 1920s, leased urban and suburban outdoor facilities, too. Ads appeared on billboards, trolleys, department-store windows, stalls, walls, skyscrapers, train stations, and showrooms; brand advertising images inundated suburban and urban environments (figures 1.2–1.7).[2]

Ad images contribute surplus information in ways no other evidence can because they so publicly communicate the shock of the new. The AMCO-GE bulb ad presents a charming visual image to sell a commodity, but it also defines the scientifically produced commodity and urges people to "become consumers," to buy products with "AMCO" or "GE" or "BAT" (British American Tobacco) on them, rather than local objects or some

1.2 Nanjing Road in Shanghai, 1930.

1.3 Rickshaw stand at the Beijing railroad station, 1930.

1.4 Moving-board advertising in the French Concession, Shanghai, ca. 1920.

1.5 Studebaker brand showroom and gas pump, 1931.

1.6 BAT cigarette billboard in the suburbs.

1.7 Coca-Cola ad and Chinese soldiers resisting Japanese attack, 1937.

other competitor's good. Repetitive, fetishized, banal, and routinized, ad images visually proclaim and engrain into daily life an image in the now of industrial commodity life. Everywhere, yet negligibly important, ad images colored Chinese "semicolonial, semifeudal" modernity, where conditions for thinking were under construction, architecturally, but also as the commodity form itself infiltrated the environment. Commercial ephemera reiterated recognizability, legibility, and intelligibility and smudged themselves into the world, just as philosophers began to anticipate new futures. Rudolf Hilferding (1877–1941), V. I. Lenin (1870–1924), Rosa Luxemburg (1871–1919), and He-Yin Zhen (1884– ca. 1919) speculated around the edge of the coming era.

The female figure at the drawing board is an advertising agent, in the mise en abyme of an advertising agent drawing herself. Her natural, unbound feet correlate with her productive labor contribution in an integrated, professional workforce. To ensure that the viewer does not overlook the relation between enlightened women and electrification, the artist has drawn blazes of light emanating out of the bulb into the universe. At top the legend reads "trademark." Beneath it are the universally recognizable brand or legend "GE" and "Edison Electric bulbs." Running horizontally along the side is the jingle or slogan "Brilliant, Durable, and Economical. Every Electric Shop Sells It." At the bottom of the image is the double triangular logo spelling out AMCO, L460, to identify which cell of a long campaign this cartoon image is, and the Chinese name for AMCO, Shenchang yanghang, within a phrase that means "Chinese-managed" or "management company." "Please mention the *Eastern Miscellany*"; this coupon enabled consumers to get a discount and retailers to feed back social science data to their suppliers/distributors. Ads for AMCO-GE frequently associated images of light with their product, and they put advertising images in highbrow journals to further enlighten readers. While AMCO ads did not, other ads offered free samples in exchange for demographic information. The Cutex hand-care campaign used both a numbered story arc and a coupon to reach potential consumers in highbrow journals like *Ladies' Journal* and *Funü zazhi* (figure 1.8), and so did the heavily flogged Pond's knockoff cream Pond's Extract Cream (figure 1.9).

Vilhelm Meyer built AMCO using a model called "trade" that emerged when the great powers formalized the right to sell branded opium for mass consumption in Chinese treaty ports. Under the Nanjing Treaty of 1842, the British Jardine, Matheson & Company; David Sassoon and Company; and Harrison, King, and Irwin Company could import capital and commodities like opium, tobacco, and infrastructure and export Chinese tea and silver. U.S., Japanese, and French trading companies joined what became a captive commerce in a nominally national economy that had little capacity to regulate its own trade, tariffs, or banking. Then the United States surged capital into the situation, allowing Standard Oil, Getz Brothers and Company, Connell Bros and Company, and little players like AMCO to expand their corporate imperialist footprint. Huge operations like British American Tobacco (BAT) began creating markets for rolled cigarettes, but all transnational LLCs sold machine-produced

1.8 Cutex hand-care ad with coupon. *Funü zazhi*, November 1924.

1.9 Colgate Ribbon Dental Cream with coupon. *Dagongbao* 84, no. 478 (June 7, 1928).

1.10 AMCO ad touting its economy of operation. *Millard's Review*, March 20, 1920.

commodities and advertised their products to promote sales. So beyond assembly lines, steam-powered machines, and reinforced-concrete-and-steel factory architecture, AMCO popularized the industrially produced commodity. From the individual household to local counties or cities, in English- and Chinese-language media, as these examples of ads for "installation warrantee," nationwide access to machinery, building materials, insurance, and Shanghai's treaty port glamor illustrate, whatever you could afford, AMCO had a package for you.[3]

"Trade" required integrated financing and large influxes of finance capital. Peng Changxin has investigated AMCO's innovative business history, and more remains to be learned, but AMCO was one of many traders that became a full-service engineering, architectural construction, and maintenance company.[4] In 1931, in the company's corporate history for its twenty-fifth anniversary, "His Excellency H. H. Kung, Minister of Industries of the National Government of China," provided a note of appreciation about AMCO's help with "extensive industrial development which has taken place in China" and anticipated continued cooperation in "our efforts at reconstruction." Minister Kung Hsiang-hsi's enlisting the company in the "industrial awakening of China" was realistic, given Vilhelm Meyer's experience. After spending four years at the East Asiatic Company and Russo-Asiatic Bank, collaborating in building the modern Chinese banking and lending process, Meyer, who believed that "foreign trade was financed by foreign banks [because few Chinese banks] were interested in financing foreign businesses," drew on his commercial networks.[5] His company, AMCO, financed U.S. companies seeking to sell in the treaty ports and enabled Meyer to land his first engineering contract in 1908, building Mukden Electric Light Works, a power plant in Japanese-dominated Dongbei, or Manchuria.[6]

Before 1917, AMCO and GE had played no role in the Chinese treaty-port economy.[7] According to Emile Garke, that was because each nation-directed, corporate imperialist project chose to electrify its own extraterritorial real estate.[8] The Compagnie Française de Tramways et d'Eclairage Electrique de Shanghai handled the Shanghai French concessions at least as late as 1917, and the British Hong Kong Tramway Company, Limited, served Hong Kong.[9] After 1919, electricity financing shifted away from direct investment. That may be why in the early 1920s AMCO began taking on more; working directly with Gerard Swope (1872–1957), the CEO who ushered GE into consumer-credit schemes and domestic-commodity sales, Meyer began advertising GE domestic products and

1.11 AMCO commodity map spanning the nation. *Dongfang zazhi* 17, no. 22 (November 25, 1920).

1.12 AMCO ad for building products. *Dongfang zazhi* 20, no. 11 (January 10, 1923).

1.13 AMCO ad for industrial factory materials. *Dongfang zazhi* 12, no. 8 (April 25, 1923).

1.14 AMCO ad for mechanical engineering import insurance. *Dongfang zazhi* 19, no. 23 (December 10, 1922).

1.15 AMCO ad for factory machines. *Dongfang zazhi* 19, no. 19 (October 10, 1922).

1.16 AMCO ad for York brand machines. *Dongfang zazhi* 19, no. 23 (April 25, 1924).

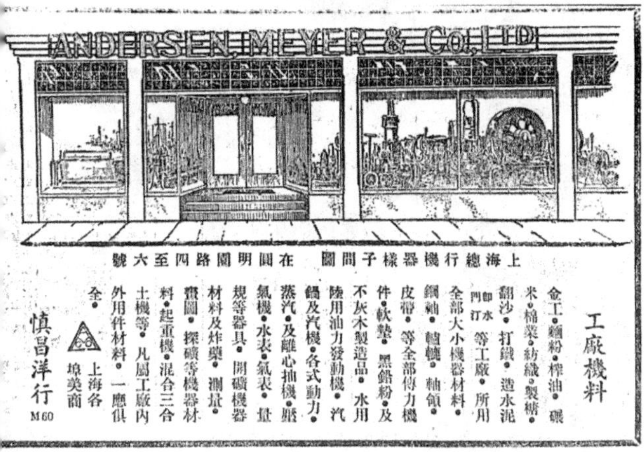

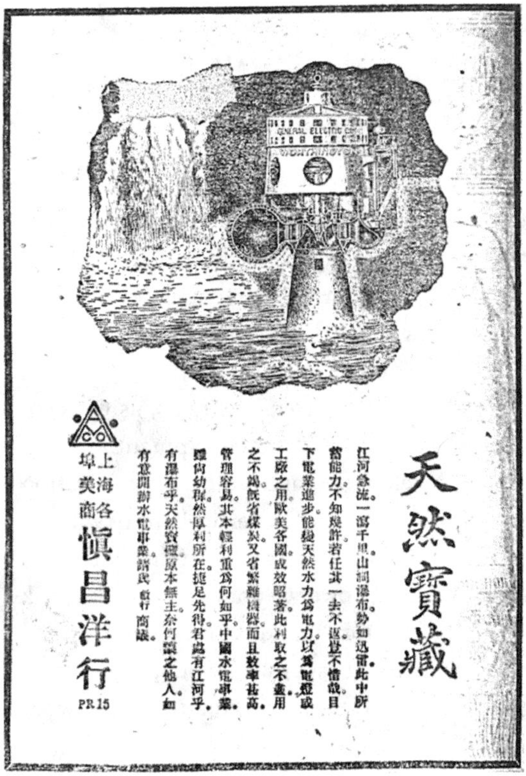

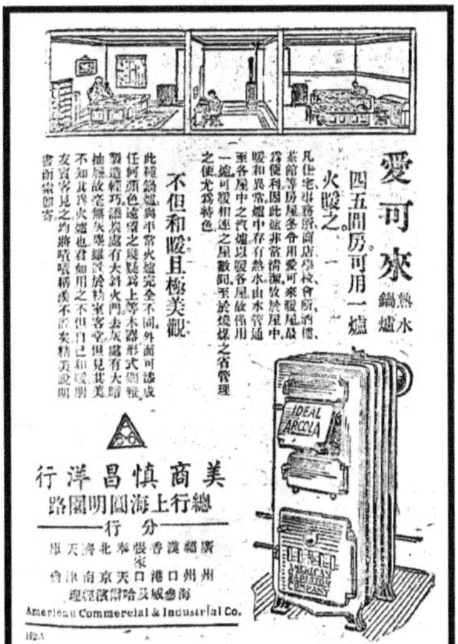

ANDERSEN MEYER & Co. LTD.

工廠機料

慎昌
洋行
上海各
埠美商
M60

上海總機器樣子間閣在聞明園路四至六號

約克
機器

商美

慎昌
洋行
總行上海聞明
園路分行各埠

天然寶藏

上海各
埠美商
慎昌
洋行
PR.15

愛可來

不但和暖且且極美觀

美商 慎昌洋行
總行上海聞明園路
分行
廣福漢香俊北天津埠
海威德哈爾濱天口京南
Americon Commercial & Indusurial Co.

1.17 AMCO ad for machine-generated hydroelectricity. *Dongfang zazhi* 19, no. 15 (August 10, 1922).

1.18 AMCO ad for an Arcola brand radiator. *Dongfang zazhi* 18, no. 22 (November 25, 1921).

general services in Chinese electrification projects.[10] Eventually AMCO conducted large-scale trade in "total packages." These included a feasibility review, scouting for location, financing, architectural design, engineering, installation, and fine-tuning of fixed capital, such as condensers at power plants. Any government could buy AMCO road-construction packages, for instance, to engineer vehicle-friendly streets, using earth rollers, tractors, caterpillar equipment, and "wagon equipment." By 1931 AMCO offered air, water, telegraph, telephone, and radio-communication technology and resembled a "prewar *zaibatsu*," a vertical entity with affiliated holding companies, interlocking directorships (e.g., with GE), overlapping stockholders, and financial power to draw commercial bank credit.[11] A naive assumption that categorical markets preexisted branded commodities or are naturally occurring spaces where people gather to extract profit is not adequate or historical—nor as interesting as what actually happened.[12] Chu-yuan Cheng's history of Standard Oil Company of New York (SOCONY) shows how marketization actually worked. The company decided to open kerosene markets because they wanted to extract microsurplus out of poor communities and kerosene was efficient and cheap. No fuel market existed because the commodity had not previously been available (people used grain oil for light), but SOCONY strategists aimed at a low return. Once the global economy shifted, however, and kerosene prices became unaffordable for villagers, SOCONY began importing automobile fuel, again to build a market that had never existed before.[13] Cheng emphasizes that after its first market-building effort paid off, SOCONY sank financial capital into what it correctly gambled would become a lucrative auto industry. Thus, SOCONY and AMCO incrementally financialized using what Mira Wilkins and her collaborators William J. Hausman and Peter Hertner call *international finance* and theorists Hilferding and Lenin called *financial capital*.[14]

Financial capital flooded newly emerging commerce—this is what colonial modernity is—to naturalize an infrastructural revolution. When Kung, a Chinese official, and an individual known as I. Andersen, a U.S.-based finance broker, agreed to use AMCO-packaged GE generators to develop the nation, the evidence actually shows two parties, one the spokesman for a fragile state and the other a middleman selling and maintaining large-scale corporate imperialist hardware, installing and stabilizing uneven development. Their strategy comes to life in everyday environments, in commercial graphesis like that shown in figures 1.20–1.23 and featuring SOCONY.

The logic is important. Initially, SOCONY had gas but few markets in Chinese treaty ports for autos or auto-related services (figures 1.24 and 1.25). Even drayage or short-distance trucking requires paved roads that, in turn, entail significant changes in financial rationality, investment, and informational advertising media. The company could pivot and resituate its market-building credit operations and financial-package operations because, like other LLCs featured in this chapter, it thrived in conditions where extraterritorial international business law, tariff manipulation, and unequal trade treaties *were held in place* by a succession of fragile Chinese states. More bluntly put, Chinese governments protected foreign direct investment. They guaranteed commercial firms and businesses the legal right to sell. Laws also granted exclusive brand copyrights. Particularly the latter empowered economic entities, from the new advertising industry to

SOCONY TRADE MARK

美孚行

STANDARD OIL CO. OF NEW YORK

The Mark of Quality—known all over the world as the trade mark of the STANDARD OIL CO. OF NEW YORK whose reputation for its high-quality petroleum products reaches every home in China.

美孚商標環
球馳名美孚
石油出品質
料之佳標獨
皆知故中華
人民家庭無
不有美孚出
品也

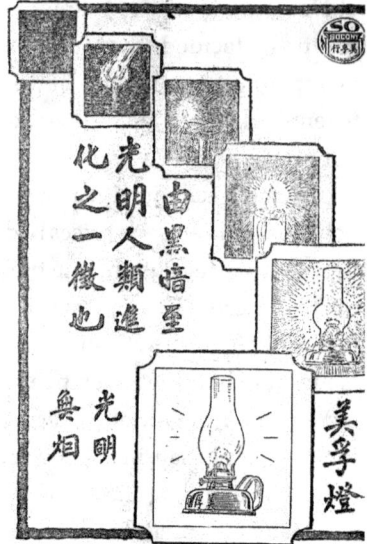

由黑暗至
光明人類進
化之一微也
光明　無烟
美孚燈

點老美孚牌蠟燭
老美孚牌蠟燭質料堅淨白潤冬
夏不變燃之經久明光與泉不同
每包六
支分九
兩十二
兩二種

君之汽車或用汽油或用電力
而汽車油則不可一日缺
君若用過美孚汽車油
則君必知美孚汽車油為最有
效最省費之汽車油因其保護
機件轉動迅速修理之費遂能
減少至最低度
君若尚未用過美孚汽車油則
請早日用之用過之後定知上
述之不虛石繼續用之不已也
美孚行謹啟

1.20 SOCONY brand established. *Dongfang zazhi* 22, no. 1 (January 10, 1925).

1.21 SOCONY ad claiming that kerosene helps humanity evolve. *Dongfang zazhi* 22, no. 1 (March 10, 1924).

1.22 SOCONY candles and female enlightenment. *Dongfang zazhi* 24, no. 1 (January 10, 1927).

1.23 Ad for SOCONY auto gas. *Dongfang zazhi* 18, no. 8 (April 25, 1921).

1.24 SOCONY service station at Rotary Fair, Tianjin, 1930. MADspace #35191.

1.25 SOCONY motor gasoline truck, 1931. MADspace #35024.

purveyors of goods and services, to manufacture and distribute identifiable small and large commodities like medicines, soaps, packaged food, menstrual products, hygienic products, light fixtures and flashlights, alkali, house paint, towels, and cigarettes. Domestic electronics from AMCO sold under Swope's guidance, as Swope made electrification attractive.[15] GE cartoon ads seen in figures 1.26 through 1.30 reinforce electricity's arrival. The map showing the GE logo stretching from the US all the way to China counterbalances a tiny scene of Chinese people enjoying a GE electrical fan.

The symbiosis between AMCO and GE typifies what Hausman, Hertner, and Wilkins call global multinational-enterprise financing of light and power, which they date from the late 1870s. Eventually, GE became

1.26 AMCO-GE ad promoting the company as offering one-stop shopping for all electrical implements. *Dongfang zazhi* 17, no. 22 (April 25, 1921).

1.27 AMCO-GE ad for electric domestic fan. *Funü zazhi* 8, no. 5 (May, 1922).

1.28 AMCO-GE ad for all-purpose electric fan. *Dongfang zazhi* 23, no. 11 (June 10, 1926).

扇電異奇國美
(衣之燿亦)

異電扇一轉涼風習習精神倍奇
興致家中商界學校工廠均不可少。

商

奇
異

各電料店均售

標

夏日酷熱身強神旺得奇

身體涼爽
精神百倍

中國總理
美慎昌洋行

F69

1.29 AMCO-GE ad claiming that an electric fan cools you off and raises your spirits. *Funü zazhi* 22, no. 12 (1925).

光明
耐用

(赤燿之衣)

奇異·安迪生
燈泡

各電料店均售

中國總理美商慎昌洋行

1.30 AMCO-GE ad for electric lighting. *Funü zazhi* 22, no. 2 (January 25, 1925).

China's leading provider of fixed machines, engineering, facilitation, personnel, and sales for electrification.[16] Meanwhile, AMCO facilitated the technology transfer. While AMCO sold GE packages and products intended to link China with the capitalist world, marketers failed to mention that industrial and communications technology becomes obsolete quickly, so that buyers must regularly pour in new capital or take out more loans to keep utilities online. Projecting a market, in other words, and selling the package do not mean that GE performed well or, more to the point, that Chinese and other buyers got what they paid for. Frederick Brown's *The Statistical Year-Book of the World Power Conference, 1933/34* listed China as last except for the French colony of Tunis in the percentage of the population living in areas supplied with electricity, and the per-capita output of electricity in China was so insignificant in these years that it did not even register in Bouda Etemad and Jean Luciani's statistics in *World Energy Production, 1800–1985*.[17]

AREA, CAPITAL, AND THE TREATY-PORT SYSTEM

Defetishizing the woman-centered GE bulb ad has restored to legibility a complex business history and a framework, the commercial capitalist financing of modern infrastructure under conditions of unequal development; later discussions show how and why generic ads appeared, what ads established, and how commercial graphesis conditioned political declarations made in light of these newly discovered modern truths. So far, the GE bulb ad has graphically condensed and made visible a trading company, AMCO, which financed light-bulb distribution and profited from mechanization-related sales and services. Defetishization or ideology critique, however, is a start because the ad also put a new thing into the environment. Ad epistemology paved the way for new stories about the evolutionary rise of humanity, electricity, modern enlightenment, and sexual selection. In this respect, advertising icons like the GE bulb ad agent or the modern woman using Cutex hand-care products highlighted physiologically mammal, natural-footed, menstruating cartoon women and girls in advertising at the center of commodity fantasies about light bulbs, electricity, and electrical generators. Over the half century of its existence, AMCO domestic-commodity ads linked its products and the modern woman figure, an aspirational project of women's liberation undertaken in the name of economic development.

"Treaty portification," Robert Bickers has argued, was an incremental, systematic process that corporate imperialists built in physical space. The Nanyang Brothers Tobacco Company (NBT) and BAT, like AMCO and GE, created "China markets" when they localized finance banking and infrastructure engineering and built factories, and piers. *Bunding* was, Bickers shows, a process of finding a prominent embankment, or *Bund*, along a riverbank or inlet and building a predictable skyline of bank facades, public parks, and trading buildings to expedite activities like inviting in a British Maritime Customs official to negotiate trading concessions from local Chinese elites and enclaving European-style neighborhoods (called *concessions*) for the exclusive use of foreign entrepreneurs, their real estate developers, and so on.[18] In fact, Bunding created a marketing-communications feedback system, with strategic investment planning, knowledge, and management techniques. Advertising was one component in this system, and these ad images for cars, trucks, and tonic medicines are typical images which gratuitously drew in the background new urban or Bund skyscapes (shown in figures 1.31–1.33).[19]

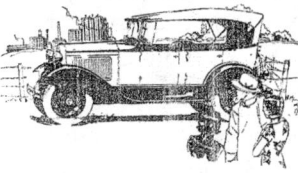

1.31 Ford sedan against the Bund skyline. *Funü zazhi* 22, no. 2 (January 25, 1925).

1.32 Dr. Jayne's Modern Urban Profile. *Dagongbao*, March 1, 1919.

Considering the treaty port to be a functional political and financial system sheds more light on corporate imperialism. Lately, historians less concerned with the drama of sovereignty have focused on how business law in particular worked in a practical sense. The treaty-port legal regime regulated not just torts and criminal law but finance, trade, banking, shipping, landing laws, weights and measures, and contract disputes—the entire gamut of regulations needed to build a capitalist infrastructure, including branding. Treaty-port courts adjudicated international business, particularly investment, to legitimate in political terms who controlled capitalist production and distribution systems. Chiara Betta, Robert Bickers, Jonathan Howlett, Stacie Kent, and Anne Reinhardt, among others, show how, in a context of *ambiguous* sovereignty, economic relations in treaty ports drove the legalization of trade and consequently new commodity product circulation.[20] Finance capital built AMCO and other companies, and the finance-dominated, treaty-port, capitalist political economy thrived because Chinese national sovereignty was so tenuous.

So, when the "area" of area studies is not a culture or a nation or state, one can also envision it as composed of companies operating globally from fixed offices in Chinese treaty ports or linked to

New York, San Francisco, London, and other financial capitals. The Republic of China was forcibly entered into the Westphalian state system late and under unequal diplomatic and economic conditions. This created a conundrum around Chinese sovereignty. Political efforts to *establish* (in the 1911 Nationalist or Xinhai Revolution) or *disestablish* (the 1931 Japanese puppet state of Manchuria) China's national boundaries were one important part of the picture. Another important part was treaty portification by corporate imperialists and local businesses. These components—stated objectives, corporate imperialism's institutional and ideological performance, LLC technologies for pushing financialized colonial markets at the beginning of the twentieth century—formed the arena Mao Zedong termed "semifeudal, semicolonial China."[21]

Ever-present commercial advertisements and commercial ephemera drives home the homely everydayness of this bigger picture. In Hausman, Hertner, and Wilkins's definition, the preferred or multinational twentieth-century financial firm was a business that mobilized foreign direct investments to influence or control foreign activity in which the company invested for strategic goals and expected a return not only from the investment but from the business "package," including technology and its application: "Multinational enterprises are able to concentrate knowledge. Their investments abroad are far more than financial flows [because t]hey involve managed resources."[22] No matter how vociferously the nationalist republic argued that national products protected national capital, in reality, as Hausman, Hertner, and Wilkins show, managed economies are not free to develop their own national strategies or to forge international relations with transnational corporations. Chinese political debates introjected themselves into corporate imperialism, known also by the name twentieth-century multinational financial firm.[23]

Figure 1.34 is an advertisement for the Japanese brand Jintan and encodes information about the company's resource management and technique for building local markets. Similar in allure to the AMCO-GE bulb woman, this ad woman is sitting at a desk surrounded by a cornucopia of commodities, including an electric lamp. She is writing Jintan's brand name in romanized letters. Electricity, light, modern women, commodity culture, and ambiguously named brand products (a "Japanese" product has a "Chinese" name) are presented in the expectation that all elements

1.33 Chevrolet with Bund backdrop. *Shengjing shibao*, July 1922.

1.34 Jintan ad showing a modern liberated woman writing at desk. *Dongfang zazhi*, January 1922, 19:1.

will reinforce each other and associate science, eugenic perfection, high intelligence, the biomorphic female body, commodity culture, and stylishness. The Jintan Corporation was a modern firm, part of the Taylorist Osaka school. Its public profile had a militaristic tone, but its advertising psychology did not vary from that of corporations like AMCO, GE, and BAT. Even more than most Japanese corporate imperialists, Jintan followed the army. Originally selling an herbal digestive, the corporation sculpted product ad campaigns to emphasize the tonic's ancient origins and modern efficacy: after all, the pills are a machine-manufactured, modernist, scientific innovation. A later chapter provides a more detailed corporate history, but here note that the entrepreneurial, technology-savvy Jintan executives advertised a world where free modern people benefited from Japanese commodities. Hausman, Hertner, and Wilkins's analysis helps consolidate evidence that these markets were *extranational yet areal* in the sense of areas formed of similarly organized corporations and imperialist authority. And sitting comfortably on top is the healthy, literate, socially competent, liberated, organically female, consumer and producer woman. Sophisticated, patient, agglomerative, and policy driven, Jintan survived or failed to survive on the basis of its capacity to measure circumstances and put into action strategic profit-making schemes. But large-scale change does not announce itself as a totality. Buried in ephemera are conditions delivered piecemeal, still available to be used in the effort to explain why people and businesses thought what they did and how graphic association worked.

THE NATION FETISH VERSUS MANAGEMENT KNOWLEDGE

Earlier I proposed that LLCs formed the sine qua non for corporate imperialism, so what about Chinese corporations? Sherman Cochran's comparative study of Jintan and the Chinese Ailuo brain-tonic brands has indicated that nationalist appeals for commodities produced in China, in factories that Chinese people owned, did little to divert Chinese consumers who showed a marked preference for GE, Jintan, or BAT cigarettes.[24] No Chinese national brands among the national and nationalist companies selling medicine, drugs, cigarettes, and other domestic commodities succeeded in wresting market share away from the corporate giant Jintan, and none ever created an advertising chimera as powerful as Brunner, Mond & Co (China) Ltd., a European chemical alkali fertilizer conglomerate.

The importance of management or organizational technology also seems clear in the more famous and successful case of Nanyang Brothers Tobacco, NBT, founded in 1906.[25] This brand has not been extensively studied as a modern LLC, perhaps because it is so frequently presumed to have represented national (or ethnic or racialized) capital and partly because it brings contradictions to the surface, as Robert Gardella, Jane K. Leonard, and Andrea McElderry have noted.[26] The company exemplifies why the LLC and advanced business methods sold so much more product under conditions that Cochran called a Sino-Western "rivalry" and I am calling corporate imperialism.[27]

A consortium of overseas Chinese living in British Malaya, directed by Jian Yujie (1875–1957) and Jian Zhaonan (1870–1923) and registered under successive Chinese governments and the colonial state in Hong Kong over the course of its checkered existence, NBT was a joint-stock LLC.[28] It seems to have operated like other cigarette companies, importing tobacco from the United States, soliciting capital from funds around the world, and marketing heavily in Chinese and Southeast Asian cities.[29] Its singularity lay in its dubious claim that it represented Chinese sovereignty. Elisabeth Köll, summarizing the work of historians like Rajeswary Ampalavanar Brown, Parks Coble, and Karl Gerth, shows that the original founders, who were brothers, adopted the pattern of multinational sourcing (Hong Kong, Malaysia, and Japan) and pioneered rolled cigarette markets primarily in areas free of taxes and monopolies, such as Thailand, Malaya, Indonesia, and Borneo. When NBT tried to enter China, it went head-to-head with BAT, and it bombed. Rather than back out of the trade competition, NBT reconsolidated. In 1918 it registered itself with the then Chinese government under warlord Duan Qirui's puppet president, Xu Shuzheng. Interestingly, in the post-1927 White Terror, the Chiang Kai-shek coup to exterminate the Chinese Communist Party, Chiang's Nationalist Party put forward its political apparatchik, T. V. Soong, who forced NBT to appoint him as the firm's CEO. After the civil war, the People's Republic of China nationalized NBT and licensed it to sell the popular brand Double Happiness.[30] Here the nation plays a fetishistic, not a substantive, role because claiming NBT is nationalist or represents national capital has proven untrue. Certainly, ethnicized and racialized Chinese migrants ran the corporation, but it, like all firms linked to finance capital investment, obeyed the same requirements that made corporate capitalism profitable, NBT's self-presentation and nationalist charisma notwithstanding.

National brands and faux national-brand cigarettes like NBT traded on the same set of clichés as imperialist brands like BAT. In the tobacco advertising I have seen, nothing particularly nationalistic appears in national-brand iconography. Figure 1.35, a Colleen Moore–style, short-bobbed flapper invites everyone to smoke high-quality tobacco as she gazes out of the window of her wallpapered mansion, perching on a modernist chaise lounge and gazing speculatively at a billboard for her favorite tobacco brand, White Golden Dragon, seemingly set in a landscaped garden. In figure 1.36, the smoker is presumed male, while the female icon enhances the pleasure that smoking brings. This is not to say women did not smoke, for they obviously did, and ads sometimes addressed women; rather, much advertising slanted toward a consumer who desired bio-women. Figure 1.37 is branded the Beauty. According to the ad copy, these cigarettes are colorful and luscious, fruity and kissable, and worth the money a gent pays to smoke the yummy Beauty brand, a national-product cigarette: the ad ran regularly in the trendsetting, cutting-edge, progressive cultural journal New Youth (Xin qingnian). In this advertising fantasy a female smoker interrogates a mustachioed gentleman sitting on a cushy sofa: "Sir, do you love beautiful women?" she asks. It turns out that it is natural to love beautiful women but that such women have drawbacks, including being scary and ill-tempered and expecting to get showered with jewels and luxury goods. Yes, the fantasy woman responds, that is true. However, when you buy a packet of the Beauty brand, you can cuddle it, spend almost nothing on it, avoid balefulness, and be assured of "timeless never-ending love." What is nationalist about this ad?

Perhaps the global economy just was not hospitable to national capital. For instance, Man Bun Kwan's case history of the Yongli-Jiuda Salt Company shows that this Chinese company overcame (that is, took major market share away from) the British-owned Brunner Mond Corporation only when Yongli-Jiuda began selling "Chinese" chemicals in Japan, which means profits came when Chinese owners sold products to the national enemy. In other words, his intricate case history presents a situation in which a Chinese national product achieved superior market share over its British competitor in East Asia but only in Japan's home market. To take the lead in market share among corporations vying to maintain China's weak sovereignty may or may not be considered a national capital.[31] Moreover, large transnationals like Brunner Mond (aka Imperial Chemical Industries [ICI]) competed against other giant

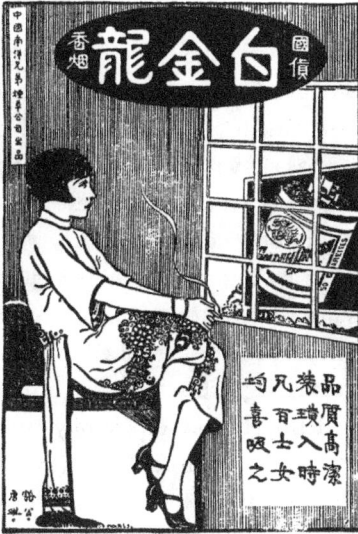

1.35 Nanyang Brothers brand cigarette ad showing a Colleen Moore–style bob-haired girl smoking. *Dongfang zazhi* 24, no. 23 (December 1, 1927).

1.36 Nanyang Brothers ad showing a kissable girl smoking. *Dongfang zazhi* 25, no. 9 (May 1, 1928).

1.37 Nanyang Brothers ad claiming that smoking is better than sex. *Xin qingnian* 4. May 1918.

請問先生！
你也愛美女麼？
那是自然，但是娶女有三件事。
很可怕，你知道麼？
第一美女會老。第二美……
女會鬧脾氣。第三美女要有金珠鑽石和那一切奢侈品的供應。
你這話誠然不錯，但是你要避免這三件事，可以每天去買
一盒美女牌香煙吸吸！你瞧他盒子上那位絕色美
女，不是你的懷中愛寵麼？他又不會老，又不要金
錢揮霍，又不會撒嬌嗔怨，一輩子廝戀著你，愛情永遠
不滅，這有多麼好呢。

烟中自有顏如玉

中國南洋兄弟煙艸公司

multinationals (IG Farben, for instance), not little ones like Yongli-Jiuda. During the period of Kwan's study, Brunner Mond's major competitor, the German-based transnational IG Farben, was already a colossus, dividing Europe and its colonies and situating industrial chemical production in a global economy. China's colonial markets played a trivial role in World War I, although, as Mark Metzler has shown, the relation of the liberal economic order and Japan's leveraged investment in Chinese colonies floated on the back of the unstable London gold standard.[32]

In any case, Madeline Zelin, William Kirby, and other scholars cited here have strenuously argued that it is not possible to determine what is or is not a Chinese company.[33] Zelin in particular established that beginning in the seventeenth century, "informal legal structures" regulated Chinese contract law. Shares of trusts were bought and sold, family capital rationally invested, business management had a professional (extra-kin-based) grounding, and unjust business practices were punishable in courts of law. According to Zelin, the Qing (the Manchu and final Chinese dynasty, 1644–1911) government had a legal platform capable of accommodating the LLC and, by the eighteenth century, offered merchants legal options similar to the capitalist firm. As dynastic authority and its legal system collapsed in the nineteenth and twentieth centuries, the four categories of allowable business companies—"co-partnership, limited company, joint stock company, and joint stock companies limited"—held firm even before the advent of international business law. This makes the question of how business concerns were or were not Chinese even more complex. Since there was no Chinese way of doing business, why, Zelin asks, "*once provided with the option of limited liability,* did few Chinese firms choose to register?"[34]

Only two of these many contradictions are pertinent here. First, NBT never qualified as a Chinese company to begin with, and, second, given that it was an LLC, its failure to outcompete BAT may have nothing to do with national or ethnic origins. In both its organizational structure and the remarkable extrasovereign sources of its manufacturing material and investment capital, NBT took its profits in complexly transnational commodity chains, selling industrially produced, machine-rolled cigarettes. By extension, although there were individual Chinese-citizen titans like Mu Xiangyue (1876–1943), who translated and popularized Frederick Winslow Taylor's *The Principles of Scientific Management* in Chinese, and advertiser and entrepreneur Huang Chujiu (1872–1931), who also had tremendous business acumen and amassed a fortune, "Chinese business" is not a coherent category, and Chineseness does not register in business terms.[35] This is a loaded argument. Others have pointed out that Chinese Maoist reconstruction hinged on belief that national capital could be captured and nationalized, its profits diverted into building a national economy. How delinking worked under the dictatorship of the proletariat lies beyond my scope at this point. This much is clear. Understanding how commercial capital linked to international investment funds and their internal organizational technologies may be a more effective way to understand corporate imperialism in China than nationalism or sovereignty.[36]

AMORPHOUS BRANDS, SOCIAL LOGIC, AND PUBLIC SCENES

Ambiguous cultural or national identity in relation to business law, capitalist accounting methods, aggressive marketing plans, and graphic images used in branding speaks to the dissimilarity between semiotic analysis and historical reconstruction. Semiosis does not make something happen, and it does not construct itself. It also does not construct a nation or "China." That said, graphesis conveys historical truths, and it behooves us to figure out how. Often underappreciated, the late nineteenth- and early twentieth-century commodity advertising campaigns pivoted around brand marks and cartoon brand building. In publications and out in the urban world, branded commodities communicated visually; they invited viewers and consumers to enter into a modern society. Figure 1.38 is a microexample of how commercial art branded the commodity and synced the commodity to the society.

In the Silver Shell oil ad, the viewer sees poetic copy hovering in the sky: "Air is so fresh in the deep green space [of the boulevard] / The new gas auto goes down the road quickly and lithely / Without Shell brand APC gas / Finding a smooth ride is not possible." The image's style comes from lithographs like the famous images published between 1884 and 1898 as the *Dianshizhai huabao* (literally *Illustrated News of the Dianshizhai Lithographic Studio*) presenting Shanghai's foreign concessions and celebrating their European-style parks, gardens, and trees; paved boulevards; vehicles; and people walking, riding bicycles, and going to pleasure halls or out with their courtesans. In this reupped contemporary image, the artist has used a European-style, central-vanishing-point perspective to graphically open a gateway to society. The Asia Pacific

1.38 Silver Shell brand ad. *Shengjing shibao* 74 (May 1906).

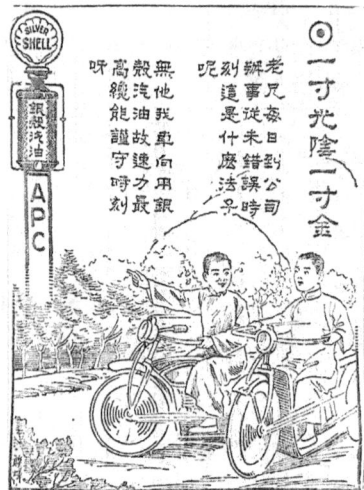

1.39 Silver Shell brand ad. *Dagongbao,* November 13, 1929.

Company (APC) distributed Silver Shell–branded gas, using stoplights and gas pumps to form a literal gate onto the parkway as pictured in the SOCONY images (see figures 1.5 and 1.24). Here, studying visual forms for their latent precepts helps show where philosophy is dug into the environment and where dormant and inert visual epistemology can be blasted out of the past. In figure 1.39, the same brand and the same ad artist have two friends extolling the efficiency of APC gas stations on their way to work.

Commercial and legal processes put brand images into circulation in treaty-port environments. Zuo Xuchu's history of modern Chinese trademarks and copyright law dates the standardization of trademark registration to 1904. Zuo argues that between 1911, when the dynasty fell, and 1927, when the Nationalist Party seized the state, the history of law is fragmented. Piecing together what he believes to have been turning points, Zuo shows that the Beiyang military junta of 1913 established the trademark registration system on May 3, 1923.[37] Regardless of which state claimed sovereignty at the time, the *Trademark Gazette* (*Shangbiao gongbao*) continued registering brands throughout the Beiyang and Nationalist periods. Zuo helps clarify a legal process that saw corporations from all over the world focused on industrial brands as tools to carve out sales territories. To achieve and register their commercial rights, business organizations disarticulated and reassembled their relationships to regional language, orthography, quotidian clichés or norms, national origin, and nationality into repeatable, recognizable, literate, and interestingly distilled and aggregated marks that formed the face of the brand.[38]

The legal (not to mention the commercial) status of branding means that ads are not representations. They are not merely racist slogans frozen into coded form but rather epistemic (and ideological) truths about actual existing conditions. However latent in the environment, these figurations provide information about where the investment capital came from, and how modern capitalism worked in treaty ports since corporations were usually headquartered in metropolitan areas outside the Chinese mainland. In this regard, brand-marked commercial ephemera induced contemporaries to participate in an emergent, financializing, twentieth-century cultural life. Among its many registered or copyright-protected ad elements, Brunner Mond touted this "moth-eyebrow moon" along with a double axe and a thumbs-up sign. To protect brand identity during what they anticipated would be a long period of market development, gargantuan corporate imperialists registered each element of their mark. Figure 1.40 is a good example, a registered Brunner Mond (Buneimen) ad element. These elements combine variously to create lovely posters, like the following image which shows an internationally fashionable woman standing in a field overlooking a pond and a manor house (figure 1.41) and another showing a young girl holding a cabbage, wearing a European red dress, and smiling at the viewer (figure 1.42). These ads recycled brand mark elements and feature remarkable, lovely women, but also focused attention on internationalism, which is another way to reference the colonial world. Thus, for instance, while Brunner Mond relied heavily on images of a classic, sexy Shanghai modern-girl icon, the British H. C. Dixon and Son yarn ad portrayed a mosque, which in the British Empire signified the alleged oriental or "Turkish" treatment of the tobacco. A Japanese corporation produced Washington-brand resin and another the widely advertised Novonol brand (no Japanese language name provided) gonorrhea remedy. In other words, female image often organized the ad design, but female cartoons are only one element of the composite "international" advertising image.

1.40 Brunner Mond fertilizer ad illustrating how the brand registered elements of its advertising art in the Brand Registry.

Counterintuitively, the corporation's putative nationality and cultural coding on brands rarely coincided. Great examples of this tendency to fabricate cosmopolitan brands are the neotraditional or "Chinese-style" advertisements associated with foreign-owned companies; the German corporation Norddeutsche Wollkämmerei und Kammgarnspinnerei tried to copyright the most famous neotraditional story of female devotion ever told, that of Mengzi's mother, who changed her domicile three times to ensure the boy sage would have morally upright friends. La Compagnie Optorg Corporation (a French-registered company selling woolen textiles in the 1920s but originally a Russian-based multinational or colonial conglomerate, still in existence today, and selling agricultural machines) recycled old clichés about neotraditional Chinese feminine beauties.[39] National products, producers, or companies that identified themselves as making patriotic goods did not hesitate to do the same. Perhaps these images were to indicate stylishness over race or nationality. In any case, copyrighted images show a preference for American and English cultural codes and an association of European visual and language references to "civilized" commodities. Perhaps Chinese-owned small companies over-internationalized their images, while Japanese firms Americanized theirs, perhaps to avoid Chinese anti-Japanese boycotts. Clearly, however, though brands indiscriminately

1.42 Brunner Mond fertilizer ad with a girl holding a cabbage. From the collection of Tani Barlow. This image is crinkly because it came out of a mattress. When political movements demonized commercial advertising images, rural people took them down and put up colorful pictures of Chairman Mao. They crumpled up the old commercial posters, and made them into insulation.

1.41 Brunner Mond fertilizer ad showing stylishly dressed woman in front of pond. From the collection of Tani Barlow.

borrowed national markings, these compounded images were anything but casual. The *Trademark Gazette* clarifies how seriously corporate imperialists took future-market planning. SOCONY registered "Pine Brand" and "White Rose Oil" trademarks for kerosene and associated kerosene products, which appear to be different names for the same commodity; it never reached the market. In addition, SOCONY trademarked the names Spinrex, Turex, Darex, and Cylbrex for types of oil and oil-burning accoutrements, in anticipation of market advertising. No images accompanied the brands, and the company appears never to have used these names or marked commodities under them.[40]

Trademark icons saturated the visual field, as pioneering historian of advertising Roland Marchand argued a generation ago when he demonstrated that U.S. advertisers were "apostles of modernity." The "social tableaux" in the United States featured a newly minted housewife-subject taking command over her scientific household laboratory to solve all the novel (and imaginary) problems that modernity could throw at her, such as disease and sanitation, including her own bodily excretions (smelly armpits and so on). The new housewife's problems could be solved with new products, whether vermin-vanquishing DDT shot into hidden crevices or GE household products that liberated her from (redundant, newly invented) labor in the newfangled kitchen.[41]

Chinese treaty-port advertising graphesis played the same role but with a difference. Treaty-port advertisers drew *social scenes* in black-and-white cartoons. Treaty-port images focused less on housewification and more on the procreative couple and particularly on the female partner. This happened at every level of graphesis. For instance, while eighteenth-century Chinese iconography might show a marital bed in a large family dwelling, twentieth-century ads situated natural women and men in living in their own private houses and socializing in the workplace. Small or nuclear families were not the preference in nineteenth-century Chinese family theory or practice, and the nuclear or "stem" family had only the marital bed (figure 1.43) in the larger family, not their own house or even necessarily their own room. Commercial aspirations for private small-family spaces abruptly and visually reinforced a modernist sociological truth: that the nuclear family is the basis of society, and the woman is a copartner in modern family life (figure 1.44). There is nothing intuitive

1.43 Eighteenth-century marital bed. Origin unknown https:// commons .wikimedia.org /wiki/File:China _Marital_bed .jpg.

1.44 Dr. Yan's brand medicinal tonic ad with an image of a modern marital bed. *Dagongbao*, March 17, 1919.

1.45 AMCO ad selling Pacific brand bathroom appliances. *Dongfang zazhi* 21, no. 11 (June 10, 1924).

1.46 An ad for Éclat toiletry products showing mother and child in bathroom. *Funü zazhi* 10, no. 1 (1924).

1.47 Colgate ad showing a modern woman's boudoir. *Dagongbao* 386 (April 7, 1922), 60.

about this truth, as I will show later. Not surprisingly, however, ad culture promoted nuclearization when it hawked hardware for indoor flush toilets and running water; the modern bathroom (figure 1.45)—an AMCO package—and the nuclear couple enjoying modern partner marriage in a dreamscape of house, sexually appropriate accoutrements, and personal auto (figure 1.46). Ads show fantastic scenes of private bathing and interiors of intimate, domestic family life, depicting the new bourgeois order of the wife, who appears at her vanity table (figure 1.47), the husband, and the children in their own quarters (figure 1.48), sans parents, in-laws, cousins, friends, and servants. Later chapters elaborate the sociological assumptions showcased in these ads, set out in public graphesis. Here the point is balder: imaginary forms of value expressed in advertising cartoons, the other scenes of use value, reinforced the new platitude that humans live in societies of their own making and that one progressive evolutionary option is commodity purchase and use. These ads are sociological and not by accident. Corporate ads conveyed a component, women, who like the GE light-bulb girl, herself an ad agent, live in society by virtue of natural rights, education, and social evolution.

The event of women is confirmed in these corporate imperialist commodity ads starring ordinary (which is to say not courtesan or sexually compromised, like movie actresses) women who have legitimately left the chaste women's domestic quarters to play public social roles in a new, marketized world. Marketized, commercialized conditions would situate women at the nexus of the modern advertising industry, critical and empirical theories of society, and the early twentieth-century theory and practice of commercial capital. The corporate story of BAT shows this nexus: BAT was like AMCO but bigger, and because BAT sold industrially rolled and packaged cigarettes under multiple brand names, it is famous for creating a market in products that have no use value; their value lies in the fantastic scenes or dreamscapes that advertising technology enacts. According to Howard Cox's celebrated monograph *The Global Cigarette: Origins and Evolution of British American Tobacco, 1880–1945*, BAT imported tobacco produced around the world, trained a racially mixed staff and advertisers of many nationalities, and financed a sociologically based market-building technology.[42] In what became a pattern, BAT first bought a medium-size, regionally significant, Chinese-owned advertising agency, Wing Tai Vo (WTV) or Yong Tai He. Now when the news media markets opened, this Chinese-owned business advertised

1.48 GE brand electric fan ad showing a happy man in a nuclear-family setting. *Dongfang zazhi* 18, no. 13 (July 10, 1921).

its own advertising services in the financial newspaper *Shen Bao*. But Cox shows that BAT wanted WTV's local knowledge of potential consumers, learning how WTV targeted consumers and what accounts it handled.

Then, interestingly, BAT not only suspended its native-informant policy but also authorized a WTV employee, Zhang Bozhao (1861–1951), to market his own brand, called Great Britain (Dayingpai). It is unclear whether or not Zhang's product was a rebranding of BAT's Ruby Queen. The adaptation by BAT of a local Cantonese nickname for a product that literally means "Red Tinfoil Package" and the long campaigns to establish Ruby Queen suggest they might have been two brands. In any case, Zhang copied BAT's business plan and engineered a way to make WTV tobacco services a subsidiary of BAT, the larger corporate imperialist. By one chronology, Zhang had also sold cigars and raw tobacco that he purchased in the Philippines, so while the ad arm remains relatively mysterious, the tobacco sales record makes sense. If this story bears out, then Zhang was a subimperialist working in the same commercialized commodity streams as BAT.[43]

Although BAT and AMCO sold different commodities, they had the same internal finance and accounting technologies. The difference is that BAT excelled in market formation. It not only relied on WTV but assimilated it. It transformed Chinese-owned firms, and while keeping those brands viable, BAT aggressively branded, marketed, distributed, and leveraged itself and its technologies to form an umbrella over all of its acquired or new, market-tested brands. In figure 1.49, the artist has drawn bats flying in the sky, thus presenting two jokes. The Chinese national language makes the noun for the flying bat a homonym for the character *fu* (branded as *fuk* in Cantonese pronunciation), or good fortune, so the brand is literally called *fortune*. Not every viewer would automatically see this language game, but in the early 1920s, a period of linguistic and visual hijinks brought the potential buyer to "an omen

1.49 BAT cigarette ad showing literal bats indicating good fortune. *Dagongbao*, March 29, 1922.

of prosperity," referencing the bat's role in Chinese popular arts and drawing attention to all the brands BAT sold. Mirroring BAT's iconography, a literal flying bat, "bat" in English is a homonym for "good omen" in Chinese, which might have been a funny bit of news in the coming commodity order.[44]

Dreamscapes of word and image are epiphenomenal in BAT's actual practices, which made native informants and punning secondary to sociological market building. Traveling salesmen of all nationalities used BAT's Form 163 to report pertinent sales information back to BAT headquarters. The fill-in blanks included the name of the town or village, population size, names of local tobacco dealers, location of merchandise depots, brands currently on sale, currency exchange rates in any specific locale (allowing BAT to undercut competitors), income stratification in the village, and questions about the likely consumer base. Granular sociological information meant BAT-China established one of the most innovative marketing-management systems in the world.[45] Its basic profit generator was signed contracts with local agents who put up sufficient collateral, meaning the company risked nothing. It extended credit to a vendor in the form of BAT-packaged cigarettes. If products sold, then BAT profited; if not, it lost nothing and apparently retrieved the product. On the basis of its social-data feedback system, BAT had figured out how to organize just-in-time tobacco delivery and stabilize inventory. The feedback loop allowed BAT sales outlets to adjust accounting and management to localities and to open possible profit each step of the way.

According to Cox, BAT managed a full-blown distribution mechanism of its own making: it retooled existing Chinese trading companies along these modern social logics and economic rationalities, "instituting an administrative framework that brought within its organizational compass a great many of the established trading firms that were already serving the traditional Chinese economy and by allowing certain of the elements within this distribution mechanism *to compete against one another*."[46] So, repeating the trick mentioned earlier, where the LLC grafted itself onto older mercantile practices, BAT grafted U.S. and European financial methods onto an already networked population of mercantile companies and expanded the rolled-cigarette market into rural China using sociological surveys. In that regard, BAT resembles the Japanese Southern Manchuria Railway Corporation, or Mantetsu, which also conducted detailed village sociologies as it laid railway service in Japanese-occupied Northeast China. The graphesis of BAT, its remarkable ability to convey ideas and associations in graphic form, also gave it a leg up. In at least one case, a BAT subsidiary trade company branded "New York" learned through failing brands that girl images were the sine qua non component in successful advertising. In the New York brand's advertising images, only three (out of forty-plus images) pictured female figures, and all of them were bound-footed kin in the segregated women's quarters of a large, patrilineal family dwelling.[47] Figure 1.50, one of these, shows cloistered women looking decidedly unsexy, engaged in conventional women's work sewing cloth shoes. The Two Gorgeous Girls cosmetics brand would test for gendered images, too, before founder Nakamura decided on an all-girl-icon blitz campaign. Whether BAT also field-tested brand images in the market before it settled on the social-woman image has not yet been established, but it is probable. Tested or not, precedent drawings in a 1900 edition of the twelfth-century *Family Regulation* (*Zhuzi jiali*) by Zhu Xi (figure 1.51), a Martin Luther equivalent in the history of Chinese thought, suggest how ads and old texts were generically the same, modern and compatible.

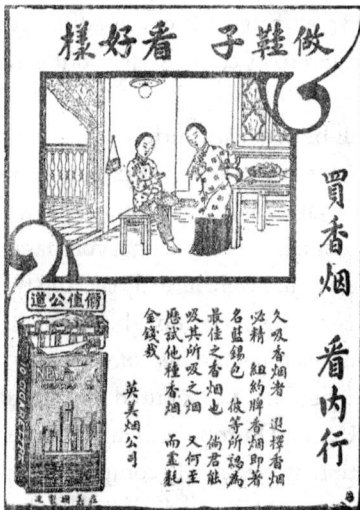

1.50 Ad for New York brand showing cloistered women being hectored by patriarchal family man. *Dagongbao*, June 5, 1919.

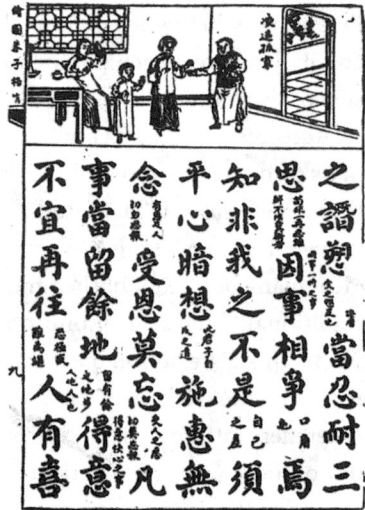

1.51 Image from a 1900 republication of twelfth-century scholar Zhu Xi's *Family Rule Book*.

Conditions for thinking about the future, the ground for the struggle over whether China would remain an adjunct to corporate imperialism, a national brand rather than a chimerical, sovereign capitalist nation, are scattered here, immanent in commercial ephemera and their situated histories. The various relationships of national capital, corporate imperialism, sovereignty, colonialism, and anticapitalist or revolutionary organizing suggest that the logic of the nation and the logics of commercial capitalization are not possible to completely disentangle. Not only is the "area" in area studies unusable in this context, but sovereignty itself is just one of many elements conditioning thought, business models, investment strategies, and profit seeking. Visionary prophets from Mu Xiangyue, promoter of Taylor's *The Principles of Scientific Management*, to He-Yin Zhen, an anticapitalist feminist anarchist, were not parochial, or just national, or even regional in a physical, geographic sense because they were, in theory and in fact, *extra*national.[48] By the same token, so was Rudolf Hilferding, who in 1910 coined the term *finance capital*.[49] Just as Lenin and Rosa Luxemburg had, Hilferding figured out how to explain anticipated changes just unfolding in his lifetime. All wrote in the future anterior and anticipated totalities that we now clearly discern with the benefit of hindsight. Hilferding began his analysis of changes in industrial capitalism with these words: "The most characteristic features of 'modern' capitalism are those processes of concentration which, on the one hand, 'eliminate free competition' through the formation of cartels and trusts, and on the other, bring bank and industrial capital into an ever more intimate relationship."[50]

Hilferding described corporations like AMCO that organized business planning around financial funds, banks, and holding companies. For instance, AMCO had struck a relation with the Pacific Commercial Company of Manila, which at one time had owned it (at least on paper) and actually financed AMCO's expansion, exactly illustrating Hilferding's point. The creation of surplus value valorizes capital, and valorizing capital, he recognized, was the whole point of capitalism. So, when AMCO or BAT traded in promissory notes and credit, they transformed how goods were exchanged. Under capitalism, there are use and exchange values, the labor process that produces and the value-creating process that commodifies human labor and produces money surplus. Credit is one way to marketize money capital. Gerard Swope did that in the early 1920s when he expanded GE's capacity to market consumer or domestic appliances and extend consumer-credit services. In these times—for Hilferding the first decade of the twentieth century—capitalism showed tremendous change. Financialized industrialization was accumulating what he termed "idle capital," or money capital that was not circulating, was not producing surplus. Entrepreneurs like Meyer captured this idle, unproductive money capital and started marketizing it, or lending it out in the form of financing for a steam engine or, à la BAT, collateralized machine-rolled cigarettes sold in tins.

Hilferding describes a banking system in which banks lend one another idle capital at short-term rates. This is the promissory note or extended credit that BAT developed in its rural markets. Based on survey information, BAT invented a new credit cycle at the micro or village consumer/distributor level. Once survey agents had established how much discretionary capital was available to men in villages, the company set an affordable price for Hataman smokes, for instance, sometimes undercutting their own profit margin or undercutting another BAT brand, Ruby Queen, and forwarded inventory to the village distributor. For Hilferding, this is how banks and financial or lending institutions became the arbiters of the business cycle. They, too, measured the long-term sales arc for capital itself. Financial entities stepped in when there were shortfalls in commodity production, shortfalls in payment of the notes, or any failures to make good on a loan. In the larger system, Hilferding points out, extension of intramural cash into caches of idle money meant consolidated capital would end up in the hands of larger corporations and transnational corporations on the international scale.[51] Again, we see this in action when BAT assimilated WTV and GE assimilated AMCO. Hilferding points out that when financing gains importance in a business cycle, transnational corporations become viable in a new way. However, the historical moment immanent within capital requires specific historical conditions to materialize, and that is precisely what AMCO achieved. And with regard to how we understand conditions of thinking, these ongoing events in commercialization and banking histories, philosophy, and political economy set the framework of intelligibility. Commercial ephemera and their material contribution in Chinese treaty-port societies help to evidence what those historical conditions actually were.

Adapting Hilferding in this context helps to clarify the general conditions that commercial capital would come to involve. To bankers, commercial researchers, and writers in Chinese treaty ports at the turn of the twentieth century, the German theorist's points were not philosophical at all. On the ground in Shanghai, for instance, theorists were explaining and anticipating changes as they comprehended them. Srinivas Ram Wagel, a Sikh business reporter working at the *North-China Daily News and Herald* in Shanghai published an important analysis in his 1914 study *Finance in China*. Wagel reflected a similar point to Hilferding, extrapolating in a negative sense that native banks did not keep reserves in silver or gold and that meant they could not be productive or financially sound. Wagel explained that Chinese financial infrastructure had lagged behind the international system (no standard, no silver-to-gold market, no capital reserves in native banks, no silver mines in Mexico, and so on) since the global shift in the mid-nineteenth century to the London-based gold standard. China had remained on its wobbly silver standard, but it had never addressed the question of abstract value since its old-fashioned commercial networks had worked on trust relations rather than universal exchangeability. The greatest anomaly, Wagel thought, was that Chinese banks and financiers did not float value. "The values of commodities in China being in silver, and the values of commodities in other parts of the world being in gold," he argued, was part of the problem.[52] A more profound concern was that neither metal stabilized as the measure of value. In the native Chinese economy, gold and silver were both commodities, though silver had more universal value than gold. Because gold and silver were both fundamentally commodities and not what Wagel called "measures of value," the abstract quality of the metal could not be extricated from its simple value as a thing, a preindustrial commodity.[53] This led to instability at the economy's core because "gold . . . is simply a commodity while silver, although it is still considered a commodity, is also a measure of value" that can be depreciated (silver from Mexico) or devaluated back into a use value (dowry jewelry). In a capitalist manufacturing economy, instability and interchangeability of value and commodity got outproduced by a massive inpouring of commercial capital. Lacking its own financialized money, the local economy lost ground to international forces. This argument led Wagel to conclude that "the fundamental difficulty with all industrial progress in China, as in most of the Asiatic countries, is the lack of capital."[54] And Wagel was by no means the only local capitalist economist theorizing treaty-port conditions.

J. D. Edkins, a former missionary and researcher, approached the question of value from a deeply localist perspective and seemingly sought to advise Chinese banking officials in the late Qing period. His 1905 *Banking and Prices in China* frankly described the role that financialized capital was playing in the great economic transformation he saw emerging. In particular, foreign banks, which he also called "colonial syndicates," poured surplus money into urban infrastructure, building the real estate market and the commercial outlets and financing factories (flour, cotton, silk, concrete), and this financialization changed the Chinese economy beyond recognition. Commercialized money capital, pouring in from national banks and fly-by-night capital-holding companies all over the world, valued capital in relation to the gold standard and put local, relatively inflexible merchants and banks at a disadvantage. Edkins more than Wagel outlined in tremendous detail how the gold standard worked and what role gold played in stabilizing colonial economies; banks in Hong Kong, India, and Australia participated in the financialization of banking in Chinese treaty ports. These national banks played a role in national economies and in international commerce because they provided the necessary metal collateral, gold in most cases. Not only did China not have a national bank, he pointed out, but it also barely had a mint because metals serving as tokens of exchange could take the form of a lump and did not require a banking imprimatur.[55]

Wagel, Edkins, and Hilferding were prescient and knowledgeable. Ji Zhaojin's recent general history of banking in China notes that the rise of foreign commercial banks began in 1847 and that over the next half century commercial capital overwhelmed the banking and investment conditions.[56] Only in 1895, with its government under unbearable stress, did the Qing state finally establish a national bank that stabilized Chinese currency, leaving the government prey to unpayable loans in durable, predatory currencies. After the Xinhai Revolution, the political successors seized control over banking systems, but this also collapsed when the ruling party stacked the national bank with apparatchiks. Here intellectual history and the local theorization of ongoing events lay out the conditions for understanding what the commercial capital, its commodity culture, and its ephemera mean historically. The range of goods and services AMCO offered fits Hilferding's description of how finance capital made specific commodities viable in a place like China in the 1920s and 1930s. His model also helps explain how the advertising business mushroomed into a profit-generating industry. As I develop in later chapters, very large firms like the British-owned Millington, largish companies like Shanghai-based C. P. Ling Company, and smaller players like Carl Crow were all intermediaries for major global business advertising accounts (Ford, Coca-Cola, Colgate Palmolive, Lever Brothers, Heinz, Parker Pen, Gillette Industries, etc.). C. P. Ling, Millington, and Carl Crow (all ad agencies using information surveys; Crow had particular interest in newspaper publication) played a central role in the commercialization of commodity markets.[57] Financialization of village-level cigarette consumption depended on branding BAT cigarettes with easily identified icons and packages. C. P. Ling studied the social science of advertising sciences and was, like Nakayama Taichi, founder of the Nakayama Taiyodo, or Club Cosmetics Company, deeply involved in theorizing advertising.

While Hilferding was a German Marxist economist writing a decade before Chinese colonial modernity had fully formed, he would have had no problem grasping how AMCO, GE, BAT, Standard Oil, Yongli-Jiuda Salt Company, Brunner Mond, Nakayama Taiyodo, Jintan, Toyoda, or NBT was organized. "The most characteristic features of 'modern' capitalism," Hilferding anticipated in his analyses and futuristic speculation, "are those processes of concentration which, on the one hand, 'eliminate free competition' through the formation of cartels and trusts, and on the other, bring bank and industrial capital into an ever more intimate relationship."[58] The history of BAT particularly illuminates how an imperialist corporation strategically crowded all potential competitors out of just-then-opening markets: buying mercantile companies, raising and lowering brand-differentiated product costs, and extending financialization to the ground-level consumer.

To Marxists as well as bourgeois political economists, the existence of an economy presumes the category of society. Actual businesspeople, for their part, had to survey and measure potential consumer communities. They had to adjust prices so that even the poor consumers in a community were able to buy cigarettes and buy on credit. The LLC distributed risk and invited capital investments from groups, banks, and individuals globally. But this desire to buy and to consume, particularly household commodities, also had to be created, and it had to be explained. The alleged instinctual need to evolve forward expressed itself in the new thing known as *society*, but society, at least in bourgeois economic theory, was a constellation of potential consumers. Hilferding put into abstract analytic language a transformation that even the poorest urban villager would feel and might understand; that is, the AMCO or BAT brands reached that person only after creating a market and drawing on social information provided by embedded operatives. Information drove technical changes like the rationalization of labor in relation to the Bonsack cigarette-rolling machine. The logic of commercial capital affected millions of people, including my mother-in-law, an upper-middle-class housewife in Shanghai during the 1920s. Mrs. Chuan-hua Gershom Lowe moved through a landscape saturated with billboards, trolley ads, and movie posters; she consumed magazines like *Liangyou* (The young companion) and stories about movie stars, foreign and domestic. She bought large quantities of the branded antiseptic Listerine, and she lived a modern, hygienic life. Created markets meet actual consumption in the everyday life of people I have known, like my late husband's mother. The bodies Mrs. Lowe kept clean, sanitary, healthy, fashionable, acquisitive, and enlightened were in historical terms precisely where generalizations about branding and financialization meet.

GRAPHESIS AND THE BRAND IN THE EVENT OF WOMEN

Advertisements shape our perception of everyday life and document the charisma of the commodity form. But early twentieth-century advertising images also tell historians where corporations opened their headquarters, where they established branch offices, and where consumers could find retail outlets for anything from light bulbs to steam engines, right down to an outlet's street address and telephone number. These data lead us outward. The modern business firm is not a mystery or a theory but a praxis that changed both physical and emotional landscapes. Commodities received in treaty ports often circulated through them, from one port to others. With the exception of Japanese corporate imperialists, lower in profile so they could work from the hinterlands and mask their militarism, most firms established flagship offices and began the work of creating markets around these centers. This pattern of commodity circulation and marketing gives the event of women a non- or unnational quality since corporate imperialism played such a central role in establishing the conditions for acting on the truth of women. Women images figured centrally into the ads. The new landscape delivered truths about physiological women (fitted clothing, natural feet, unbound breasts, hormones, menstruation, birth control) and consequently conditions indivisible from politically inspired actions that would install truth in human praxis.

In other words, one cannot remove capitalism from the truth of women because an event is a politically inspired action to install a newly discovered truth. The evidence strongly suggests that the corporate imperialist advertising industry delivered the natural woman into everyday life. At the conclusion of this chapter, He-Yin Zhen's polemics will help us understand how a political theorist installs an event of women; recognizing a newly discovered truth, she cantilevers a critique against finance capital and the patriarchy and solidifies women's natural rights. Other nationalist figures—Qiu Jin comes to mind—would also contribute politically inspired actions to install the same truth.[59] But here my point is to demonstrate that under Chinese modern conditions the event of women exceeded the tremulous nation state. Of course, national advertising campaigns create national visual aesthetics aimed at selling commodities and setting up local or indigenous female commodity markets, styles, manners, and so on, but the event of women was not national. The arena where political theorists perceived a new truth of women turns out to be the same area that multinational enterprises established to manufacture and market their products. These are *areal*, not national, markets, societies, collectivities, and so on. Companies such as AMCO, GE, Jintan, and so many others exploited the tenuous Chinese sovereignty. They reinforced international trade law as they installed "national" commercial aesthetics. Under conditions of financial capitalism, the truth of women, appearing in ad iconography, collaborated from inside an expanding formation.[60]

Walter Benjamin's point about the image being dialectics at a standstill and historical truth being eternal yet never timeless helps when we consider corporate imperialism's contribution to the conditions for material history. Benjamin also remarked, not unkindly, that historical truth being material is therefore "far more the ruffle on a dress than some idea."[61] Yes, and more scientific—proving that humans are mammals—than nationalist. That is, in advertising graphesis, the woman is always a universal (a mammal), *and* she is always part of something labeled the larger society. This is true because women's truth lies in discoveries about human biology and the physiology of sexual difference. But it is also true because the political motivation to install a truth about physiological difference and human social life was integrated into the economic and political conditions outlined here. Social logics are part of what Benjamin obligingly attributes to Karl Marx, the notion that research "has to appropriate the material in detail, to analyze its various forms of development and trace out their inner connections."[62] With that research underway, I find social logics in play because everyone from evolutionary philosopher Yan Fu to Chinese Communist translator and cultural revolutionary Qu Qiubai recognized that all sentient beings, even insects, live in societies.

The truth of human social interaction and social nature lies in the beating heart of marketing efforts and in graphesis, which always features women in society. So *things* (commodities), the *commodity form* (modern relations of producers and purchasers), *ideas* (e.g., economic theories), *technologies* (the LLC), and the female advertising icon are inseparable. Since truth, in another Benjaminian aphorism, "is not, as is often thought, to instruct by means of historical descriptions or to educate through comparisons, but to cognize by immersing itself in the object[s]," the GE bulb ad has allowed me to build a stable set of historical truths.[63] I have situated the ad at this central point. The study mounts hundreds of advertising images to materialize political theory and voluntarist acts. The companies that marketed the light bulbs, launched the advertising campaign, brokered the relationship to GE, and negotiated with capital funds to commercially subsidize investment in products from trolley systems to electric fans have left material traces. There is no comparative framework in this argument. Nor is this a particularly descriptive history because I have argued a point rather than describing a constellation of objects. Immersed in objects—commercial advertising ephemera—we can cognize evidence left behind in the trash, crystallized in the amber of the past.

IN THE EVENT OF WOMEN

In 1903, three years before AMCO was founded, seven years before Hilferding's masterwork appeared in German, and twenty-three years before Li Da wrote his pathbreaking *Xiandai shehuixue* (Modern sociology), the Chinese anarchist feminist He-Yin Zhen published a series of declarations about the natural rights of women.[64] She began from a new truth, presupposing women to be physiological, natural rights–bearing, erotically motivated animals because natural, organic body rights in-here in women's and men's mammal being. As do all mammals, women must express their sexual destinies, erotic desires, and reproductive needs. She and all Chinese anarchists struggled over the ethics of so-ciobiological interiorities. She held that natural woman was a universal category and that all over the world women in societies were suffering similar impediments to the ones she experienced when she sought to ex-press her natural rights. Recollect that an event is called when someone arises out of the latent totality of the conditions of historical possibility, to politically act on a new truth. He-Yin was by no means the only per-son to notice. Theorists of all kinds, respectable aspiring cosmopolitan women like Mrs. Chuan-hua Gershom Lowe (née Sharon Nieh Hsien-en), martyrs like Qiu Jin (1875–1907) and Tan Sitong (1865–1898), and avant-garde consumers invoked international anatomical and physiological truths and integrated them, placing the rights and the corporeality into a subject, women. But He-Yin is by far the most trenchant and politically insistent.

He-Yin's writing vividly showed global capitalism delivering nonne-gotiable conditions. The truth of women under oppressive conditions could only be agonistically expressed, since while evolutionary theory had revealed women's animality, commercial capital constrained our ef-forts to act ethically on the basis of our human truth. Painfully, she set out an agonizing rationale. Women, a biosocial collectivity, she argued, had had their natural rights and rights to subsistence violated through-out patriarchal history. The solution required Chinese women to kill. She knew that capitalism was the culprit in her time, the fundamen-tal cause of human misery, and that men, like women, suffered under its regime. But she was simultaneously aware that patriarchy had done its work even before capitalism. Her own violent disposition led her to state that "every single man," under capitalism and under Confucian pa-triarchy, "has contributed to the oppression of women to the point of [women's] death."[65] In this, He-Yin raised the promise of modern femi-nism, that a self-declared woman can speak for all women and can claim her experience to be normative. This is a true subject, a woman, forward-ing herself, declaring her truth as a woman to be natural, universal, and grounds for a community of women. Yet in the event of women, nothing is so simple. Why, she asked rhetorically, as men "started to treat women as their private property," did there emerge "extreme . . . differentiation" between women and male subjects?[66]

And with that query she raised the specter haunting her oeuvre, sexuality.

He-Yin named the event and participated in it. Philosophically, for an event to occur, there has to be in the environment a superfluity, what in Alain Badiou's language is *a multiple*, and there has to be a subject. In theory, the tricky part is that those who can recognize a truth emerge, anomalies, out of normal multiples, ordinary groupings or sets of things. The characteristic that makes He-Yin singular is that she not only recognized what the Badiouists call the "evental site," and what I am calling here *the conditions for thinking*, but also guided and shaped the outcome of the event of women. She not only expressed her loyalty or, again in Badiou's language, fidelity to an event or evental site but actually nominated women herself. To nominate in this philosophical world is to determine politically what actually exists, yet has not yet been recognized or realized. To nominate is to ontologize truth, and in He-Yin's manifestos lies the constitution of the event of women, a realization that women are humans. This is no mean feat. Of course, the conditions that enabled He-Yin to denominate an entire class of subjects, women, are themselves complex, and this chapter has just scratched its surface. But in addressing the conditions for thinking, it is also keenly important to note how voluntarist declarations shape the world. In an exegesis, one of Badiou's most compassionate critics, Quentin Meillassoux, puts it this way: "The subject intervened not only in the labor of fidelity to the past event, but in its very constitution, since without nomination, the event itself could not occur."[67]

When I claim that the event of women is a politically inspired action to install a newly discovered truth, I am revising Badiou's formula and voicing another point in prosaic, nonphilosophical language. It turns out that minor figures, sloppy thinkers, ragged people, and even *women* also mobilize politically inspired action to install newly discovered truths. There is, for the record, nothing in Badiou's great oeuvre to preclude me from legitimately (and under his patronym) making such a claim.[68] Simply put, the political act is more common than philosophers imagined. One need not be a Mao Zedong (politics), a Paul Celan (poetry), a Paul Cohen (science), or a Jacques Lacan (love) to do this or to know truth. In fact, an event surrounding a truth that is absolutely not obscure but, on the contrary, obvious to all readers—popular science comes to mind— spreads like wildfire, like a prairie fire. He-Yin saw this multiple as an event, and she nominated it politically on the basis of her still queasy insight that human beings are mammals.

This actually *is* new news, and in He-Yin's hands, sexuality became the primal social and physiological force. Her writing pivoted around the allegation that sexuality is a mammal drive. Unnaturally repressing female sexuality (i.e., cloistering elite women) leads not to virtuous chastity but to hypersexualization and, consequently, to women's chronic sexual misconduct. The claim that feudal society represses women is obviously easier to defend when sexuality is understood to be naturally and biologically innate. And this is even easier if being a good mammal means sexual selection, the social act of choosing an appropriate mate, and the claiming of natural rights, including the rights to one's own sexuality and bodily existence. To demonstrate that the more elevated and elite the Chinese family, the more disgustingly licentiousness its women, He-Yin gave lots of historical examples of female sexual transgressions to show that "the intended consequence [of cloistering] is to encourage women to indulge freely in sexual fantasies even though the original intention was to deny them freedom. In other words, the prohibition of sexual transgression . . . encourages sexual transgression in practice."[69] On the other hand, sexual conduct among so-called liberated women leads to "self-indulgence" or "blind passion" and logically (if we take He-Yin's suppositions to their conclusion) to self-degradation.[70] Her primary point is that overthrowing capitalism and men is a realistic option, because the historical record of women's violated natural rights cannot otherwise be resolved.

Not only was He-Yin a pioneer in feminist philosophy, as Lydia Liu, Rebecca Karl, and Dorothy Ko, her translators, editors, and interpreters, have argued, but He-Yin put into play a liberated female subject in a filthy capitalist world. She could imagine that the truth of women's physiological difference from men forced self-nominating women to walk a tightrope: in pursuit of her natural sexual expression, a woman might cave to the patriarchy or auto-degrade herself. In contrast, the age-old "chastity cult" that rewarded widows for refusing to remarry also, according to He-Yin, gave Chinese women a potential leg up in the struggle of the liberated. Why? According to He-Yin's speculation, after killing all the capitalists, Chinese old-world sexual discipline might protect Chinese women from turning into Euro-Americans who live under conditions where "the moral prohibitions are far more lax than in China [and where] it is not shameful to prostitute oneself."[71]

One prominent and fascinating part of He-Yin's political act of recognizing the truth of women is her ambivalence. Resting her argument on anarchist theorists Kaneko Kiichi (1875–1909) and Tazoe Tetsuji (1875–1908), He-Yin proposed that the unequal distribution of wealth was the main reason women had so few options. Even being visible in a corrupt capitalist society required women to submit to marriage and acquiesce to "the combined humiliation of being both prisoner and slave," which meant, in political terms, inflicting abjection on oneself. "This situation cannot but lead to a point where the idea of woman itself is rendered utterly inhuman," she wrote, so that to be individuated, to claim the truth of being a woman in a political sense, meant being responsible for the consequences of one's actions.[72] To make a living wage yet avoid prostitution or slavery (self-abjection), women had to overthrow capitalism.[73] Touchingly—in what was really the only position possible, given her logic of innate oppression and ethical sexuality—He-Yin figured that "if we want love to flourish, then we must first abandon money. . . . [W]hatever tendencies toward brutalities or lingering licentious customs remained, these could be rectified expediently. *Therefore, a woman's revolution must go hand in hand with an economic one.*"[74]

He-Yin argued that repudiating the commodity form would be impossible without social revolution. In a passage that appears to argue either that women are human but do not recognize our humanity or that we have not yet become visibly human, she wrote, "Suppose we are granted our humanity? How will that square with *our historical record of passivity*? How can we tolerate this oppression day after day *and not think about resistance?*"[75] He-Yin often used a rhetoric that complicated the relation of women subjects under natural law. That logic is: *If* I am a natural woman mammal, *then* how should I act ethically and socially? This is an evental claim in a world that will struggle violently to shape acceptable behavior. She goes to war over the fact that women are a universal physiological and natural rights–bearing category of human beings, yet in capitalist, patriarchal society are *in*visible because men and capitalists deny women's innate natural rights. She wrote to authorize women to be women, but her positioning was complicated since she both stated the truth of women and anticipated complications stemming from women's truth being denied. Whether women are commodities, consume commodities to improve their value in sexual selection, or repudiate the commercial world of women's sexualization, she argued in an ambivalent rage, the only option was to "do away with governments" and to return to the "possibility of communally owned property."[76] Like Minerva taking flight at dusk, He-Yin, a supremely gifted logician, critic, and polemicist, theorized just at the time when an aspirational Chinese bourgeoisie was on the rise. Under these conditions, she could not avoid walking into the snare that other advocates have tripped. Are women abjects or subjects?[77]

RETHINKING CONDITIONS OF THOUGHT AND THE EVENT OF WOMEN

The extranational area of the treaty port and the forcefully installed corporate capitalist markets did suture together a rough totality. Rapidly spreading financializing and privatizing corporate marketing systems, however, turned national insignia into branding fantasies, since in the case of the Chinese mainland, no viable nation-state could forcefully brand the nation as such. The strange advertisement in figure 1.52 conveys the dilemma. The Jintan general, a national brand for Jintan and for Japan itself, watches over a parade of clown-like male figures, each carrying a shield with the general's visage and each one branded Chinese. What did the designer intend? I have recently found a photo image of a group of men dressed this way and touting the product (figure 1.53), but that does not explain what the performance intended. After years of thinking about and showing this image, I still do not know. At the very least, it clarifies how corporate imperialist Japanese zaibatsu and small commodity companies cashed in on the strong and militarized Japanese imperial state.

My point is that forces and facts may feel like abstractions, but they are not. On May 27, 1920, the *Shanghai Times* ran a story under the title "A Dual Mishap—Tram Collides with Motor Car."[78] It concerned a Chinese man who was alleged to have gotten in a verbal fight with foreign passengers on Tramcar No. 175 shortly after two in the afternoon. When the tram braked on Nanking Road between Chekiang and Fokien Roads, a car carrying "a foreign occupant" rear-ended it. No note was made of the brand, but the car belonged to AMCO. The person in the car might have been Mrs. Meyer, who had designed the ubiquitous triangular AMCO brand trademark. The fight took place in a foreign-produced, machine-tooled tramcar and involved Shanghailanders, the term foreign residents preferred over imperialists. The news article does not say

1.52 Jintan advertisement showing clown-like Chinese men holding Jintan general image boards. *Shengjing shibao*, March 14, 1933.

1.53 Photograph of the actual parade event pictured in the Jintan ad. From Sanger, *Advertising Methods in Japan, China, and the Philippines*.

whether the Chinese man was arrested or whether he appeared before a foreign judge in a Shanghai-based extraterritorial court. This inconsequential nonevent, reported to an English-language news organ that foreign residents consumed, played out in everyday life all the forces described in the preceding: corporate imperialism, mechanization of mass transportation, treaty-port Shanghai, cars and car culture, and, indirectly, a professional journalist at a for-profit venture whose salary was paid in part by AMCO ads. Until forces at play are written into histories of the moment, we risk historicism, idealist representations, and claims that effectively paper over ruptures, novelty, voluntarism, and our own capacity to act.

Everyday life and massive political economic changes are inseparable; for me, they are latent in ephemera. Known historical actors like Meyer and He-Yin, writing at the moment Meyer founded AMCO, situated philosophy and machines and ideologies in the self-same framework. Hilferding, Wagel, Edkins, He-Yin, and the others belong together in the future anterior because they envisioned society, each from their own disparate horizon. The GE light-bulb girl and the Jintan desk-lamp girl are epistemological twins, residing in a commodity world linking female physiological bodies to theories about life in society. They are present or are, as Benjamin put it, latently caught in the amber of the past, for us to blast awry and to reanimate.

It is not for me to declare how the logics of a world are; theorists of a past day are reliable-enough sources at this point. Theorists illuminate the conditions and logics as they were barely intuiting the new things entering the world, flashing out danger that they, not wholly comprehending, nonetheless declared. An event is a politically inspired action to install a newly discovered truth. He-Yin was among the first to anticipate the possibilities emerging in her era and to install that truth politically. In fact, truths ripple through political communities, instigating acts of various kinds. Anticipating in her theoretical work the political conditions for militancy she felt were latent in her moment, she politically planned to act on her sexual difference, to be an avatar for other women becoming conscious about their compromised position in feudal and capitalist patriarchy. The rise of the commodity-girl icon in commercial advertising would confirm He-Yin's anticipation: her anarchist political position is cruel and accurate. Anarchists were repelled by the conditions that would make their subjective lives possible and their personal ruination probable. Philosophically, He-Yin recognized that under capitalist conditions, the ethical, even the sociological, question of women's autonomous, willed, erotic, and social lives is thinkable, and yet it had not arrived with a mandated subject. Even if patriarchy was extinguished overnight, women would still remain problematic because their natural rights remained latent. In contrast, when latency is politically transformed into militancy, the militant may still lose the struggle, because the conditions that animate militants—He-Yin and Jiang Qing come to mind—also give rise to the modern girl, the commodity girl, and bourgeois women, to slaves, masochists, and whores. According to He-Yin, sellouts misrecognize what and who they truly are and willfully degrade themselves socially. Though anarchist philosophy barely predated full-blown commodity culture and the steep rise of the advertising industry, He-Yin's foresight anticipated the contradictions these social conditions would bring to thinking about new truths. As early as 1900, the struggle over the event of women had begun.

CHAPTER TWO

Foundational Chinese Sociology

Chinese modern thought is overwhelmingly convinced that humans
live in societies. The conditions of thinking sketched out in the previous
chapter also situated social philosophers' commitment to the categorical
imperative underlying intellectual revolution: all beings live in society,
and I do, too, but society robs me of my natural rights. The BAT business
model sent sociological agents to collect information and turn villages into consumer societies for smoking rolled tobacco, which makes
marketing into innovative social theory in the sense that it rationalizes
human labor to anticipate profit or surpluses. As variously positioned
as they were, He-Yin Zhen, Rudolf Hilferding, Srinivas Ram Wagel, and
Vilhelm Meyer shared this sociological outlook. Li Da and Qu Qiubai's
calling asked them to explain how our group-oriented species evolves
socially and how establishing social justice is congruent with biosocial
evolution. Chapter 3 considers other social theorists. But while all shared
the social logic that Qu and particularly Li developed philosophically,
Chinese Marxism has a political impulse to install the truth of women's
humanity at the heart of human science. If the truth of humanity is sexual
difference, in the event of women political acts make revolutionary sense
of what truth has revealed to us moderns.[1]

And these philosophers are modernist in the cosmopolitan sense.
Initially, for instance, Li Da intensively read Gabriel Tarde, Georg Simmel, and Franklin Henry Giddings, as well as Wilhelm Wundt and

Charles A. Ellwood, before moving into the socialist camp. Li's mature work still embraced emotion's importance but packed zoology and sexual difference into Marxist exegesis, where he found explanations—sexual selection and psychosexuality—for human natural and social origins. Qu Qiubai died before he had an opportunity to revisit his early preoccupation with sexual difference. But we know from various sources that Qu's commitment to August Bebel's sex theory was unchanging. Qu's other significance in this chapter is his thesis on language and representation because, like He-Yin Zhen, he felt language had to accommodate and subsume reality, including sexual differentiation. He wanted mimesis, the presupposition that language represents truth because it reflects a realistic or mirror image of the "objective" world. Mimetic prose sustains the self-evidence of the social in the social sciences.[2] Difference turns out to be a truth, part of our mammal nature. But justice, denied or fulfilled, demanded that new truth be embraced. He-Yin never moved beyond a painful ambivalence regarding women's natural rights in relation to women's social responsibilities, although she took the truth of physiology and society as givens. So did the new corporate imperialists and their social science of commodity advertising. All of these theories rest on a reification of communicable, mimetic new truths, society and life.[3]

SOCIOLOGY AND INTELLECTUAL REVOLUTION

Once upon a time, Chinese people had believed in an epistemology that situated humans between the heavens and the earth. It took sixty years of translation and debate to dislodge this ontology. In its place, intellectuals established a newer "real truth," that human beings had actually just dreamed up the old triadic epistemology. It was a wrong ideology or false apprehension of reality, according to sociologists, because all people, including Chinese people, actually live in society. Society is categorically universal because human life, no matter how barbaric or sophisticated, cannot survive in its absence, yet societies all have different cultures. Culture is the way that social beings understand themselves and their habitat. These are sociology's basic truths. Given the magnitude of these claims, relatively little has been written in Europe or the United States about the role of human and social science in Chinese intellectual life.

In the People's Republic, however, academic intellectuals are definite about the ideological revolution. Histories of sociology include Yang

Yabin's three-volume, comprehensive *Zhongguo shehuixue shi* (History of Chinese sociology), documenting disciplinary sociology in Chinese universities before the state suspended formal "bourgeois" disciplines. Yan Ming's 2004 history of Chinese treaty-port sociology departments tracked the influence of U.S. pioneers in China like Robert Kulp and Sidney D. Gamble, Clarence G. Dittmer and Edward C. Hayes, and their Chinese disciples. Yan's survey also reviewed Christian-inspired social surveys in early twentieth-century institutions like the Young Men's Christian Association (YMCA), Princeton-in-Peking, Yanjing University, and Peking Union Medical College, as well as departments in the modern new university system Christians helped to set up and finance. This is not to say that foreign machinations caused a national intellectual revolution. Generations of Qing exam-system trainees and successful scholar-officials had long been agitating to reform examination criteria. During the National Revolutionary movement that culminated in the 1911 Xinhai Revolution, many Chinese institutional players—including provincial power holders, reform-minded local elites or gentry, Christian churches, business concerns, and so on—agitated for new schools. Before the Qing administration abolished its formal exam system, local power holders and government officials tried all kinds of methods to attract intellectually able youth into political service. Tsinghua and Peking Universities were the consequence of decades of local agitation, the Qing state's weakness in relation to the imperial powers, and a general frustration among educated people about schooling. Between 1901 and 1919, major national postsecondary schools, in theory Chinese owned, responded to mandates from big international players like Theodore Roosevelt's Boxer Indemnity Scholarship program, the Rockefeller Foundation, and other foundations. Yung-Chen Chiang's 2001 *Social Engineering and the Social Sciences in China, 1919–1949*, establishes two significant facts: missionary organizations spearheaded institutional reform and graduates from U.S.-style sociology departments in particular moved into Nationalist Party social engineering projects.[4]

More recently, Yao Chun'an's remarkable critical research, expanded with a preface by fellow historian of sociology Sang Bing, evaluated China-based research since the 1980s. Both stress how historians struggled to figure out what the discipline of sociology was in the early twentieth century and what kind of logic structured its philosophical burden and core assumptions.[5] Yao's book is particularly valuable because it distinguishes, for instance, what a discipline is or means, how the struggle to define sociology in relation to other social or human sciences like anthropology and ethnology took place, and to what degree the philosophical content of Chinese sociology is European and American philosophy mediated through secondary sources in Japanese. It also presents a "history of the present" for sociology in China today.[6]

Qu and Li excelled in the old and the new education. Most intellectuals coming to national prominence in the 1920s knew the scholastic tradition and spent their lifetimes negotiating intellectual revaluation. Some became "New Confucians"; others sought to reconcile old aesthetic and knowledge systems with Kantian aesthetics and natural teleology, for instance; and still others, such as Qu, sought to overthrow and destroy an amorphous new entity they bundled under terms like *feudalism, tradition,* and *Confucianism*.[7] Yet when educated Chinese translated or discussed new philosophical categories and ideas, it was not just in relation to their local origins but in relation to long-unsettled intellectual dilemmas in Europe and the United States, too. No one had a lock on categories of modernity, realism in scientific representation, or sexual difference, which means Qu and Li were translating *problems*, not solutions; theories, not foundations of scientific socialism; and contradictions that modernist intellectuals on a global scale were confronting.

A good example of how this double problematic worked is Yan Fu, the father of Chinese sociology. Yan reposed the question of why bees have societies but do not evolve socially. Why do only humans appear to have thrown off physical and psychic constraints and evolved naturally and socially? He noted that in the beehive physical bodies do not change, and the hive is an overly specialized and static society. Yan anticipated sociological studies in China before their consolidation into formal disciplines. Like He-Yin Zhen, Yan was a polymath and had both a conventional Qing education and an avant-garde course in "Western learning" (algebra, arithmetic, astrology, chemistry, English, geometry, navigation, physics, and trigonometry) before becoming nationally significant. Intellectuals in Qu Qiubai, Li Da, and Mao Zedong's generation read Yan's pathbreaking, eccentric, interpretive translations of Thomas Henry Huxley's *Evolution and Ethics*, Adam Smith's *The Wealth of Nations*, John Stuart Mill's *On Liberty*, Montesquieu's *The Spirit of the Laws*, and Herbert Spencer's *Study of Sociology*.

Yan opened what became a century-long argument over human evolution and the social role of communications, tool making, organization, class hierarchies, and ways of organizing human life. He was prescient in the sense that he believed humans evolved like plants and that humans, like plants, left sympodes, or irregular zigzag growth patterns.[8] He was better educated than U.S. sociologist Lester Ward (1841–1913), but he laid the ground for next-generation Chinese intellectuals who then read Ward's influential lecture "Evolution in the Vegetable Kingdom." In this multiply translated lecture, Ward noted that, like the evolution of vegetables, human evolution consisted of a crisscross unfolding of inherent evolutionary possibilities; this is a general logic of the sympode. The instructive difference for Ward is that vegetables lack self-awareness and thus have no *society*. Vegetable evolution suggests that we humans have evolved as we have because we have the capacity to communicate within our species. A sympodial human society, say a primitive tribe, is an offshoot and may be devolving, but human societies will devolve or evolve because humans are beasts with a species-being highly evolved in its capacity to draw on unconscious drives, conscious emotions, mass emotions, individual motivations, criminal impulses, and so on, to mediate between nature and culture, or between physical inheritance and social development. That is why, according to Ward, the social scientist and specifically the sociologist must disaggregate social and natural factors using intermediary ideas like social psychology.

Yan's translation project, like younger generation intellectuals' obsession with Lester Ward, is an urbane version of evolutionary philosophy, launched in an already fertile field. By the 1830s, Chinese scholars were collecting information about Europe, obtained primarily from Christian missionaries. The most famous example is Lin Zexu's (1785–1850) 1846 acquisition of Abraham Rees's (1743–1825) *Cyclopaedia; or, Universal Dictionary of Arts, Sciences, and Literature,* published in 1819–1821, and his 1834 acquisition of *An Encyclopaedia of Geography* by Hugh Murray (1789–1846), which Lin ordered translated.[9] By the first decade of the twentieth century, a generic "encyclopedic dictionary" came into circulation among Chinese readers, rooted in the technique of the German taxonomist Friedrich Arnold Brockhaus and the Chambers Brothers' pioneering 1857 genre of the "people's encyclopedia" showing ordinary readers the branches of knowledge that the people most desired and used. Although, historians point out, the Chinese world of letters had had its own massive information-processing and taxonomy systems since the early 1770s, the Western encyclopedia movement transformed, not so much the content of information as such, but knowledge's boundaries— by including physical, chemical, and natural sciences and highlighting new, different categories. Data got shifted from the older *leishu* (Chinese encyclopedic) order to an alphabetic or phonetic retrieval system that filed new data according to scientific formulas.[10]

As early as 1902, a foundation situated theorization of society, sociology, social logics, and the situation of physiological or gender relations in evolution. The encyclopedia movement justified the Guangxu or Qing Reforms and consolidated the position of politicians like Kang Youwei, who sought conservative change and a constitutional monarchy on the model of the Japanese Meiji Restoration. The compilation, translation, and innovation that resulted from the influx of European-style Chinese encyclopedias merged to become, in the end, what Milena Dolezelova-Velingerova and Rudolf G. Wagner call a "modernization package."[11] What they mean is that information was codified into a general framework where specifics reinforced generalizations. For instance, by 1855 educated Chinese readers could know that the mature human body has 206 bones, not 360. Philosophically, a number has no meaning until the life sciences of physiology demonstrate how the living body is born with 270 bones and over the life cycle fuses bones, activates glands, floods the gonads with sex hormones, and motivates the drive to sexual procreation. Actually, it turns out, the "fact" of 206 bones is intimately related to the *theory* of human physiological evolution. Building on this relation took time, particularly because the earliest translators and commentators were largely producing newfangled source materials for Chinese diplomats stationed abroad. The diffusion of systematized information from Western knowledge sources (later a massive inflow of Japanese-inflected and translated social science) inserted the concept of modernization into the intellectual world of all Chinese elites. On the basis of these massive publication events, Liang Qichao and his cohort could build cheaper and friendlier distribution media and advocate for newspaper publication to transmit the modernization concepts and teleology.

Following the failure of the constitutional-monarchy movement in 1898, many educated people awakened to the philosophical dimension of European learning. Intellectuals like Kang had not fully investigated key extra-Confucian philosophical terms (such as *sympode*). Also, at a certain point, advanced Chinese intellectuals realized that Spencerian social and natural evolutionary theory lacked explanations for human intentionality and rationality, or will and emotion. This insight led social scientists like the psychologist Pan Guangdan, two decades later, to embrace a version of Freudian psychoanalytic theory. Pan, whom I discuss in more detail in chapter 5, worked under the assumption that the liberation of individual and mass sexual energy freed people to make intentionally good reproductive choices that unintentionally forwarded eugenic evolutionary development. Like Sigmund Freud, his major influence, Pan knew that considering humans to be "social animals" meant philosophers, practitioners, and analysts would have to reassess and recognize the entangled social and mammal mixture in people. Chinese intellectuals educated in China, Europe, or Japan were engaging with this conundrum, which lies at the heart of Spencer, Huxley, Charles Darwin, and others' theories: the social and natural sciences obey the same scientific laws but are distinct, though entangled, domains of *reality*.[12]

Nonetheless, even as late as 1902, Chinese editors, publishers, academics, translators, and diplomats had "little sense of something now called 'society.'"[13] In his intellectual history of Yan Fu and Nakamura Keiu's foundational translation of Mill, historian Douglas Howland found a pattern in the philosophical awareness of translators and interpreters of early social science into Japanese, too. Saito Tsuyoshi, for instance, exhibited almost no comprehension of "society" in his Spencer translation. The founder of the Marxist tradition in Japan and a pan-Asian intellectual force, Nakamura Keiu (Nakamana Masano, 1832–1891), who was Li Da's teacher, remained "without an expression for 'society,'" which, Howland points out, limited what Nakamura's translation of Mill's *On Liberty* could express. Howland takes pains to say that Nakamura did not mistranslate or actively misconstrue Mill. Neither did Yan. Requiring a stable calque (new word or neologism) for "society" limited Nakamura's philosophical compass, and making a calque to cogently express a concept is extremely difficult. "An abstraction like society is, after all," Howland writes, "a difficult concept in any language."[14]

Wang Rongbao (1878–1933) and Ye Lan's (1875–?) *Xin Erya* (New Erya), a text aimed at the high school market, defined key terms, or historical catachreses, or philosophical calques, that were restructuring twentieth-century Chinese thought. Wang and Ye were familiar with earlier Chinese and Japanese encyclopedia collections, but their volume is more declarative. Among the terms defined are *society* (in both proposed calques, *qun* and *shehui*), *economy*, *law*, *physiology*, *logic*, and *natural science*. *New Erya* defines *society* as follows (paraphrased): When more than two persons live together, that body is called a *qun* (group) or a *shehui* (society). Those who do research on qun rationality or laws are called qun-ologists or sociologists.[15] These specialists share the same object of study. The content of the object of knowledge, intrinsic or extrinsic, is considered as a question in such research. *The object of study for sociology is the qun/shehui, and sociology is all about group or sociological problems.* There are many different methods appropriate to this study, but two are basic, the empirical rational strategy and the experiential or inductive logic. All kinds of methods are appropriate to these two modes of research.[16]

This clear but circular definition says that humans require specialist knowledge in order to understand themselves in their social relations. It continues on in declarative sentences to outline distinctions in sociological research: the qualitative and quantitative methods, the inferential and the deductive modes, idealism and imagination, statistics, and so on. The point of these various studies is to extract the *wuzhi lifa* (the logos of things) from the social world. To do so requires objectivity and subjective appreciation for the manifold objective world or *shishi* (reality). *New Erya* explains how sociologists become self-aware, become conscious or self-conscious, which allows the investigator to be open to the principle of objectivity. In other words, social science logic sets off a process for the study of society that requires a shifting relationship between the investigator and the investigated. The implication seems to be that *ziwo zhijue* (self-awareness) occurs as one is *doing sociology.* Indeed, sociology and the logos of things lead toward socialism, and communism is the natural outcome, because this natural and social process of self-realization makes it possible for actualized sociologists and their readers to throw off oppressive social relationships.

The sociology discussion references natural conditions that made possible the physical separation of humanity into social groups and categories, the basic laws of the horde. In the past, when men and women lived together, they did so under conditions of promiscuity, where the mother of children was known but not the father. This condition led eventually to regulation and to the emergence of the *jiazu*, or kinship group, a "natural" basis of society; but Wang and Ye also do not spare details. In a separate section, they write explicitly about the sexual relation. In primitive times, unlike the present, humans mated with one another by force of sexual desire and need for gratification. They sexually selected one another. Then various violent forms of capture emerged, and marriage was instituted, with power shifting from female to male hands, and kin avoidance in marriage was required (incest taboo). This signaled the end of the matriarchate and the rise of patriarchalism, or the primary relation of fathers and sons. Sexuality drives evolutionary development.

Consolidating these terms has an impact that cannot be overestimated. Wang and Ye set into a simple story all of the reductive empiricism of the human and natural sciences. Their origin story includes the natural genesis of primitive humanity and the social world of the species-being. It does not distinguish the origins of *Homo erectus* or protohumans from the concept of humans as social animals; these two theories merge into one set of maxims. The key is how primitive sexual intercourse drove social animals into groups or societies. The authors of *New Erya*, published first in 1903, had studied the Darwinian argument about the ascent of humanity and no doubt knew the social evolutionary debate over the direct ape-to-human theory that Huxley and Richard Owen steered after Darwin's studies were published. By 1902, erudites had for the most part accepted even the most distasteful part of Darwinian theory (at least until Friedrich Engels, Bebel, and Marxist sociology came up with a more compelling argument about labor power): that natural and sexual selection was the motive force in human social and anatomical evolution.

This is not random storytelling but an origin philosophy that proposes the mammal and social evolution of all humans, not just one clan or state or tribe or race. In this regard, Wang and Ye consolidated among other key terms a conceptual reality, society, which would stand no matter what Chinese word eventually got assigned to it. Once conceptualized, society is an irrefutable fact, a concrete abstract. It is a first symptom in the larger movement toward the social scientization of Chinese modern thought. Yan Fu and Zhang Taiyan had scholarly reasons for preferring the *qunxue* (the study of qun), and Yan tried hard to express his understanding of Mill's *On Liberty*. Yan was steeped in British debates over social evolution, individualism, social logic, and the sociology of utilitarian value. Unlike the subsequent generation, Yan read and wrote English and had lived and studied in England. He never aligned with younger people in Japan struggling over which Chinese word best described social logics and philosophy, and politically he ended up in the royalist camp. Later intellectuals came to understand Enlightenment sociological philosophy as a package. In the end, the Sino-Japanese term *shehuixue* (sociology) became standard, and translations of Meiji- and Showa-era social science interpretations flooded the Chinese media market. Wang and Ye had demonstrated that the name was less significant than the categorical, society.

When thought is social-scientized, the term *society* arrives with unanticipated problems. Most fundamentally, the logic of social science philosophy is representational, rooted in theories of mimesis. The premise of mimetic scientific exposition à la Francis Bacon is that, of the human sciences, sociology most accurately represents material, social, and natural human reality. This Baconian stance is obvious in a polemic that Liang Qichao wrote, in which he argued that Chinese people's inability to think beyond the monarchy had hindered China's social-cultural evolution. In his view, Chinese people were literally blinded to *reality* because they did not think scientifically.[17] Liang was no sociologist, but his insight was prophetic. He argued on the basis of his own rationale that pre-social-scientized intellectuals failed to discern that humans *do not* live "under heaven" but rather exist together in an objective platform or structure called society, where as individuals and citizens they accept or repudiate social contracts. Society and the science of society, sociology, according to Liang and the Chinese vernacular sociology that would follow him, enable us to see reality beneath our illusory thoughts. We can finally, Yan Fu had suggested, grasp the objective realities of our natural evolution and our human natures.[18] The presupposition of reality and realism flowered philosophically and critically in the development of Chinese dialectical materialist philosophy and Marxist sociology. In other words, one need not fetishize the individual scholarly debates that created, debated, or circulated social science neologisms, because the conditions for thinking were so much larger than the efforts of any one intellectual, even any one giant, and the general conditions for thought were, by the turn of the century, so deeply unsettled. Sociology is a way of thinking in an Enlightenment or scientific or social scientific tradition where society, as Liang observed, is the scientifically presumptive condition of human existence.

CRITICAL SOCIAL THEORY AND SEXUAL DIFFERENCE

Young social theorists Qu Qiubai and Li Da began their careers translating major texts directly addressing sexual difference. In Qu's time, international debates pivoted around sexual selection, evolution, and individual choice; natural scientific determinism; and social scientific voluntarism. The mother-right debate, for instance, asked how humanity had evolved so quickly into highly differentiated labor power with oppressive social relations that trapped female humans in humiliating social degradation. Arguments about sex difference and the origins of society were so intense that most European philosophers had something to say about social versus natural essence. What we consider the international socialist heritage was part and parcel of high philosophical debates among Schopenhauer, Mill, Kant, Huxley, Freud, Wundt, Tarde, Spencer, Ernst Haekel, Thorstein Veblen, Mill, Georg Wilhelm Friedrich Hegel, René Descartes, and Baruch Spinoza. Thus, Qu and Li entered existing discussions over evolutionary temporality, sociality, physiology, and the relation of social evolution and species evolution amid this disagreement over reality and language.

Qu rendered into Chinese a Russian translation of Bebel's German version of *Women and Socialism*. Li brought into Chinese a 1904 Japanese translation of American sociologist Lester Ward's famous statement in *Pure Sociology*, "The Gynæcocentric Theory."[19] With these actions, each entered the debate over female-centered primitive society. As Gong Yanhong and Liu Shipeng have established in a comparative study on Li and Qu, both men were trying to analyze the *fact* of human sexual difference. Gong and Liu write that Li was struck by the Kantian argument that a true social individual is both sexes, male and female. That is a philosophical observation that reinforces the scientific fact that it takes ovum and sperm to create a human fetus. Society is thus "the world of male sex and female sex participating together."[20] Gong and Liu also summarize the position that Qu took, which is fundamentally a mix of Bebel's *Women and Socialism* and Engels's *The Origin of the Family, Private Property and the State*.[21]

Both Chinese sociologists began from sexual division, physiologically in reproductive biology and in relation to social forms. Each was also embroiled in positions other Chinese intellectuals were contesting, but that discussion is deferred for the moment, because when translators read Bebel, Ward, or Havelock Ellis, they were accessing the breadth of European social science philosophy.[22] And perhaps even more important, Chinese intellectuals were caught up in the same debates that wracked European social theory. Temporality, sociality, physiology, and the relation of *social* evolution and *species* evolution show up in all of these intertextual debates. A core question that the physiology of sexual difference imposes is what role sexual difference has played historically. Bebel, the German socialist revolutionary; Ward, the premier American academic liberal evolutionary sociologist; and Ellis, the British founder of social sexuality studies, all became available in Chinese translation from Japanese by 1913, and all fixated on this question.

Perhaps it will eventually be possible to demonstrate that the Chinese debates placed relatively more stress on female voluntarism and women's centrality to social development—more, that is, than other socialist sociological traditions did. That remains to be determined. What is manifest already is that the Chinese debate over society and sexual division assumed that woman is *the* central figure in human evolution. In my terms, it means that Qu and Li were participants in the event of women. Li emphasized Kant's point that human individuals combine male and female. He also read Japanese sociology of sexuality, which emphasized women's evolutionary primacy. And given the alleged central reality of sexual selection, it seemed that human women ought to be choosing their own partners for procreation, as all other mammals did. There simply was no alternate position to take given the evolutionary logic and the mammal evidence.[23]

According to Zhong Shaohua, the early Chinese intellectuals promoting the natural and evolutionary social sciences in the Western learning agenda often misrecognized the central role philosophy played in Western science, technology, and social science.[24] Zhong does not mention that social logics in the human sciences are rooted in theories of evolution, so there really is no avoiding the dilemma women and sexuality posed. If there were no other explanation for human natural and social evolution than sex itself, then it seems intuitive that better social conditions for human sexual selection would accelerate evolutionary social development. How was the breeding capacity of human mammals reflected in or integrated into the social evolutionary factors that propel the species forward? What happened in the long-term processes of sociobiological species evolution when women's range of activities was severely constricted? How could females *not contribute equally* to evolutionary development when each sex contributed genetic material to sociobiological progress? As the New Culture Movement began its focus on philosophy and theoretical technologies that earlier entrée points had ignored, the role of mammal relations in social evolution became a starker problem.

Atop a churning theoretical crisis over social theory and the logos of sociology, early twentieth-century Chinese scholars, strategists, political theorists, and government officials implemented eugenic population control, gender and social development policy, and theories of history that began with the assumption of matrilineality. Women's liberation took a role in all theories of civilizational stages that arose on the basis of natural science. In other words, in the human and natural scientific revolutions among Chinese intellectuals, a women's revolt or liberation movement had evolutionary predicates and implications. The assumption was that a feminist uprising has a forward or progressive role to play in social, mammalian evolution. It is consequently important to see as clearly as possible the foundations—fundamental philosophical assumptions—revolutionary philosophers made then. Ensuring women's social liberation has been, for better and for worse, an article of faith in socialist traditions, and the political implications of historical materialist ideas require explanation.

QU QIUBAI: SEXUAL DIFFERENCE AND SCIENTIFIC MIMESIS

Qu Qiubai introduced historical materialist philosophy into Chinese debates. He was also a theorist of translation working to establish a social scientific language rooted in the promise of mimesis. He presumed with others in Europe and elsewhere that a mimetic or representational language was necessary to give Chinese intellectuals and ordinary readers access to reality. Qu grew up in an intellectual culture already familiar with botany, anatomy, the evolutionary study of flora and fauna, the encyclopedic array of technical and scientific information, and the formalization of sociological categories à la the *New Erya*. In 1919, however, the twenty-year-old Qu Qiubai and his fellow Russianist Geng Jizhi (1899–1937) joined up with polymath Zheng Zhenduo (1898–1958), later educated at Columbia and Yanjing Universities; Xu Dishan (1894–1941), who was educated at Yanjing, Columbia, and Oxford Universities and became a religious scholar; and Qu Shiying (1900–1976), a translator who would obtain a PhD in education from Harvard and join the James Yen Rural Reconstruction Movement in later years. Given his manifest talent, Qu had a second-tier education compared to his peers, and yet he mastered Russian and achieved competency in French and English. Together, these gifted intellectuals founded the journal *Xin shehui* (New society) under the auspices of the Social Progressive Association and started bringing into Chinese the names and basic ideas of European and American sociologists like Tarde, Simmel, and Charles-Marie Gustave Le Bon on the masses and Ward, Giddings, and Charles A. Ellwood on social dynamics. After *Xin qingnian* (New youth), *Xin shehui* was the second most influential journal of ideas during the 1920s.[25]

This intellectual cohort focused on the social implications of translation and philosophy of translation. Qu's contribution stands out because he voiced early concerns about China's written language, Han graphemes (or logographs or *hanzi*). He concluded that the Chinese written language had been *culturally* corrupted. His short scholarly life (he became a full-time Communist Party translator and activist) focused on changing the Chinese written script to make it, in his view, capable of accurately representing material, social, and natural human reality, including the core relation of the sexes. He took a leadership position in the Communist Party, proved completely inept, and was eventually captured and shot to death by the Nationalist government in 1935 at the age of thirty-six. Among his first essays, "Zhishi shi zangwu" (Knowledge is stolen goods) begins with the question, "What is *zhishi* [knowledge]?" Addressing his own rhetorical question, Qu argued that zhishi in its written form inverted class moralism and knowledge of the real. This led to a catastrophic notion in current linguistic norms, that a Chinese person with no knowledge is a moral "inanimate" (*muou shixiang*). Obversely, moralistic Chinese *obscured* what social scientific logos clarifies to be true.

Qu was the first Russian-competent, left-wing Chinese intellectual to study Russian in the USSR. Among his other duties after returning to China in 1923 was setting up a sociology department at Shanghai University under the umbrella of the two major competing political parties (on the left the Chinese Communist Party and on the right the Nationalist Party) under the USSR-sponsored First United Front (1922–1927).[26] Although he spent inordinate amounts of time translating party communication, his university assignment meant he created social theory himself and taught curricula in the new Sociology Department and burst onto an already roiling debate over modern Chinese textuality with other intellectual leaders of his day. These included Liang Shiqiu (1903–1987), Fu Sinian (1896–1950), and the father of Chinese modern literature, Lu Xun (1881–1936). Lu and Fu took the position that the Chinese language could be transformed and improved in the process of translation because bringing linguistic change, that is, ideas from the world, would shift its matrix, allowing for the systematizing, stabilizing, and regularizing of a written language that could be read aloud in mass media and would provide a satisfyingly literary alternative to inherited genres. In Qu's case, the ideal written language could mimetically represent the social as such, starting with the question of sexual difference. These aspirations placed Qu firmly in the camp of those who agonistically struggled with a tension in origin stories between natural science and social science.

Qu embraced an Engelsian version of dialectical materialism that stressed "a material reality subject to the laws of dialectics, and of practice as the kernel of a correct epistemology," views later reinforced in the philosophies of Georgi Plekhanov, Vladimir Lenin, Li Da, and Mao Zedong.[27] It meant grasping the origins of materialist philosophy in the Greco-Roman, European tradition and developing political strategies based on this alleged materialist reality. Absorbing Plekhanov required valorizing the real. In his writing on sociology and social revolution, Qu wavered, as historians have pointed out, over the question of the superstructure (read: society) in the same basic way that Russian Marxist philosophers Plekhanov, Lenin, Abram Deborin, Mark Borisovich Mitin, Leon Trotsky, and Nikolai Bukharin did. Qu seemed, in the end, to think that Marxist dialectical materialism was "a determinist, [though] not a fatalist, theory" and mobilized his poetic imagination and powers of invective against the Chinese language, which to him propped up a culture of decrepit obfuscation.[28] He appeared to assume that the prevailing Russian orthodoxies and his own scholarly tendencies coincided and that the socially organized human had the capacity to force social change. On the one hand, this made him pessimistic and reckless; on the other, apparently because he agonistically devalued the beautiful Chinese literary heritage, his voluntarism and openness to cultural revolution were wildly optimistic and presumed that such a transformation of thinking and written expression was possible.[29]

As a consequence of coming so early to explicit Marxist debate, and of his own intellectual orientation, Qu's Marxism was a philosophical version of sophisticated global human sciences. Moreover, a core problem particular to his circumstances was not one generally scrutinized in social theory elsewhere. The question he spent his last years engaged with polemically and philosophically was why the Chinese symbolic written system had preoriginated and then claustrophobically subjugated mass speech to itself. This is the inverse of the question raised above: How can the Chinese written script be forced into mimesis? Qu's affirmative question became, Can Chinese revolutionary intellectuals collaborate with the masses to create a written language capable of voicing the reality of social life and, thus, the people's real social conditions? As already mentioned, his discussion was part of the larger debate over the relative autonomy of the superstructure and resurfaces in the work of Li Da, who lived longer and was more productive in a scholarly sense. But during Qu's final underground Shanghai years, working with Lu Xun and for a time advising on Mao Zedong's experimental cultural revolutions during the Jiangxi Soviet period of 1931–1934, Qu recommended the revolutionary overthrow of previous Chinese worldviews and written languages so that a language of realism, a *real language* that described real social realities, could be forged, a language that illiterates could comprehend when it was read aloud to them.

In a late essay, "Marx, Engels and the Literary Realism" (Makesi, engesi yu wenxue xianshi zhuyi), Qu argued that Marx and Engels advocated literary realism because it reflected society; thus literature could represent reality.[30] Quoting Engels's letter to the English writer Margaret Harkness in which Engels praises Honoré de Balzac, calling his literary realism "a most wonderfully realistic history of French 'society,'" Qu noted that Engels and Marx were not opposed to literary realism per se but only literature that distorted reality, "paraded around selfish individuals," and "raped logic [*qiangjian luoji*]."[31] In any case, he reasoned with Engels, there were two Balzacs: one was a realist writer and the other the darling of the French establishment intellectuals. Qu joined what he saw as Engels's anti-identitarian position, meaning Balzac could not be classified or dismissed as a bourgeois writer or a Catholic writer, nor any other situated partiality, because he was a great realist universalist (*yuzhouguan*). Balzac was a writer with the mind of a sociologist.[32]

His claim that Balzac could see around personal perspective and write a universal language parallels Qu's persistent interest in real sexual difference. Among his earliest works, mixed into Russian realist novel translations, are his articles "Women at the Center of the Proletarian Movement," "A Teensy Question: Women's Liberation" (Xiaoxiao yige wenti—funü jiefang de wenti), and "Goodbye to Women's Literature" (Gaobie funü wenxue), published in his own journal and others, like *Liberation and Reform*, and *Debates of Women*. It would seem Qu embraced theories of sexual difference without equivocation: his conditions for thinking and capacity for invention, mashed together mimetic representation, physiological and social scientific truths, to conclude that in truth women are embodied, socially oppressed natural humans. Qu sought to describe social problems truthfully. That is why we see him agonistically struggling with hanzi like *nüzi*, one of three major Chinese words corresponding to the English noun *woman*. He read Russian novels in part to expand his vocabulary, but it is said that he chose this route to fluency because the novels gave him insight into the universal social incarceration of women. Qu sought to answer the question, What is the fundamental origin of women's oppression? But his work includes an additional dimension. Qu advocates Bebel's position not just because women's liberation means that women are analogous to the proletariat in social reality but also because a revolution undertaken in the name of social reality will show the truth of sexual difference and the joint contribution of both sexes to social and species evolution. It is simply physiologically not accurate that women are inferior to men![33]

According to Chen Tiejian, Qu was rare in the depth of his commitment to the question of women's oppression and to finding in Bebel the fundamental evolutionary and social reasons for women's apparent universal oppression.[34] It helps, therefore, to know what Bebel was promoting as truth. To Bebel, women and the proletariat are the most socially oppressed in modern or bourgeois society—and the female even more so than the working class. Drawing on a mixture of Henry Lewis Morgan's anthropology and Engels's and Johann Jakob Bachofen's theory of the rise of patriarchy and private property after the prolonged primitive matriarchate and the subsequent enslavement of all women by propertied men, Bebel showed that women's apparent social backwardness was in fact a social evolutionary productive contradiction. By objectifying women and making them property, men obscured women's zoological nature, meaning women's responsibility to sexually select male inseminators, and forced women (and men) into social devolution. In Bebel's naturalistic scientific view, sexual desire and sexual intercourse are mammal activities and have supported the social evolution of humans to this point. Bebel's most aggressively argued version of his thesis is in chapter 7 of *Women and Socialism*, "Woman as a Sex Being—the Sexual Impulse," which shows Bebel deeply involved in the effort to distinguish natural and social science:

> Of all the natural desires that are a part of human life, beside the desire for food in order to live, the sexual desire is strongest. The impulse of race preservation is the most powerful expression of the "will to live." This impulse is deeply implanted in every normally developed human being, and upon attaining maturity its satisfaction is essential to physical and mental welfare. . . . The so-called animal instincts are not inferior to

mental requirements. Both are products of the same organism and are mutually interdependent. This applies to both man and woman. Hence it follows that knowledge of the nature of the sexual organs is as necessary as that of all other organs, and that the same attention should be bestowed upon their care. We ought to know that organs and impulses implanted in every human being constitute a very important part of our existence, that they as a matter of fact predominate during certain periods of life, and that therefore they must not be objects of secrecy, false shame and complete ignorance. It follows furthermore that among both men and women knowledge of the physiology and anatomy of the various organs and their functions should be as widely diffused as any other branch of human knowledge. . . . [W]e decry knowledge pertaining to those matters that are most closely linked with our own "ego" and are at the bottom of all social development.[35]

On the question of bridge-building between natural physiology and social development, Bebel cites Mill and Kant. The first stated that marriage was a legal form of enslavement, and the second, as noted earlier, that the full human is a fused man and woman. But Bebel had his own singular positions. As society has progressed, Bebel said, men have evolved to the point where they desire an intellectual partnership in their human sexual love. Invoking Schlegel, Bebel claimed that the intent of nature is the intellectual erotic congress of women and men in social bonds of marriage, freely entered on the basis of love, intellectual compatibility, and sexual desire.[36] (He gave no nonheterosexual option.) Since it is the intent of nature for human social action to perfect the social or marital bond, the progress of humanity is not unlike—and in fact is analogous to—the evolution of the vegetable kingdom. Echoing Ward, Bebel argued, "The same laws that apply to nature apply to human life," particularly when, in his opinion, "to-day it is in human life as in plant life."[37]

There is always another twist in this tense, long-enduring argument. According to Bebel, social teleology means class and sex dependency are progressively resolved. This development must be scientifically true because nature is a constant readjustment in an ongoing natural and social progress. That is why one will never find an enduring master-slave dialectic in nature. A processual understanding of natural evolution is a block against foolish fears that women may reverse the current order to avenge themselves and oppress men. *Nature* is the brake on social oppression in sex relations. Social instruction, including sex education, is the way to learn about your nature, but justice and *égalité* (i.e., equality of difference) are part of natural law. Nature is benign because it is not only self-righting but also subliminally an extension of the potential that humans and all mammal species possess. Anyway, the "men and women of future society will possess far more self-control and a better knowledge of their own natures, than men and women of to-day," because society will (apparently naturally) evolve better education! Bebel ends *Women and Socialism*, "Man should no longer regard himself an exception to natural laws. He should finally strive to recognize the laws underlying his own thoughts and actions, and should endeavor to live in accordance with these laws. He will eventually learn to arrange his life . . . according to the rational principles derived from an understanding of nature. Politics, morals, law . . . will be shaped according to natural laws. An existence worthy of human beings, that mankind has been dreaming of for thousands of years, will become a reality at last."[38]

SOCIOLOGY, SEXUAL DIFFERENCE, PHILOSOPHY: LI DA

Li Da, who survived the wars to become an influential theorist of Mao Zedong Thought and interpreter of Russian and Japanese Marxism, also began his career translating a canonical work on sexual difference. In the preface to his Chinese translation of Sakai Toshihiko's Japanese version of the most famous chapter of American liberal sociologist Lester Ward's book *Pure Sociology*, Li Da stated in *Nüxing zhongxin shuo* ("On women's centrality"; what Ward termed "gynæcocentrism" in a chapter in *Pure Sociology*) that Ward's insight into sexual difference and gynecocentrism was on an intellectual par with Copernicus's explanation of the solar system and Darwin's theory of evolution. This was not too farfetched at the time, since Ward was one of the three most influential philosophers of sexuality and sexual difference in Li's Sino-Japanese intellectual world. The other two were Havelock Ellis and Edward Carpenter, whose works were translated and circulated regularly. The Ward translation was by no means Li's only publication on the woman question, either. "*Nüzi jiefanglun*" (On the liberation of women), published in 1919, and other works mirror Wang Rongbao and Ye Lan's definition of sexuality, sexual difference, and sociology. Li's work is suffused with the understanding that human sociality is partly motivated by sexual procreation, although he would resolve in the end the tension between social sciences and natural sciences that he inherited.

When Li embraced what he called Marxist or materialist philosophy, he realized that philosophy is "the science of sciences" because Marxist philosophy synthesizes truths derived from the physical and the human sciences. While he did not stay with Ward's simple argument about sexual reproduction, and his grasp of Marxism deepened into a realization that the means and social relations of production and of labor power were the evolutionary generative force, he never subordinated the insight that had struck him so forcefully, that women formed the root of human existence. As did Qu Qiubai, Li had an enduring interest in gynecocentric theory, and a residue of the argument he translated from Ward occurs in a more Engelsian form in his first major book, *Xiandai shehuixue* (Modern sociology).[39]

Ward, for his part, claims to be the originator of the theory of female superiority in human evolution. Like socialists' and Marxist sociologists' emerging consensus, Ward believed sexual difference was central to social evolution yet difficult to explain because it entangled natural and human science. The basic problem in "The Gynæcocentric Theory" is to figure out how our species created binary sexual reproduction. Fundamentally, this is a zoological question, but in those times the distinction between the physical, or natural, and the human, or social, sciences was porous, and the origin of sexual difference was also considered part of a social science investigation. Organic human evolution requires the ability to secure variation. Many species reproduce by producing single-cell (parthenogenesis) clones of themselves; multicellular individuals may divide or may simply release sperm and ova for haphazard fertilization, so the result may be a better-adapted individual. From the nineteenth-century physiological and biological evolutionary position, the question appears in the following terms: How does protoplasm generate enough nutrition to enable not just the mixing of sperm and ova but the ability of the human mammal female to retain the growing fetus inside herself?[40]

Ward's "The Gynæcocentric Theory" claims that, funnily enough, scientific evidence supports a theory that the human species began as female. Ward drew on Darwin, Charles Lyell, Herbert Spencer, John A. Ryder, Edouard Van Beneden, and other zoologists to support this alleged scientific fact. In Ward's view, the Arachnida, or spider, class is not an evolutionary perversion but an ancient form of reproductive exchange in which the female extracts sperm and consumes the sperm donor. Ward then contests the popular view that the human male, male mammals generally, and male birds are superior to the female and that the female is a form of "arrested development" in the human species, where males evolved more quickly than females. Ward's comments are ingenious. The female, he argues, represents the normal condition, while the condition of the male is *abnormal*. In species terms, females must remain the center of gravity in all biological systems and must select for variation; males just provide it. Ward interpreted sexual selection as nature's mechanism to continue the female-centeredness of reproduction and preserve the female's status as the "hereditary trunk" of what we now call DNA and RNA. Though the female is the ancestral trunk in humans, unlike other mammals, the sexes choose each other on the basis of different, functional, evolutionary mandates.

Consequently, while females are the original humans, males began as an extrusion to make it possible for a single, female, human host to extrude a human sperm, and it began at the instigation of females. In Ward's imagination, the evidence presented a situation in which female humans sexually selected for rationality, rather than for strength or good looks, in what over time emerged to become men. Indeed, women started to accidentally breed men who were superrational, and that led to the tipping point, the gender power imbalance. Ward is careful to say that both sexes in humans *possess* rationality. But he is more interested in how an evolutionary speedup, an increased rationality in men, enabled them to seize control of children from mothers. Rationality in men had led to the overthrow of the mother right and the establishment of patriarchy. Luckily, of course, an evolutionary redress to this injustice was already in process. Men abuse women not because they are hateful, strong, stupid, or brutish. Men have simply not yet evolved the capacity for empathy that women have. As women begin to sexually select men for empathy, the most egregious abuses of the patriarchal present should resolve themselves, and women will have bred a superior group of mates.

Several questions arise out of Li's preoccupation with Ward: (1) To what degree did Li bring "the gynæcocentric theory" into his sociology, and (2) is the fascination with the animal origins of sexual selection and social evolution a shared socialist tradition, or is it particularly pronounced in Mao Zedong Thought? Like Qu Qiubai, Li was drawn from the start to the philosophical implications of dialectical materialism. He felt attracted to translating and publishing core Japanese social science theory as well as basic works on land and politically strategic analyses of economy and society. An itinerant Marxist philosopher, he taught in universities, always in danger, always outside of yet dependent on his Chinese Communist Party connections. He survived, was readmitted to the party after Liberation (the end of the civil war in 1949), and worked closely with the orthodox strains of thought that would culminate in Mao Zedong Thought until he was murdered in a hospital in 1966. As Nick Knight points out, what binds Li to the Marxist project are his certainty that philosophy has a political purpose, his preoccupation with how to diagnose social problems in order to grasp social change, and his struggle to resolve the tension between natural and social science. He would eventually adapt his thinking to Engels's position laid out in *Dialectics of Nature*.

Like Qu Qiubai, Li was superbly intellectual, and he opened up ideas that motivated revolutionary commitment and action. Li knew international socialist and Marxist debates very well, including ongoing philosophical contentions in Moscow. He was not isolated. His work is not "sinicized" or particularly "Chinese," because it was preoccupied with intricate Soviet Marxism. For instance, in the 1920s a debate broke out among Mark Borisovich Mitin, Emmanuel Semënovic Enčmen, Bukharin, and Deborin over the degree of relative autonomy that the superstructure and human volition played in politics; in the early 1930s, a similar debate was revived among Stalin, Mitin, Pavel Yudin, and Vasily Raltsevich. While Li had to rely on Japanese texts to access ideas from the USSR, these were abundant, and Li selected Deborin and Mitin, who, although hostile to one another, concurred on the centrality of contradiction in the dialectic; both agreed on a social etiology for sudden developmental leaps or historical events and also agreed that the unity of opposites was a *natural* law, as well as a sociological truth. This was true because the unity of opposites had been resolved in the science of physics.[41]

To what degree did Li continue to fold into Marxism the question of women's centrality in social evolution? Over the 1920s, Li's grasp of Russian materialist conceptions of history and Marxist theory of social change developed in relation to changes in Moscow and the cycles of Sino-Japanese translation. By the 1930s, Li was emphasizing the "causal primacy within the forces of production, and in particular within its sphere of technology," but at the same time balancing this formula against his persistent and initial appreciation of the relative powers of the superstructure.[42] As early as the 1926 volume *Modern Sociology*, Li considered the relation of sub and superstructure to be a feedback loop in which developments in one would be translated into actions carried out effectively in the other. This is a standard dialectical position. Rooted in economic determination in the last instance, Li put politics in charge as he wrote and translated volume after volume of exposition on the dialectic, on the materialism of social relations, on the possibility of land revolution, and so on. In his *Outline of Sociology*, he would further develop an immanent critique that places causality within an "internally generated motion."[43]

In his major work, *Modern Sociology*, Li distanced himself from major nonsocialist tendencies in the study of society. The mission of sociology, he wrote, is to grasp and change the thing called society. Making Ellwood his straw-man bourgeois theorist, Li shows Ellwood placing sexual reproduction at the center of social theory and animating reproduction with instinctive drives but in the end reaching a theoretical impasse because this simple theory cannot address social injustice. Sociologies rooted in instinctual drives cannot reach beyond reformism, according to Li, since they revolve around the question of what is natural to the species. This short-circuits the relation between animal drives and social habits, confusing the two and appealing to change on an individual ethical level via self-restraint or legal enforcement. While Li criticized sociologies rooted in European contract theory and natural rights, he is more emphatic about psychological forms of sociology than abstract ideas of contracts and rights. In terms of social essence (*shehui benzhi*) and the alleviation of injustice, then, European contract theory, biological sociology, and sociology of emotion are at best ameliorative.

Yet Li was not reactive. After sketching out the weaknesses of sociological traditions that make law, biology, or emotion the central motive force in theories of society's origins and its laws of change, Li defined historical materialism around those same questions. In other words, it is not that law, procreative physiology, and emotional life are bad or worthless objects of study. But when measured against the relations of production and productive forces, they are not strong enough to sustain a plausible general theory of reality. While Li, to my knowledge, did not directly address the question of scientific representation of reality, he presumed what Qu Qiubai had sought to demonstrate, that the advantage of the social sciences was that they described and analyzed the reality of social relations and the ways social change could be understood and channeled. That is why Li seems to take most umbrage against Ellwood, who relied heavily on instinctual and emotive ethics to approach what he called social problems. The social-problem focus entangled natural desire and social factors in an unsustainable mixture, according to Li. This led to excessive individualism in the theory because if Ellwood argues that sexual desire is the origin of society, then society is naive and unself-reflective; this "bourgeois" origin story puts the brakes on social awareness and social or political action. It is a fundamental problem with all natural science–based instinct theories that cross the line between the natural and the social sciences. It does not admit human consciousness into its framework. And without consciousness there is only reformism or devolution. Indeed, Ellwood's theory of evolutionary reform and poverty amelioration left control of society in the hands of the most conservative stratum of the ruling class. Thus, for all Ellwood's vaunted interest in social problems, in Li's reckoning Ellwood's direction was not an appropriate one for Chinese materialist sociology to take. Like social contract and emotion-driven theories, amelioration is restricted to existing minority power elites, and they have little reason to change the stasis. From the perspective of Chinese historical materialist sociological theory, Li argued, the emotions and physiology and the law of contract appear but in a different guise, in a different relationship to the motive force.

Sociology, Li stated, must use historical materialist methods to explain social essence. Historically, society had not required contractual relations to form itself. Society also did not emerge out of human imagination or emotional attachments, and it was and is not the sum total of organisms operating unconsciously in relation to subliminal natural law. Only when people enter into production relationships does society or social essence appear, for those who do not work do not eat. Humans started as a horde and lived by satisfying immediate natural desires for sex and food, but even in primitive times, the ancients began to regulate their animality because, using the materials they had at hand, they began to realize the efficacy of systems of exchange, systems of social relations, and eventually incest taboos; this led, in turn, to economic advances, and humanity left the natural environment's restraints behind.[44] The tension between our social self-consciousness and our ability as social beings to augment and change our selves and surroundings was never a repudiation of our mammal origins but rather a leave-taking. Unlike the bees or the vegetables, humans became self-aware human animals.

Put another way, Li's *Modern Sociology*, which became the period's best-selling introduction to historical materialism and was constantly reissued, asserted that biology, physiology, anatomy, and the natural sciences crystallized into a scientific worldview situating natural science inside social relations of production. In the various social processes that Li described in his lyrical classical Chinese, the natural or mammal human could not but eventually be dominated by its own creation, society, the sum total of all social relationships of production, exchange, and reproduction. As differentiation of work occurred and space and circumference of exchange widened, mutual relations of work drove social evolution forward. But where theorists of desire or emotion had argued that mammals are driven by either evolving sensitivity to variation or aesthetic pleasure or appreciation of rationality, Li argued that in the process of material production, a spiritual culture arises out of the material productive relations, causing pleasure, improving the productive forces, and stimulating social evolution. Social progress is the progress of the productive forces.

In his book's short chapters, originally designed to be lectures, Li incorporated much European nineteenth-century philosophy of rights, instincts, sexuality, and sexual reproduction into his explanation of the relation between the economic base and the superstructure. He carefully illuminated the significance of politics and law in class conflict, relations of class under the state, and the current global economic and political conjuncture. But then he moved toward a consideration of what he would call the spiritual elements of human social life. Ethics holds the same status in social evolution as does instinct, he argued. Embedded in the human animal, ethics evolves out of herd integrity because an individual human will sacrifice themselves for the species.[45] The major world religions are just versions of ways that human societies have organized themselves historically and spatially, to ideologize herd integrity. Art is the concrete expression of our social lives. And, definitively, the superstructure, the place where human creativity and will are expressed, rests dynamically on an economic base consisting of the relations of production and productive forces.

In his culminating statement on the role of the superstructure, Li struck a note that is important for a number of reasons. First, he asserted, the object of philosophy is to understand completely the axiomatic relation of humanity and nature. In his first great synthetic work, the philosopher sought to bridge the problem evolutionary theory had posed, which is that human sexual reproduction is both mammal *and* social behavior, an injunction from nature and a complex social exchange and negotiation. Second, philosophical concepts must be understood to be embryonic elements of the material world, mediated in social economic relations. Always influenced by their situated environment, people will almost involuntarily turn to the exercise of intention to establish social relations. Prevailing thought is connected to power holding and to the desires of the ruling class. Most philosophies show a distinct class character. But, third, thought, in the form of philosophy, has finally evolved a position of autonomy. Philosophy is at the stage of being able to expose for social analysis natural secrets that until now had defied explanation.[46]

The role of scientific philosophy is therefore, as we saw in Qu Qiubai, the capacity to see the logos in the body. The natural sciences clarify and make real to our senses the rational secrets locked in nature. The social sciences track how the dialectic transforms social life and history faithfully. Here Li repeats the promise of mimesis, to represent accurately and correctly the reality of society in its natural-historical and its social evolutionary guises. In his long chapter on kinship, we find that his foremost instance is sexual reproduction and the extension of human society through the familiar cycles of the matriarchate, the patriarchy, the gens/clan, and the state. To bolster his argument that the clan or kinship is the cradle of society, Li invoked Engels, Bachofen, Lewis Henry Morgan (whose work on tribal nations, including the Iroquois, Marx and Engels had cannibalized), and John Ferguson McClennan, the Scottish ethnologist whom Engels relied on in his *The Origin of the Family, Private Property and the State* (1884).

Although Li does not repeat Ward's claim that humanity began with the female, he does not repudiate it either. It has become, in a sense, beside the point. It does not matter historically how sexual reproduction developed zoologically out of protoplasm; we would not exist without physiological change, but that is no longer Li's primary issue. What matters in social terms is how, once the *species-being* of human mammals' organic procreative practices was established, kinship relations evolved to support social development. One marker of the humanity of the human mammals was the species transition out of primeval promiscuity and into regulated sexual reproduction: various forms of exchange, sibling incest, group marriage, exchange marriages rooted in kidnapping, bride stealing, and other anthropological residues that ethnologists and anthropologists like Morgan postulated were the roots of modern practices. Casual sexual encounters increasingly gave way to productive roles.

That is why the current bourgeois form of exclusive marriage will not be the final solution in the continuous relation of evolution to primal nature and sociality, rooted in taste and mutual attraction, for individuals. And, most important, this is why women are at the center of the *proletarian* revolution. Born out of economic necessity and socially retained to accumulate wealth, the bourgeois marriage form and its inhuman patrilineal customs have reached an evolutionary dead-end.[47]

FOUNDATIONAL CHINESE SOCIOLOGY AND SOCIAL REVOLUTION

Stabilizing a platform called *society* in sociology took a long time. Questions of categories and referentiality, or basic assumptions in thinking and the ways that expression confirms the truth, all changed as theoreticians injected new realities into the world. The theorization required a concerted debate over specific kinds of society in specific places. By the time sociologist Chen Han-seng wrote his classic study on tobacco farming and commercial capital under U.S., British, and Japanese imperialism, Chinese and Sino-focused sociology was as sophisticated as advertising theory and its subdiscipline, selling social science. While Qu Qiubai's productive life was cut short, Li Da went on translating and rethinking how to describe Chinese society and what kinds of revolutionary action might be appropriate to the real conditions at hand. When Chinese sociological norms finally stabilized, the Marxist philosophical wing continued to theorize the ascent of humans and the role of human sexual reproduction in primitive, barbarian, and civilized societies. A U.S.-style, U.S.-educated empirical wing took up surveys and disciplinary debates. Their work was certainly loyal to the truth of physiology and thus participated in the event of women, but it made women into a demographic marker within a naturalistic patriliny. While for Li, what requires fidelity is women's priority and organic creation of the society as such, among the vernacularist empiricists whom I take up in the next chapter, women never posed a philosophical, foundational problem.

The Marxist philosophical heritage never stopped thinking about how society had emerged in the first instance and what role the human female played in social evolution. It continued to link the evolution of morals to the evolution of society and to insist that revolutionary values were an extension of the natural evolution of better women and better men. Importantly, Li and Qu never repudiated the European bourgeois sources of their inspiration. They assimilated and transformed them. There was no scholarly repudiation because sociologists in China during this period were all familiar with basic social theory. Yan Fu had translated sociological theories, and as we see in the next chapter, even ordinary readers, elites, and nonsociologists read vernacular sociology and published their comments in short articles or opinion pieces. While professional American sociology was a major presence in Chinese universities during these years, Li and Qu had no contact with it.[48]

Thus, there is little intellectual overlap between pioneer Marxist sociologists and major empiricist, university-oriented intellectuals like Sun Benwen (1892–1979; doctoral degree from New York University), Tao Menghua (1887–1960; doctoral degree from the London School of Economics), and Lin Yaohua (1910–2000; doctoral degree from Harvard University). Empirically minded scholars—students trained in these programs and by American sociologists like Sidney Gamble, with funding from U.S. foundations and universities—became a wing of the Nationalist governing apparatus. Social engineers participated in the rise of the new universities I noted briefly, which found support from local Chinese power holders, Chinese governments and party states, and particularly religious organizations and entities like the Rockefeller Foundation, the YWCA, and other Christian-inspired, progressive groups. Empiricists who remained in China after Liberation in 1949 fell under suspicion, and the new government of the People's Republic of China abolished sociology departments, calling the academic discipline a tainted bourgeois pseudoscience.

Revolutionary urgency and the real conditions of their fugitive lives meant that Qu and Li did not form a school of sociology. The basic divide in social theory was philosophical. These and other wings of Chinese social science did cotheorize the event of women, however. In the end, a cosmopolitan Chinese Marxist philosophical tradition addressed the problem of physiological woman in biological and social evolution. The event of women in China had multiple sources. Marxists and, as I indicated highlighting He-Yin Zhen's philosophy, anarchists made the event a mainstay question and continued to loyally present true evidence of women's origins. In their view, the zoological ascent of the female of the species was a new truth, and the political struggle to install it took a long time.

In the chapter that follows, I analyze far less sophisticated disputes about the status of the female human in society and remedies, large and small, for alleviating the social exploitation of women's labor and reproductive capacity. So-called vernacular sociology was a form of scientism, or popular, degraded, aphoristic use of categories like instinct, sexuality, social role, social problem, and so on. But here the point is that Marxist and anarchist social philosophy rested on theories about the horde and the ancient matriarchy and consequently made female social contributions a sine qua non of evolutionary sociology. Ideologies generated and chosen by ancestral humans arise out of the relations of production and not only change over time but also, at the beginning and the end of the teleology, hold out the promise of *equivalence in difference*. At issue in Chinese Marxist sociology are truth and evolutionary urgency, human praxis, and also the promise that liberation is achievable. Li contributed to the theorization of the social relations of production, and Qu to the principle of mimesis in scholarship. Their insistence that the origins of human society lie in the procreative act joining together women and men is a scientific claim. The event of women is indisputable in natural science.

CHAPTER THREE

Vernacular Sociology

Vernacular sociology is a tremulous amalgam of natural science, social science, and mimesis. Previous chapters have shown corporate imperialist marketers harnessing social surveys to construct commodity markets. I also showed that commercialization normalized the idea that in society people should buy branded commodities. When advertisers built business models to accelerate surpluses—Vilhelm Meyer, commercial advertising mogul C. P. Ling, and corporate imperialist Nakayama Taiji were all speculators in this sense—they anticipated future profits. They sought to borrow cash money and invest it under conditions of limited liability, to get surplus the next year and expand their productive capacity forever; that is, theories about how capitalism works reinforced the future anteriority expressed in sociological reasoning. Readers familiar with the European debate between Louis Althusser and Adam Schaff will immediately recognize my position. Schaff argued that all philosophy is written in the future anterior, because theory is, or equates to, disciplined speculation about a future rooted in a correct appreciation of a present conjuncture, while Althusser, like Michel Foucault, actually discounted subjective time (human voluntarism), recognizing only breaks, gaps, and disruptions in a geologic historical temporality.[1]

This chapter underscores the notion that popular generalizations also embed futurity. Unlike Marxists, however, they canonized assumptions about animals, including ourselves, who form societies and relationships on the basis of instinctual drives. Associative rather than analytic, vernacularists proposed that since (in relation to insects or fish) our physiological makeup makes our bodies more flexible, our natural instincts drive us to form procreative couples. Arguing that monogamy is instinctual and yet it needs to be instituted in China's future society is to claim both a sexually distinctive origin story and a return to the future, but, spurious or not, this argument opens a transvaluation of values. The modernist thought revolutions we know as the New Culture Movement (ca. 1915–1930) or the May Fourth Movement (ca. 1919) sought scientific, and modernist ethical foundations to repudiate the large-family system. More than most turn-of-the-century sociology discussed in earlier chapters, vernacularists made the fabulous accusation that plural, polyandrous, child, and polygamous marriages were *unnatural* and impeded Chinese social and natural or racial evolution. This is not a natural rights argument or even an ethical insight; it is a popular adjustment of social Darwinian logic to the desires of an aspirational bourgeoisie.

In fact, at the time these contradictory and teleological theories emerged in the late Qing period, a consensus still held that procreative family only existed to fulfill patrilineal expectations that everyone produce sons, fathers, and grandsons. Late imperial procreative relationships could be arranged in a huge variety of ways (marriage, concubinage, polygamy, polyandry, household women, contractual conceptions, etc.). As historian Francesca Bray shows between the fourteenth and nineteenth centuries, a gap had opened separating procreation from kinship relations and reifying an elite domestic hierarchy, in which ritual first wives took exclusive maternal possession, becoming the primary mother of all the husband's children. Any plural sexual relationships the male family members struck up with second wives or concubines and maids all had legal standing, but the biological mothers of resulting children could not claim the children as their own. Ritual kinship order trumped gestational biology.[2]

Mainstream May Fourth social theory and youth culture in the 1920s revolved around what intellectuals called *social problems*, or *shehui wenti*. Thus, the woman problem, the youth problem, the rural problem, the language problem all were identified and sociologically defined. To reiterate, a fulsome eugenic stance on individual sexual selection underwrites this notion but it is internally inconsistent. Vernacular sociologists' progressive temporality promised to remake social relationships to approximate what it posited were "natural" ones, or humanity's instinctual order. This suggests that what they meant by social problem measured aberrance in relation to allegedly social scientific norms and therefore natural truths. So besides positing Chinese culture's relative "unnaturalness" this ideology promoted the truism that animal instincts drive individual people to form families, that push humans into sophisticated, highly articulated societies where, in evolutionary theoretical terms, we often encounter developmental problems. While this formula has difficulty differentiating what is social from what is natural, that is not a reason to disregard it since vernacular sociology excited popular imagination and introjected itself into the textbook market, as Peter G. Zarrow has shown. The conventional elite big family with its multiple wives, its subordinated women who did not own their own children, got attacked for being unnatural, socially backward, not able to consume or evolve appropriately, and immoral.[3]

Commercial ephemera played a role in establishing the "social problem" paradigm. A 1931 Sincere Department Store advertisement (figure 3.1) standardized the notion that consuming modern products is a *zoologically* reasonable act in a capitalist society. The text suggests that buying commodities renders a service to society, because the more you consume, the more your race, nation, and culture progress or evolve. This is vernacular sociology expressed in commercial terms. It asserts that society's substrate is biological and that biology's expression is not only social but, since it is social, also commercial and by nature commodified and acquisitive.[4] To repeat, while sexual and social evolution are never easy to disaggregate in modern thought, in this drawing a girl figure chooses the most modern industrially produced commodity to buy and thereby magically adds potent energy to the nation. High-end product advertising glamorizes acquisition while providing a social scientific justification for a class fantasy.[5]

There are three overlapping, discernible cohorts in the vernacular sociological stream. First, there are vulgarized versions of Yan Fu's British empiricism. In contrast to Chinese Marxists, who pioneered dialectical logic to explain social evolution, vernacularists in the Yan Fu school argued allegorically: they were sensible, but they were not reflexive or interested in considering the problems their own thinking raised. The second group consists of Japanese contemporaries like Ariga Nagao, whose works translated from Japanese into Chinese underwrote late Qing dynastic reforms. Ariga, like so many contemporary Japanese intellectuals, read European social theory and brought ideas into Japanese

3.1 Ad for Sincere Department Store with an iconic modern girl gazing in awe at her mail-delivered commodities. *Funü zazhi* 17, no. 8 (August 1931).

circles for many reasons but among them to legitimate Japan's imperialist projects. Japanese theorists who entered into this stream of Chinese-language translations aligned social evolutionary theory and instinct to generalize about the struggle of the fittest nations, races, and imperial projects. The third group are a younger, vernacularizing May Fourth cohort that Tsing-song Vincent Shen calls the "social science humanists" and Wang Xiaodan terms "the new intellectuals."[6] Shen's characterization rests on a joke, which is that humanists like Ma Junwu (1881–1940), who, over the course of his lifetime, translated the entire corpus of Charles Darwin's works (and Zhou Jianren [1888–1984], who also translated Darwin and wrote eugenics for mass audiences), were literary translators.

To put this bluntly, social science humanists had no social science background. Vernacularizing social science became a sideline occupation for educated Chinese during the first half of the twentieth century, and the reverse also proved true: literary scholars with no literary backgrounds emerged out of the natural and social sciences into general popular or vernacular social theory. Significant numbers of educated men who started or even completed degrees in new science disciplines like economics (the literary pioneer Yu Dafu), medicine (the writers Guo Moruo and Lu Xun), and military engineering (the cultural theorist Cheng Fangwu) ended up champions of the human sciences. An excellent model of a social science humanist is Zhang Ziping, who, to support his cultural activities, began as a professional geologist and is remembered for his pioneering role in the modern small-press movement. As historian Ling Shiao has shown, small presses competed with the three big, capital-intensive national presses—Shangwu, Zhonghua, and Shijie—when the topic was vernacular social science.[7]

YAN FU'S SCHOOL OF VERNACULAR SOCIOLOGY

Yan Fu's most widely read book was Thomas Henry Huxley's *Evolution and Ethics*, which Yan reconfigured into a best-selling "translation," *Tianyan lun* (On evolution); but his *Shehui tongquan* (Full account of society) also interpreted William Stanley Jevons and John Stuart Mill on logic, Montesquieu's *The Spirit of the Laws*, and Edward Jenks's *History of Politics*. Yan was a complex figure, and the Huxley meditation had an enormous impact, but he was a generation older than the New Culture Movement vernacularists, and for all their strangeness, his interpretations ruptured norms in a way that no one had before and opened the floodgates for a younger cohort. Shen notes that in "Yan Fu's translation, [Huxley's] hypothetical sentences become categorical assumptions, while the descriptive sentences become involved with emotional and affective interpretations."[8] This holds true generally in vernacular sociology, but Yan can serve as the exemplar because he insisted that "science" is a true theory about tangible evidence and therefore a picture of reality; that is what scientific mimesis promises. So the allegorical logic that Yan developed in his Spencerian Darwinism does precisely what professional sociologists like Fan Jichang railed against; it turned a hypothesis into an assertion. In 1924, in "Shehui kexue he benneng de wenti" (Social science and the instinct problem), Fan was already calling out the idea that physiology motivates social progress.[9] Whenever inept social scientists cannot resolve something, Fan acerbically noted, they call in so-called animal-instinct theory to back them up. "Social science should basically get rid of talk about instinct," he wrote. "Instinct theory in psychology was originally an 'as if' proposition, not a fact. Hypotheses [*jiashe*] in science are often an absolutely necessary tool used to explain and analyze actuality. But a hypothesis can never simply be used indiscriminately to explain a phenomenon."[10]

That said, according to Yan's text, there are three levels of *empirical* truth: the astral (the Copernican revolution in space and modern astronomy), the bio (physiology, natural selection, sexual selection), and the socio, and each is a revelation because they are demonstrable and tangible. At the astral level, atomic theory and chemistry demonstrate truth; at the biological level, readers have the truth of natural selection ensuring the survival of the human species; and the social sciences prove humans build increasingly complex social worlds inside nature. This last dimension gives social science its scientific gloss.[11] Yan's argument— remember that he is speaking through Huxley and Darwin, voicing his own opinion—goes like this: As humanity learned to invest its animal essence in nature, the achievements of socialized humans accelerated, and the global population expanded, forcing Europeans into colonization projects. Given the historical propagation of European colonialism, humanity confronted problems. Humans, unlike worker bees in the beehive, become more human and less animal as an effect of living in groups, but it is not ethically or zoologically feasible to breed humans in the way that humans breed insects, plants, and animals. This is an obvious dilemma if one is being colonized. More positively, however, unlike bees or other social insects, humans, even when facing a necessarily imposed oppression, have no physiological constraints on their ability to actively change the environment and their own being. Only humans continue to evolve *socially*. In Yan's interpretation, imperialism, colonialism, overpopulation, and racialism played a salutary role in China's social evolution.

In the chapter of his *On Evolution* titled, "Human Society," Yan directly invoked society as a category to address the philosophical question of the humanity of human animals. In his version, humans are the zoological or biological elite because social groupings (*qun*) facilitate our species development. Like Li Da and so many other Marxists and vernacularists, Yan also situated sexual difference at the center of human existence. Because humans improve at the level of our biological substrate and through time in the process of our social differentiation, the astral level of knowledge is increasingly open to human empirical scientific understanding and to ontological speculation. That is, socially advanced people can grasp all levels of reality. Unlike other animals, particularly insects, our physiques make it possible for us to develop socially and intellectually *as we also evolve biologically*. Evolution itself has made it possible for us to understand the reality of nature, geologic time, and social forces and even gives us the capacity to understand reality. This was a foundational epistemic move and is probably the reason that Yan, despite his eccentricities and willfulness, is a major contemporary intellectual figure.[12]

THE POLYMORPHOUS ORIGINS OF CHINESE VERNACULAR SOCIOLOGY

Late Qing scholar-officials had turned toward social science seeking the intellectual roots of power after China's 1895 loss to Japan in the First Sino-Japanese War. While Japanese imperialism had caused the catastrophe, Qing and post-dynastic intellectual radicals seemed less interested in positing Chinese singularity than in learning from social scientific styles of writing translated from Japanese into Chinese. In other words, they did not dwell on what special characteristics of Chinese culture had led to failure (although this would later become a standard part of Chinese intellectual culture) but rather presented translations that, while obviously chauvinistic and clearly Japan oriented, made universalist claims. The vernacularists not only did not nationalize international social science but did the reverse, setting into circulation their own interpretations of theories and theorists wherever they found them. This was the shortcut around Europe, which Chinese social science advocates concluded lay behind Japan's successful intellectual revolution during the Meiji Restoration.[13]

Wang Xiaodan's history of Chinese social science translation illuminates this seeming obliviousness to nationalist perspectives. First, Wang notes that vernacularists were indiscriminate.[14] Second, Wang sees a cohort of these new intellectuals carving out a fresh modernist profile in Chinese intellectual history, and, third (Wang's core point), the vernacularist wave, as we saw in the case of early Marxist theory, went for social science epistemology.[15] Vernacularists shared with social science a belief that natural science opened the door to accurate, objective or mimetic representation and that the social sciences could do the same with appropriate methods. Social sciences held out the promise of a universalist language in which all of humanity registered their own local particularities.

Figure 3.2 shows an ad for Japanese Ajinomoto cooking powder that ran perennially in Chinese-language newspapers. The cartoon shows a modern Chinese city. In between the sketched-out blocks of tall buildings is a skyscraper-size package of the taste-enhancing cooking powder, or MSG (monosodium glutamate). Skyscrapers and Ajinomoto—one a part of a modern cityscape, the other a chemical compound—belong in the same imaginary universe of a commodity-rich world that popular sociology rationalizes. The ad's ordinariness, despite its multilingual orthography, indicates that it participated in naturalizing social life, vernacularizing what are actually complex new ideas. Why put a box of amino acids into a modern landscape? The answer is that advertising condenses knowledge into graphic form and displaces the world of the senses with a future imagined world of plenty. Life, it turns out, is chemistry! Also, a newly discovered social unconscious (analyzed in chapters 4 and 5) meant that graphic and linguistic displacements were endless. Japanese ads and Japanese-language translations of European Enlightenment philosophy that were then translated into Chinese became omnipresent, prosaic fixtures in Chinese vernacular society, graphesis and popular sociology.

For instance, between 1902 and 1915, two translations of Japanese Sinophobe Ariga Nagao's *Shehui jinhua lun* (On social evolution) appeared in Chinese.[16] Repeated translations and multiple reissues suggest that the text was profitable and popular. The primary questions are, first, why readers liked it so much, given Ariga's position on what he called the double obscurantism of Chinese civilization and the disparaging term *Zhina* that he used throughout and, second, how deeply texts like this one affected Chinese readers of vernacular social theory.[17] *On Social Evolution* appears to have offered readers the same quality Yan Fu's texts did. Analytically speaking, in the world of ideas and new cultural movements, the Chinese were translating the universal social epistemology seemingly without concern about Sinophobia, so maybe they appreciated Ariga's attack on the same old Chinese thinking that they would oppose in the New Culture and May Fourth eras.

These are intriguing concerns because Ariga was situated with Inoue Tetsujiro and Toyama Shoichi, who also authored major attacks on so-called Chinese learning in Japan in the 1880s.[18] As they turned "away from Asia and toward Europe [*Datsu-a*]," Japanese scholars repudiated *Japan's* Confucius school and established epistemological positions expressed in German and French philosophy. Although Ariga's reasoning

3.2 Ajinomoto ad showing a cityscape. *Dagongbao* 7 (July 21, 1923).

differed from Qu Qiubai's theory of historical residues, *On Social Evolution* also postulated that the Chinese language was expendable and that people would be better off without it. He believed it relied "on physical form to indicate the abstract"; physicality restricted the Chinese intellectual's ability to generalize, to "describe abstract relations and hence to develop science and foster progress."[19] Of course this is Sinophobic and absurd, but its perspective is philosophical in the European sense. It also expressed Japanese intellectuals' worries over the alleged dead physicality of received Chinese ideas and the brake this putatively put on Japanese philosophical creativity. Not much space separates Ariga and Chinese intellectuals like Qu and Lu Xun, who feared that Chinese intellectuals would be forever caught in the retarding, deadly vise of inherited literary writing.

Whether Sinophobic or Sinophilic, late nineteenth-century Japanese social scientists had already miraculated a nameable object, society, before Yan Fu interpreted the foundations of European social science. Society in Japanese speculative work was a reified, organic entity amenable to scientific law and political praxis. However, unlike new

Chinese scholar-translators, Japanese intellectuals leveraged society to rethink Japaneseness on a new and allegedly scientific basis and to produce modern interpretations of Japan's past, present, and future.[20] Unlike the calque and concept of *the people* or even *the nation*, the term *society* opened up a philosophical and empirical proof of human agency and thereby authorized Japanese theorists' intent on controlling the general course of social development.[21] Consequently, Ariga's book opened with the declaration "The phenomenon of human society exists in truth, and it compels a rational analysis to fix the meaning of social phenomena, which is why we have sociology."[22] Sociology's special brief, the thing that other social science disciplines cannot do, is the sociology of ordinary phenomena. The sociology of ordinary phenomena does not mean particularism, however, or the worship of archaic facticity (an inherent failing of Chinese intellectual practice, in Ariga's view). Rather, phenomena are comprehensible in relation to larger or more abstract categories, which it is the central task of sociology to establish.[23]

Two points followed, according to Ariga (in Chinese translations). First, historical sociology must determine which factors have been at work in the rise of the fittest nations—Japan and Britain—and the decline, or even the incorporation through imperialism, of weaker ones, such as the subjugation of Greece to Rome (or China to Japan). Second, society is itself an agent. Although humans are social animals, our evolutionary drive and basic instincts, expressed socially in the struggle of the fittest, fold humanity into more and more complex social formations. These formations, in turn, also struggle to survive, and one of their strategies, the one that Ariga explicitly endorses, is to incorporate primitive protohuman hordes into themselves; this lays the groundwork for Japanese imperialist assimilation theory. His discussion on how society emerges historically from its protohuman form into the highly articulated relation of individuals among one another and of masses to the social whole is flexible and sophisticated. He is as conversant with the social evolution of the American aboriginal Comanches and Dakotas as he is with the Madagascar primitives, which all Spencerian philosophers had to be.[24] The motility of societies, units of competitive drives, offers the possibility of accelerating development. Given this, perhaps what Chinese readers found most centrally interesting was the logical connection Ariga drew between individual improvement, the accelerating development of society, and the need to enlarge and improve patriotism (*aiguo zhixin*) through disciplined industry, scholarship, and native aesthetics.[25]

Ariga's story about the evolutionary rise of human subjects occurs in the chapter on "groups" or "society," which the Chinese translator rendered as *qun*. As per the cliché, more than two persons living together in a group form a society. The discipline for studying people in groups or society is called either *qunxue* or *shehuixue*. The object of sociology is to address what is called a "subject of consideration," or *duixiang*. The question that sociology addresses in its objective research is called a "sociological subject," and an "item" (*shixiang*) is a social or sociological problem. And he goes on thus for pages; methods are delineated in capsule form (the rational method, the experiential method, etc.), and differences among scientific inductive and deductive or nonempirical methods are all carefully laid out à la the *New Erya*. Each element of the modernist lexicon is carefully burnished and defined.

These are no longer just vocabulary lessons but rather toeholds in a great facade of sociological comprehension to which Chinese popular elites reading and writing in the 1920s clung in an effort to valorize individual volition. The individual is a core element of vernacular social science theory. In the Ariga translation, the individual is where society and nature meet. Women are a social problem, but the male individual became an agonistic ideological subject in political struggles among May Fourth cohorts, who returned over and over to the truths of their own personalities and to the question of how Chinese people improve. Sexuality was our animal instinct: in good societies it leads to eugenic progress, and in bad ones it is repressed, leading to devolution.

THE INDIVIDUAL IN VERNACULAR SOCIOLOGY

Endo Ryukichi's *Modern Sociology*, published in Japan in 1903 and in Chinese translation in 1920, illustrates how the individual became a foundational argument in Chinese vernacular sociology.[26] Endo condensed into systematic terms ideas that became normative in advertising images, movies, personal testimonials, personal autobiographies, and the new modern fiction. In Endo's view, all interior feelings, desires, will, intellect, and mediated instinctual needs that our animal nature has imposed on us are expressed individually. Endo was concerned with both the basic theories of general sociology (which, of course, means primarily French, German, and U.S. scholarship) and with how Western social theories measured up in relation to East Asian social forms. *Modern Sociology* begins with a general introduction to the types of sociology and their contents, their materials and methods, and their major problematics and systems. It moves on to chapters on precursors, the sociological method and its relation to natural sciences, the subjective factors in sociology (desire, subject, ideation), statistics and statistical categories, the study of social development, primitive society and matrilineality, social systems, key figures in social theory (Lester Ward, Émile Durkheim, J. H. W. Stuckenberg, Herbert Spencer, etc.), and foundational problems in sociology. Endo's particular concern was the question of individual subjectivity, and within that, he singled out the problem of the human will.

Endo adapted U.S. sociologist Lester Ward's theories regarding the material foundations of human life as detailed in Ward's 1898 *Outlines of Sociology*. Having emerged out of primal matter or plasma, Ward postulated, humans are an assertive and self-evolving species. Of all the complex elements that make up individuals, the will (*yizhi*) compels and organizes action, including self-evolution. Thus, for instance, in a detailed discussion of the relationship between desire (*yuwang*) and will, Endo develops a complex argument regarding the relationship of desiring, willing, and compelling the other in relation to one's self. Each quality of personhood, willing and desiring, is a separate capacity or function inside individuals.[27] The will is exercised in relation to desire or the psychology of emotions and, very important, spirit (*jingshen*) and so on by consolidation (*jiehe*), a process that will not concern us here. In his conclusion, Endo asserts that the unit of all of these calculations is the individual (*geren*).[28] And he situates individuals in every major social collectivity (nation, race, etc.) one would expect late nineteenth- and early twentieth-century evolutionary sociology to assert, no matter where in the world one encountered it.

Endo's writing is not professional sociology, and his speculation is not philosophy in the Marxian or Hegelian tradition, either. It is loosely empiricist and vaguely notional, built on the foundation of European and U.S. sociological speculations refracted through the sensibility and concerns of a self-identified Japanese nationalist translated into Chinese and being read in Chinese in Chinese cities. Two things are concerning at this juncture. First, the connection between the natural sciences and the social sciences—or physiology and society—in vernacular sociology gave Endo's new social categories (for example, society, desire, individual, and sexual essence) not merely a universalizing (all humans are the same) but a totalizing (what it means to be a human, humans are now capable of fully knowing) quality. There is no room in these generalizations for alternatives to the logic that individuals live in society. (One obvious alternative is the theory that we became a species in the process of mutually interdependent, affective relations starting at the earliest stages of creative hominoid evolution, a Bergsonian argument.) Endo and his modernist friends recognized different social origins, races, and sexes, but to them all history flowed in one direction because beneath historical change is evolutionary progress and its reproductive biology. Endo's argument reinforced the anatomically obvious natural man and natural woman just then populating advertising images.

Standing behind the question of will and willed behavior, in the shadows, is the question of what people desire and why they need Pond's vanishing cream or BAT's Three Castle brand cigarettes (figure 3.3)—"Everything you could desire" (shishi ruyi)—rather than homegrown tobacco or another brand. The advertisement shows an iconic Chinese woman celebrating National Day. She is a self-willed, skilled consumer, and she is inviting the crowd assembled below her to do what they want and enjoy themselves in the new nation. This ad image condenses desires into a simple, pleasing image saturated with complex new ideas. Vernacular sociology imagined it could explain how people manage in their social lives to negotiate their own humanity; the question of personality (renge), which progressive Chinese feminists pursued over the next decade, does not appear in Endo's text, but the theory that human individuals live together in societies as collectivities (markets, races, nations, communities, etc.) and in exercising their individual wills forward the aims of the race, nation, community, and self does. And when Endo talked about desire or will, he included the will to purchase and consume. Of course, he also meant women's will to get an education and everyone's will to be good parents and eugenic partners. But like the advertising in figures 3.1 and 3.3, Chinese readers of Endo saw the new society, the new consuming woman, and the new nation cheering her on to strength, prosperity, and happiness for all.

The 1865 "five-fold classification" of the Caucasian, Mongolian, Ethiopian, American, and Malayan world racial stocks and races, produced by J. F. Blumenbach (1752–1840), came into Chinese circulation via the Japanese theorist Shibue Tomotsu.[29] Perhaps the young woman who translated Shibue from Japanese, Ms. Jin Mingluan, liked Shibue's theory of sociosexual agglomeration, according to which sexual selection

3.3 Female consumer holding a *ruyi* symbolizing good fortune. *Dagongbao*, 98, no. 848 (December 29, 1929).

puts the autonomous will to choose sexual partners into the brains of the females of species.[30] Shibue linked naturalistic sexual attraction and racial purification, in the tradition of U.S. feminist Margaret Sanger, who toured China and Japan in the 1920s.[31] But any contemporary popular sociology in any of these languages tells the same story: the reproductive couple is the basic unit of family formation; families have historically taken diverse but, evolutionarily speaking, progressive forms (usually the progression is from polyandry to polygamy to monogamy); family, however organized and however closely it approximates the most natural productive procreative unit of one man and one woman, is the basis of society, and society is the foundation of the nation; the modern heterosexual couple is consequently both *modern* in the sense that it liberates women to choose male partners and *primeval* because it is also the most natural dyad available in eugenic or developmental sexuality.[32]

The *benneng*, or instinct problem, occupied a space in professional social science as well as popular agita. Guo Renyuan, a Berkeley-educated physiologist and psychologist, introduced Chinese readers to Karl

Groosse and William McDougall, major theorists of instinctual drives. Guo's background in embryology and somatically rooted biopsychological issues is less significant than his popularization of C. Lloyd Morgan's *Habit and Instinct*, William James's *Principles of Psychology*, McDougall's *Introduction to Social Psychology*, Herbert Spencer's *Principles of Psychology*, D. F. Philips's *Elements of Psychology*, and Théodule-Armand Ribot's *The Psychology of the Emotions* to support his own theories and experiments in instinctual psychology.[33] Distinguishing animal and human instincts, Guo deftly laid out the definition of instinct from English (not German, where the problem is more complex), starting with Spencer's theory of innate instinct and expanding into late nineteenth-century theories about reflexive instinct and psychology, perception, behavior and emotion, physiology, and life-stage instincts, from birth to adolescence.[34] Guo postulated a term for explaining the sexual and parental instinct, which he called the *nannü benneng,* literally, the instinct of the sex-differentiated human.[35] Likewise, Chen Dingmou, who trained at the University of Chicago Sociology Department, in 1915 returned to China to teach sociology at Fudan University. In his work, "Putong xinli, yi benneng" (Common psychology, translating instinct), Chen, too, undertook to popularize core instinct theory for the nonprofessional reader. The latest thing in psychology, he felt, was instinct-driven human psychology, feelings and emotion. On top of his exegesis of McDougall, Chen introduced Douglas Alexander Spalding, who like Chen was popularizing late nineteenth-century discussions of Darwinian instincts in lower mammals. Spalding's importance to Chen lay in the question of how, since drives are instinctual, psychological states unfold in social life.[36]

This was not a local problem but a general one because there seems to be no way of figuring out what determines even our commodity choices, our instinctive animal nature, or our executive function, our feelings, or our will. Academic intellectuals like Guo and Chen leaned on U.S. and British intellectual debates because they trained in the United States, but teachers and students were all vulgarizing the same set of ideas. Taking this debate seriously a century later is essential (and deeply irritating). Evolutionary philosophy put an epistemological vacuum in middle-brow social theory, and instinct held out a brass ring. This new dogma did not go wholly uncontested, however. Yan Jibo had registered deep concern about Guo's initiative in his essay "Faming shi renlei de benneng" (Invention is the instinct of humanity), but the most formidable antagonist of the moment was the counterevolutionary theorist Li Shicen (1892–1934). Li rooted his philosophy in Friedrich Nietzsche and Henri Bergson.[37] Bergson's role in flummoxing teleologies and natural selection with notions about creative evolution, subjective voluntarism, and human emotion has morphed in our time into Deleuzean philosophy, but May Fourth philosophers a century ago used Bergson and Nietzsche to call out Spencer's teleological view of human evolution.[38]

Li and Guo squared off over what proportion of measurable emotion or scientifically ascertainable humanity can be attributed to animal instinct and what proportion to cultural or social factors. Li's points are philosophical, whereas Guo was a research and lab psychologist in the U.S. social science model. Li figured heavily into the broader philosophical debates in Chinese Marxism. Although Li was a Hunanese, like Mao, he began his intellectual life in Japanese, later becoming editor at *New Youth* (Xinqingnian) and *The People's Tocsin* (Minduo), the most avantgarde theory journals of their time. Li's preoccupation with *neibo* (Nietzsche and Bergson) informed his two major works, *Philosophies of Human Life* (*Rensheng zhexue*) and *Three Lectures on Chinese Philosophy* (*Zhongguo zhexue shijiang*), where he approached the question of affect, or materially grounded emotion, by dividing philosophical problems into inner and outer conditions. This grasp of the relation between internal life and material conditions eventually led Li into historical materialism, but the issue at this juncture is how Li embraced nonteleological, multiply explosive evolutionary philosophy and linked Bergson's thought to nonteleological Chinese thought. These fine distinctions did not resonate with popular audiences. Truisms explaining our behavior in relation to our animal selves, our physiology, our synapses, and our brain matter sold better.[39]

Guo and Chen were credentialed professors. Most instinct theorists were not. The engineer and cultural critic Gao Xian had a lot to say on this topic.[40] Yan Jibo enthusiastically declared in "Faming shi renlei de benneng" that a discovery instinct existed, so one only had to set one's mind to it and the world was one's oyster.[41] He used the trope of mushrooms (they grow exponentially), which linked him to British theorists, and he encouraged his peers to jump on the discovery bandwagon. This example is absurd, but Zhou Jianren, the brother of Lu Xun and Zhou Zuoren, also qualifies. Lung-Kee Sun has long pointed out Zhou Jianren's role in propagating eugenic sexuality in this era.[42] There is no need to retrace Sun's steps, but Zhou Jianren's neo-Lamarckian eugenic poetics reiterated vernacular social scientific truisms in literary language. He believed that the fittest races would be those among whom we find the highest levels of personal choice in romantic and erotic life.[43] Zhou bemoaned social limits on eugenic racial health (e.g., parents choosing spouses) and the consequent Chinese racial inferiority and cultural degeneracy. The woman's power to select her spouse was not just natural but invaluable because her choice improved species-being. Allowing women to assert their repressed natural rights and ensuring their civil right to choose love would lead to racial betterment. Zhou is precisely Shen's social science humanist.

There is no rage here. When He-Yin Zhen argued that women should choose because they had natural rights and human erotic desires, she threatened to kill those standing in her way. She focused on rights, not instincts. Zhou and Gao make the racist point that offloading responsibility for choice onto women would improve the race, whether they liked it or not. But that is as far as Zhou got. Vernacular sociology is not particularly coherent. This is both its weakness and its power in debates over institutions like marriage and divorce.[44]

VERNACULAR SOCIOLOGY, SOCIAL PROBLEMS, AND MAY FOURTH YOUTH CULTURE

In the 1920s, Chinese urban popular magazines published continuously on the topic of social science logic, and intellectuals wrote profusely as they struggled over natural and social science. A debate structure emerged where young people contributed short commentaries to address or resolve what I introduced earlier, the *social problem* (*shehui wenti*).[45] Lost in the historical novelty of the new sociological logic, new youth embraced the social problem to resolve their own pressing concerns. Relatively abstract arguments about the relation of social and natural sciences in evolution became, among culturally progressive youth, a titanic struggle over their own individual futures. They personalized vernacular sociology's preoccupation with the primal relationships of individual and society (the social contract), the biological roots of human sociality (obligations to oneself and to one's parents), and so on.

Readers' and writers' obsessive concern with personal social and reproductive choice formed a big part of confessional sociology in journals like the *Ladies' Journal* or *Funü zazhi*. In this venue, young men and some women wrote about themselves, their individual emotions and angst, their frustrations, and their efforts to choose social, ethical, and natural pathways for future modern life. Sometimes they wrote autobiographically in directly self-referential style, but they also wrote, as Yan Fu had, using translations to authorize their opinions. During the 1920s translators frequently listed themselves as the author of an essay and assigned what they called the "original" author an inconspicuous second billing. It seems likely that they gave themselves, as translators, first billing because they chose and valued the ideas that the first author had roughed out. Translators in this era were more like commentators or guides who assimilated the signposts that the first author had installed, and they made truths available to their peers in contemporary times. In other words, "translators" not only interpreted new, universal ideas and situated themselves vis-à-vis these ideas but were prone to working through personal stakes as they tackled a social problem.

In this regard, Wei Xin's interpretation of Charles Jean Marie Letourneau's thoughts on the evolutionary significance of divorce is a typical May Fourth commentary. The original author was Letourneau, but Wei Xin (perhaps a pseudonym) published his piece in Yan Fu's style under the title "The Evolution of Divorce" ("Lihun de jinhua").[46] Wei himself was likely facing a complex problem many confronted in the first third of the twentieth century. How could a youth remain attached, loving, and filial in relation to parents and at the same time rebuff a prearranged marriage or, in the worst case, divorce a spouse that the parents had chosen? Wei's "The Material Basis of Life" ("Shengming zhi wuzhi de jichu"), which appeared in the same year, posited the need to force intellectuals to retheorize life, or human existence, in a neo-foundational truth about the ascent of humanity, the mammal drive in human social norms. In this canonical essay, Wei argued that humans are natural beings, originate in nature, and evolve slowly into a complex social order. Our intellectual orientation must begin with the natural sciences, and the clearer theorists are about our natural origins, the more congruent and true sociological truths will become. To supplant earlier thinking about reciprocity and ritual patrilinealism, Wei began his "translation" of Letourneau by thinking about nature. Patrilineal affection is good because it is natural, but nature presupposes the emergence of agonistic human societies, so to rethink a problem like divorce or marriage requires re-grounding the social issue in mammalian evolution. Truth is eugenic, so divorce has to be measured in relation to social progress and animal evolution.

Another example, Ke Shi's essay "The Responsibilities of Women in Evolution" ("Funü zai jinhua zhong de renwu"), provides Li Da's and Ward's argument that women are the primary agents of social evolution, although Ke, like so many, equivocated about the unsteady balance of social and natural forces. He drew widely on authorities ranging from the eugenicist paleobotanist Marie Stopes to the neovitalist general or popular scientist J. Arthur Thompson, whose scientistic masterwork *The Evolution of Sex*, cowritten with biologist and sociologist Patrick Geddes, enjoyed enormous popularity all over the world. In these popular evolutionary arguments, the starting point is always the same: evolution is both natural (humans belong to the mammal family, which propagates bisexually) and social; consequently, natural selection and sexual selection should be yoked together to promote social and species development. Women must be free to choose on the basis of instinct rather than commanded into family formation by force of rotten old social convention. This, in itself, is a liberatory argument, if liberation just means choice.

These pieces comfortably invoke natural science to show how social processes work or should work in the future and why sociology is a science like chemistry, biology, and physics. Vernacular sociology belongs in the category of popular philosophy and ideology because its social claims exceed the existing science and are archaic in our times (Lionel Tiger notwithstanding).[47] Yes, vernacular pop ideas celebrated women's freedom to choose a spouse. Free-choice marriage should, according to Chinese vernacular cryptoscience, result in social advancement. But with the exception of love, marriages and divorce, vernacular sociological arguments were fragile because they could not explain freedom or social agency. Without an internal logic or scientifically viable evolutionary notion of species development, assertions about the naturalness of mammal nature envelop and finally subsume voluntarism, defaulting in the end to crude, instinct-driven erotic desire and sexual selection. Perhaps the vernacularists put the will and willed behavior at the center of their theories about individualism because of a weakness in their argument. Self-selective breeding or self-propelled eugenic development addresses only the most biologically grounded human needs. Extrapolating the human emotional or personality qualities lying beneath choice has proved far more difficult. In the end, the advocates confronted a philosophical and a simple logical problem. How can humans develop volition when their primal instincts operate unconsciously and automatically? What guarantees a symbiotic relation of good choices (volition) and good development (evolution rather than devolution)? If so-called social problems are nothing more than volition gone wrong, or bad choices, how can bad eugenic choices be overcome with good eugenic choices? And so on.

Gao Junzhe's 1930 essay in the professional journal *Shehui xuejie* (Sociology world) laid out the "biological schools of sociology."[48] Gao was a theorist and sought to reconcile the fragile logic holding natural and social science together. She highlighted a category that she called *social selection*. Darwin himself never speculated about a social selection; social selection is neither natural (the battle of the fittest) nor sexual (females selecting genes) but, in Gao's view, an in-between logic. Social selection also did not entirely replicate Spencer although, Gao argued, Spencer's organicism had given birth to theories of social selection. Gao listed three subtopics of social selection: race war, eugenics, and population. Less well-schooled commentators than Gao were already adopting popular eugenic concepts in China, as was also happening in the United States, Britain, and Mexico; anywhere one finds relations of modern domination and heterogeneous populations in the early twentieth century, eugenics also popped up.[49] Debates about women and sports, physical education, or just natural mobility (educated women getting more physical exercise, for instance) got cast in relation to popular eugenic improvement schemes.[50] Ideologically speaking, virtually no generalizations about the social responsibility of modern women seem to have lacked a eugenic or natural science justification, even love itself.[51]

This reinforces the truism here; vernacular sociology is not coherent.[52] Yet it invokes a truth of women. That truth is physiological: women's reproductive cycle is organic to her body, and her body contributes half the material of human vitality to her fetus. In the event of women, even incoherent arguments like this one contribute fidelity to the new truth. We have seen female reproductive labor invoked in foundational Marxist sociology. All modernists concurred that female procreative sexuality was the secret of human evolution. This view marked the modernist as modernist. Problems remained at the individual level, as vernacular theorists make clear. Unless society is epiphenomenal, and He-Yin Zhen correctly saw that social regulation is nothing more than sanctioned cruelty, there is oddly enough no logic in vernacular social theory to explain the existence of society at all. Social organization, social choice, and individual beings have no relevance to species evolution in eugenicist eyes since behind their argument lies the indefatigable, elastic, amorphous thing they called *instinct*. In the end, importantly and in the face of all this jabberwocky, evolutionary biology and sociology present a truth of women, wrapped around the putative fact that female procreative sexuality is the truth of all truths.

A debate between the vernacular psychologist Pan Guangdan and the sociologist Sun Benwen further clarifies this point. Pan began his rise as a vernacular critic, while Sun became a dean of non-Marxist, university-certified, disciplinary sociology. They clashed over the question of racial fitness. Pan, who had voiced the problem of Chinese racial degeneration in relation to European and U.S. "races," claimed that natural drives, heredity, and intelligence are linked to evolutionary development. He argued that no evidence supported the theory that intelligence and virtue are class related, and he rejected notional cultural capital or social advantage. His take on eugenicism was that people individually, in each generation, should be out in the social jungle competing for sexual partners.[53] In other words, when women are authorized to select their mates, like wild animals selecting the fittest for reproduction, then the quotient of superior people in a civilization will rise. The herd, in Pan's case, was the human, cultural, national society.

Sun made the stronger case. He avoided the problem Pan introduced, the paradox of liberating women to choose versus women's biological instinct. Sun did not directly address the question of how sociology or philosophy explains women theoretically. He simply stated that humans live in societies and that in all societies women play a key role in social processes, such as maternal socialization or socialization into literacy. Sun took Charles A. Ellwood's pathway, in other words. Like Ellwood, Sun argued that social work and professional social workers could resolve social problems. The job of sociology was to adjudicate social problems when, for instance, an instinct threatened to run roughshod over people's well-being. To Sun, the woman question was no more pressing than other social questions like criminality and poverty. All could be resolved through social reform and goodwill. Nevertheless, despite differences, each man made the female reproductive body the central (and in nonfeminist writing like this, largely undeveloped) ground of social existence. By 1929 the centrality of female fertility, the female will to choose, females as the switch point between the processes of human reproduction, the human sciences, and civilizational achievements was so foundational in vernacular and professional sociology that it could be safely assumed.[54]

THE EVENT OF WOMEN AND WOMEN'S LIBERATION

Vernacular sociology's circularity raised immediate, powerful doubts. The point Li Shicen, Ke Shi, and others sought to establish was that, measured against the relations of production and labor power, metaphors about bio-evolution creating species-specific human brains are an implausible theory of reality. Li Shicen criticized vernacular sociology for situating the laws of social evolution on the surface of society and charged that it fibbed about social contracts, citizenship, and "social roles." Li did not unilaterally reject the agon of physiology versus natural rights. Property law, procreative physiology, selective breeding, and emotion are important to Marxist social theory and critical social studies and to any adequate understanding of human society. Once mimetic scientific claims and realism in literary representation promise to accurately represent scientifically demonstrable nature, however, a fight over "what is real" is triggered. Li set out to demonstrate that surface-level bourgeois or vernacular sociology had failed the reality test.

Li Shicen made Ellwood his straw man. Li argued that Ellwood shared a general weakness apparent in most natural science–based instinct theories, because he and they had trouble explaining human consciousness. Ellwood had subsumed sexual desire to instinct. Alas, for the sake of consistency in his argument, instinct bypassed consciousness, where will and emotion reside. If people are instinct driven, their capacity to resist a bad reality or to change their perception of a real one will be minimal. Li-style anarchist and Marxist critical theorists held that when vernacularists defined the social crisis as a series of problems, social scientists and professional social workers became responsible for patching things up. Social problems have to be fixed. There is no inhering subliminal contradiction and thus never a need to enact revolutionary praxis. And, Li claimed, without conflicted reality, there are only two options, reformism and devolution.

Li was right. Both Sun's and Ellwood's position appeared to rest on noblesse oblige. Not just middle-class do-gooders but a tiny, evolutionarily superior social elite should resolve social issues discreetly. Their job would literally be to reinstall a credible, natural, evolutionary class hierarchy. While Chinese Marxists integrated the question of women's volition and matriarchal relations of production into a singularly revolutionary theory, Ellwoodian Chinese vernacular sociology minimized women's anomalous position in evolutionary theory and turned it into a mere "social problem." Thus, while May Fourth vernacularists reified the category of the social problem, Marxists maintained that, far from law and instinct, evolution operated materially through explosive contradictions in social relations of production, and that drove social evolution. Complicating vernacular sociology further, yet another cohort of social scientists arrived on the scene in Shanghai, Hankou, Osaka, and Tokyo. As explored at length in the next chapter, advertising social scientists and advertising agency pioneers spilled a lot of ink and a nontrivial amount of university seminar time debating the social science of selling and buying.

In vernacular sociology there is constant reference to the truth of women. In fact, eugenic philosophy rests on the fact that females carry a fetal human inside their bodies. They contribute half of all inherited material. They can choose well or force an entire civilization into decline when their natural inclination to choose a love partner is denied. Two core intellectual camps have appeared. Vernacularists argue that women's liberation was a social problem, and since no foundational reason exists to prevent it, a state run by sociologists would liberate all women, and evolutionary problems would go away.[55] Critical theorists also recognized female centrality and the biological truth of women. Their position, however, fused the biological ascent of humanity to human labor power. Society did not just happen for no reason. The logic of accumulation and the excess that labor power granted meant that no gap between social and biological forces existed. The human body itself changed in relation to women's shifting criteria for sexual selection. This put sexual selection on par with other Darwinian and social Darwinist struggles and the survival of the fittest society, nation, ethnic group, or race. Not a social problem but rather a question of continued revolutionary development and justice for beings whose natural rights are stymied, liberation is in the event of women.

CHAPTER FOUR

The Social Life of Commercial Ephemera

Two figures drawn in "public space" (*gonggong de difang*) gaze at an advertising billboard in figure 4.1, one page of a chapter titled "Advertising" in a 1927 adult literacy primer. The accompanying text declares,

> Advertising. The joint development of advertising and commerce is extremely important. Good businessmen often speculate (*chuaimo*) that using social psychology in all advertising media will expand their commercial [success]. For instance, some of the many excellent methods for drawing attention to advertisements are to publish unique new ads in newspapers, send out beautiful calendar poster ads, put lovely hanging posters on the roadside or in public places to draw people's attention, and leafleting (*chuandan*). If we take as our common objective the development of commerce, then we cannot but take advertising extremely seriously.[1]

The image includes ads for itself (*The Urban Citizen's 1000-Character Study Guide*, or *Shimin qianzi ke*), Xinhua Improved Agricultural Implements, a Newest Stove–brand coal burner, and a subscription to *New Citizens News* (*Xinminbao*) and notices about seed stock, "women's products," and commerce itself. The copy introduced fourteen new words (all complex, requiring up to sixteen pen strokes to write) and put literacy to use in advertising social evolution. Reporting to the U.S. consul in Shanghai in 1932, vice consul J. Ernest Black noted the primer since it was his job to

4.1 Pages from "Zhonghua pingmin jiaoyu cujinhui," in *Shimin qianzi ke.*

help American businesses get the upper hand over Japanese brands.[2] As Black noted, literacy was not the key to Shanghai ad culture, but doubtless consumption would accelerate if more people could read.[3]

On the other side of the world, cultural theorist Walter Benjamin had already sensed a no less fateful loosing of commercial ephemera into the world and anticipated that commercial campaigns constituted "the expressive character of the earliest industrial products" and the "actualization" of a modernist historical milieu, society, and language.[4] Social philosopher Henri Lefebvre held a similar view.[5] But placing commercial ephemera into the Chinese treaty port lifeworld took a lot of work, it did not happen blindly, and where it did occur, commercial ephemera materialized the category of society.[6] One final generalization: generically, advertising is ephemeral because ads have fleeting value. Commercial ephemera appear because a company broker buys or rents space to expose a commodity's brand. Once an ad is published, or in the case of signboards degraded by the weather, its value vanishes. That is the logic underlying Benjamin's assertions that ephemera are historically invaluable evidence of the past. It is another reason he valorizes the "sudden image"—or, in my own homage to Alain Badiou, the art event—and calls the "sudden image" dialectical. This dialectical quality means that although the conditions underlying the ads are incontestably real, the ad's relation to the past is adjacent, and it does not directly reflect a totalized past; it is not a puzzle piece. Ephemera, caught like pollen in amber, are neither a representation nor a potent genetic cause of anything. Their real can only be recaptured historically. Historians must figure out how ads got into the magazine or signboard in the first place, unearth how the advertising industry theorized, psychologized, graphically designed, and situated media campaign strategies. Steeped in social science theory, ad ephemera installed the truths of vernacular sociology, which legibly, publicly, and openly flaunted "women in society." Women in society define what Benjamin called the imagistic (*bildhaft*) materialist presentation of history.[7]

EPHEMERA DEFINED

The term *ephemera* (ἐφήμερα) is part of what in 1961 Philip Babcock Gove called the International Scientific Vocabulary, describing terms created in the nineteenth century to scientize life processes and engineered out of anglicized faux Greek or Latin stems.[8] *Ephemera* joins together a Greek term *epi*, meaning "on" or "about," and another, *hemera*, meaning "day," to indicate the short-lived mayfly.[9] C. J. Chen suggests that the translation in Chinese be *fúyóu*, adapted from the classic poem, *Shijing*, also indicating an insect's fleeting life.[10] Each of these words denotes a capacious category of objects with short-lived, inconspicuous, or transitory material and physical forms, in a specific time, in a specific place, and, when we collect ephemera, they are cognizable as metadata or categorical knowledge. The postcard is an obvious example.[11] Like the short-lived insects, ephemera are physical embodiments left in disposable media, recording the everyday lives of time-contingent, bodily remains that might not otherwise leave a trace. Historical ephemera presented in this chapter encode social objectives in material form, in fragile remains, a shadow of human touch. Ephemera generally should prompt historians to appreciate the physicality of conceptual orders. Philosophical texts, social theory, and religion all unveil potential truths; the social sciences postulated the truth of society, and ephemera are a material archive where these truths smeared into things. Ephemera—here, commercial ads—are amenable to complex archival formatting and are worth resurrecting and fighting over because if they came into the world, then they have a contingent temporality and can be ended one day. And that includes sociology itself.[12] Commercial ephemera particularly lend themselves to critical restoration because generically they build into themselves sophisticated expression and emotional logic, and they fuse past and future; we see this latter quality particularly in ad campaigns or story arcs.

THE ADVERTISING INDUSTRY AND WOMEN

The ad shown in figure 4.2 appeared in *Shenbao* on March 7, 1920. It anticipated the commercial advertising boom of the next three decades and the corporate advertising industry. Evoking Chinese boudoir paintings (see chapter 5), the girl obliquely looks into a hand mirror so that her face is shielded, surrendered to the viewer indirectly. This is a famous Pond's cold cream ad, and although not the earth-shattering accomplishment its designer claimed, it does embody professionalized and psychologized modern ad-design scenario. The text extolls "The Cosmetic Masterpiece!" that Pond's cream produces. Noting that her skin had been a "wreck" only a month before and is now white and enchanting, the fictional figure attributes her transformation to having applied a modern, branded vanishing cream each day. The girl icon in the Pond's ad had appeared over and over in print media during the 1910s as one of two new-woman images the prolific sketch artist Ding Song recurrently drew.[13] In the images reproduced in figures 4.3 through 4.5—two women using phone technology, a girl alone in an enclosed space gazing at herself, or alone painting modern Chinese women, and in the final Ding Song image, depicted leaning on a sofa chair to play with her cat— what allegedly shocked readers in 1920 was seeing Ding Song's characters appear in a commodity ad.[14]

As figures 4.3–4.5 illustrates, Ding Song drew women together. The younger one who appears in the Pond's ad often accompanies a senior modern woman. The girl sometimes raises a badminton racket or stands in front of a water hydrant or an English-style mailbox. Having seen hundreds of these drawings, I still do not see a clear distinction since the older woman might carry a bird rifle, knit looking out a window, read a newspaper in her study, and is as active as the girl. The point is that Ding Song created these stereotypes, and other artists appropriated them. In figure 4.6, for instance, the two appear in a sophisticated 1925 image selling Sunlight soap, a Lever Brothers product, in a national news media. The party responsible for placing the giant-scale Pond's ad was Carl Crow, of Carl Crow, Inc., who alongside C. P. Ling's Chinese Commercial Advertising Agency (Huashang guanggao gongsi) was one of the "big four" ad agents in Shanghai. Ling and Crow belonged to an industry that mushroomed between 1919 and 1937, when the Japanese military attacked China and drove refugees from the eastern seaboard into the interior. According to Su Shangda, writing in 1931, Ling, Crow, and Wang Wanrong (owner and founder of Rongchang Advertising Agency), as well as Vee Loo Advertising Company (Weiluo guanggao gongsi), and the Perme Company (whose owner was Italian), combined forces to accelerate demand for marketing and distribution (the two classic rationales for advertising, à la Harry Tipper) following the 1910s influx of foreign-branded commodities, including the Japanese miracle medicine Jintan.[15] Other prominent Chinese advertising figures—Lu Meiseng, Lu Shoulun, and Zheng Yaonan—founded United (Lianhe), apparently a business consortium affiliated with the newspaper Shenbao.[16] The British-owned F. C. Millington, Inc., as well as entities such as the Direct Mail Advertising Agency (Jieyun guanggao gongsi) and Chinese commercial moguls like Huang Chujiu and commercial art poster magnates Jin Xuechen and Ni Gaofeng, worked in the same business environment as the advertisers listed in English-language Shanghai directories, like M. Tanaka, Richard Chester, J. J. Chollot, and Mr. B. Rosenbaum.

Crow and Ling—like their Japanese analogues, capitalist innovators Morishita Hiroshi (founder of Morishita Nanyōdō, also known as the Morishita Jintan Company, the company producing Jintan pills) and Nakayama Taichi (entrepreneur, founder, and advertising genius behind cosmetics innovation at Nakayama Taiyōdō, known alternately as Princess Araiko and Club Cosmetics Company [CCC]) in Osaka—directly and explicitly employed advertising social sciences to promote themselves and their products, just as literacy advocates pushed commercial capitalist praxis—reading ads and buying commodities—into everyday life.[17] So while academics and industry innovators harnessed marketing, the psychology of consumption, emotions, and commodity acquisitiveness to social progress, advertisers were drawing cartoon images and writing ad copy in weirdly clinical ways, explaining how society worked. Crow's, Morishita's, Nakagawa's, and Ling's advertising images sought to enlighten potential buyers (recall how the AMCO girl advertising literalized electric light) by wrapping commodities in stories and design

4.2 Large-scale Pond's cold cream newspaper ad by Carl Crow. *Shenbao*, March 7, 1920.

to further fetishize them, as the California Sun-Maid raisin brand transformed an available Chinese food, dried grapes, into a precious health import (figure 4.7).[18]

After winning a Boxer Indemnity Scholarship, the phenomenally gifted C. P. Ling earned a second BA at the University of Rochester and a master's in the social science of selling at Columbia University and New York University. At this time the U.S. eastern seaboard institutionalized the social science of advertising, and Northwestern University and the University of Michigan offered additional programs. Ling returned to Shanghai to establish his agency in 1926 and took on exclusive accounts for Ford, General Motors, Coca-Cola, Philip Morris Cigarettes, ASPRO (an Australian brand of aspirin), KLIM milk powder, Horliks, Parker Pens, and Pan American World Airlines. By 1936 the Chinese Commercial Advertising Agency, C. P. Ling Proprietor—the official corporate title—also handled Jardine Matheson, RCA Victor Company,

4.3 Drawing by Ding Song of a woman and a girl using a telephone. *Min'guo ribao*, March 12, 1917.

4.4 Drawing by Ding Song of a girl with braid and mirror. *Min'guo ribao*, March 22, 1917.

4.5 Two drawings by Ding Song. A woman painting, and a girl playing with her cat. From Ding Song, *Shanghai shizhuang tuyong.*

4.6 Lever Brothers (established 1885; consolidated into Unilever 1929) Sunlight brand washing soap tableau. *Dongfang zazhi*, November 25, 1925.

4.7 Ad showing Sun-Maid raisin girl. *Funü zazhi*, July 1918.

Cheesborough, Heinz, General Foods, Quaker Oats, Welch's, and, interestingly, AMCO. After the Guomindang government fell in 1949, Ling's outfit moved to Hong Kong.

Ling cocreated practices in order to generate imaginary use values out of exchange. Sellers have often named their product and shared information about its virtue with potential customers. Only commercial advertising in the late nineteenth and twentieth centuries had the capacity to statistically test and poll potential consumers using social-survey methods to demonstrate an ad's effectiveness, meaning its return on investment. Advertising pioneers were early adopters of Taylorist or Fordist theories and production practices. The China-based Lu Meiseng and his Taylorist counterparts in Osaka, Japan, spread the dogma of efficiency (i.e., the difference between the capacity of a unit to produce and the projected sales of its products) by translating and circulating new philosophy and demonstrating superiority in practice. But for Ling and Crow, specialized knowledge and the consequent ability to snag international brand accounts placed them in a different world than local businesses like Vee Loo, later part of BAT.[19]

Advertisers gather information just like sociologists. "We make market surveys," Crow wrote, "speculate on what articles they [consumers] will buy, how the article should be packed, how advertised, and what merchandising methods should be followed."[20] His surveys invited consumers to learn about imaginary use values, graphesis conveying other scenes of use value, ways to procure branded commodities, and ways to both use them and appreciate their aura. Crow was a keen observer who spotted trends. This helped his business, since agencies handling corporate accounts sold directly to retail consumers in the Shanghai region and by mail order to readers all over China and Southeast Asia, as figure 4.8 advertises.

In the early 1920s, Crow was among the handful of pioneers systematizing emotional expression in commodity ads.[21] The 1921 Pond's ad associated femininity, bashfulness, inwardness, self-love, sexual seductiveness, anticipation (scientific skin care will transform my skin and

4.8 Sincere Home Delivery Service, Shanghai, *Funü zazhi* 6, no. 3 (March 1923).

reveal my personhood), and the democratic point that anyone can use Pond's white cream to become a natural cosmetic masterpiece.[22] The image featured a Ding Song girl icon set among four cold cream jar icons. Like Mickey Mouse's ears, the Pond's jar endured throughout the commodity's lifetime in Chinese markets, but the shock of the new came when Crow paired a girl cliché and scientific modernity. Since a physiological female figure is a constitutive element of modernity as such, what he intimated here, in commercial ephemera, is that the anatomical woman is *indivisible from the commodity form*. Tormented and contested as this binding of women to commodity forms became in revolutionary politics, the truth of women circled around and around the subjective possibility that generic women were not just female in a zoological relation to men (sexual selection) but became themselves by using or applying commodities; women were thus, in a sense, indivisible from the capitalist commodity.

The images in figures 4.9 and 4.10 show two versions of female cathexis to a commodity. In the Kodak Film ad in figure 4.9, a sexualized girl figure holds a roll of negatives while a male figure gazes not at her but at the film. In figure 4.10, a female figure mixes Sal Hepatica, a mineral salt laxative branded and sold globally by Bristol-Myers from 1903; it settled the stomach, cured rheumatism, and eased gout. Sal Hepatica woman stares not at the man but at the commodity, yet the scene unfolds in front of a marital bed, its privacy curtains drawn and quilts and pillows neatly stacked.[23] Theories about sexual selection made women responsible for racial health but graphesis in these ads link women not to sexual intercourse but to commodity use and thus to self-making. Social science claimed the truth of women's material physicality and chapters 5 and 6 will reinforce this point. But for now, note that female figures in these banal commercial advertisings are not other, not objects under a gaze, not psychic fantasy, or a medium for son producing; they are not a field, a farm, or a rib.

Between 1918 and 1923, the Shanghai-based Advertising Club of China met regularly to hear lectures on the science of advertising. Major venues like the industry monthly *Printers Ink* were available in Shanghai, meaning that the advertising club had access not only to advertising theory but to trade journals and organizational or operational blueprints. Influential business owners, modern business concerns, and the circulation in English and probably Chinese of the U.S. science of selling indicate that Shanghai elite ad businesses never fell behind business practices

4.9 A man and a woman see Kodak products differently. *Dongfang zazhi* 23, no. 22 (November 25, 1927).

4.10 A wife prepares Sal Hepatica for her husband in their bedroom. *Dongfang zazhi* 17, no. 11 (June 10, 1920).

like those described in the great texts of the advertising age, Walter Dill Scott's *The Psychology of Advertising* and *The Theory of Advertising*, Harry Tipper's *The Principles of Advertising*, and Harry Tipper and George French's *Advertising Campaigns*.[24] Moreover, all larger agencies working in Shanghai and other treaty ports took on international accounts. The apparently Chinese-owned Dongya Advertising Agency handled the Osaka-based CCC, for instance. The qualifier *apparently* indicates that businesses had multinational investors, were registered in the United States or Japan, or worked in partnership with larger firms like Toyota Company to create markets for Chinese citizens who owned companies or limited investments in LLCs. Ling's efforts to register his company with a Chinese government failed, for instance, and he registered under U.S. law in Shanghai's extraterritorial court system. Just as one cannot automatically attribute a nationality to capital or corporate imperialism, advertising agencies also used subterfuges to mask their nationality within a transnational community of interested, profit-seeking, modernist capitalist entrepreneurs.

The social science of selling, like vernacular sociology, presumed that women's social problems like illiteracy, dirty clothes, or dry skin, were individual and could be resolved through commodity use. Commodity allows you to modify your race-body. This story lurks behind many commercial pleas selling face creams, deodorants, hair products, milk powder, washing soap, chemicals, tonics, liver pills, and so on. Since aspirational middle-class people longed to improve the race, they appeared responsive to medicine brands like Doan's while living in an older, cheaper world of bespoke Chinese medicinal tonics.[25] In addition, advertisers were steeped in social theory of sexual difference. They quickly latched onto physiologically correct female icons. Until modern times, women did not pursue domestic consumption as a natural or gendered duty. Wealth and domestic purchases (clothing, bedding, stoves, foodstuffs) had a longer expected life span. So why would a chemical fertilizer or an electric light bulb rise into the conscious mind in association with a nubile young woman? Perhaps, reeling in shock, commodity sellers, like social theorists, returned time and again to the remarkable truth that humanity is split and that, like women on the marriage market, machine-produced industrial capitalist commodities are for sale to anyone who can afford them.

INDUSTRIAL PSYCHOLOGY AND SELLING THEORY

An event is a politically inspired action undertaken to install a newly discovered truth, something ontologically sound that did not exist previously. As ads escalated into grossly public displays of human physiology, imaginative line artists graphically expanded the truth that advanced women live in society. In 1921 Devoe's Brilliant Oil, an affiliate of Standard Oil of New York (SOCONY), was still running a pre–commodity revolution ad depicting the product, information, and the brand name (figure 4.11).

A decade later, Guangyao, a U.S.-origin branded kerosene lamp company, showed a related commodity in experiential terms: social conviviality, intimacy, familism, and heated spaces in elaborate, dynamic, eye-catching, female-dominated imagery (figure 4.12). The differences reflected a decade of work linking commodity use and human emotions. As advertising pioneer Walter Dill Scott noted, the more complex an advertising image, the more it arouses emotion and the free flow of psychological associations. The commodity must be made desirable,

4.11 Primitive ad for Devoe's Brilliant Oil, a SOCONY affiliate. *Dongfang zazhi* 18, no. 12 (June 25, 1921).

4.12 Sophisticated ad for Guangyao brand domestic lamps, stoves, and cooking burners. *Funü zazhi* 17, no. 9 (September 1931).

and the desiring subject capable of buying. Scott wrote prolifically about how people cathected, or invested their feelings into, objects, or commodities, and how this bond between the potential buyer and the commodity triggered purchasing. Scott was an amateur Freudian psychologist. In a long psychoanalysis of his own everyday life, he wrote about his unconscious associations on a walk he took, musing about his sweater. As he ambled, his mind shifted to shoes in a store window, to Theodore Roosevelt's shoes, and to generic versus specialized shoes for athletics, business, and leisure. Then he recalled Roosevelt, the 1898 Sampson-Schley controversy over who actually won the decisive battle of the Spanish-American War, Roosevelt's getaway in the Rocky Mountains, the Boer War, a local dinner party where a guest had mentioned Peking, the Siege of Peking, and then returned to Roosevelt. Analogously, the Brilliant Oil ad lacked the Guangyao brand's pattern of familial associations and the feminized, modern warmth and psychic pleasures that commodified domesticity offers.

More insistent claims would unfold in the Japanese advertising world, but all advertisers made packaging more important than the product. Ludicrously literal, a Colgate ad (no doubt a Crow invention) named its product "Gold Head Perfume" (figure 4.13). A product took its name from its own package; it appears at the bottom of the ad, nestling in its adorable box. The text declares that since the perfume is the equivalent of makeup, you should take a moment and sprinkle on some Gold Head Perfume to cover your clothing with its charming fragrance. Compared to Crow's 1919 girl gazing sideways into her mirror, this one makes direct appeals to the senses; it is even possible that, as he boasted, his studio invented the prototypical clichéd Shanghai woman sitting in front of a European vanity completing her maquillage and smiling with self-recognition—or, as in figure 4.14, smiling obliquely into a mirror reflecting not her face but just her open-mouthed, toothy smile.[26]

The Crow prototype aside, of the hundreds of iterations of the mise-en-scène, my favorite is the FLIT ad in figure 4.15. Established in 1923, originally a Standard Oil of New Jersey subsidiary, FLIT was a home-use

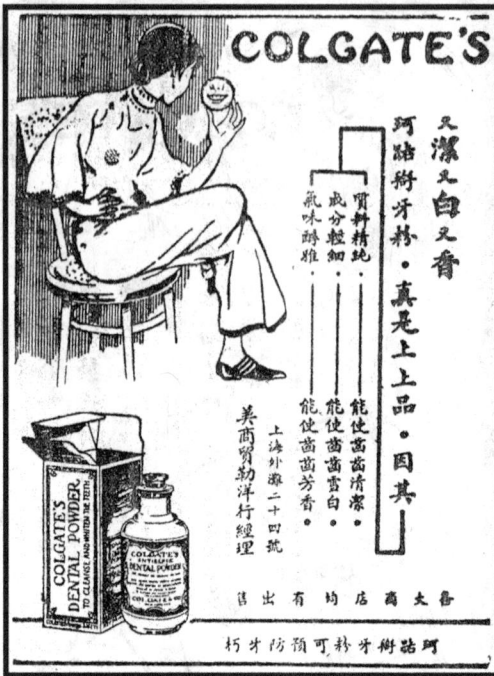

4.14 Ad showing a woman's bright teeth after using Colgate brand dentifrice powder. *Dagongbao* 85, no. 278 (July 28, 1928).

DDT product, similar to GE's home electronic appliance market.[27] This ad regularly appeared in the *Ladies' Journal*, a Shanghai Commercial Press publication, but the FLIT company distributor, Mustard and Company, had registered in Hong Kong, so the image may have originated in the Millington studio. One of the big-four agencies was certainly involved because FLIT published similar visual matrices globally using local icons, not all female, meaning Standard Oil had to employ agents with international connections. The familiar objects appear but with more elements: a Japanese robe, a French vanity table, an Anglo bed accessorized with an electric light, and a DDT "gun." The modern girl promotes social evolution and supersedes the old female figure with braids and body-obscuring pants. Hundreds, perhaps thousands, of ads like this particularly detailed one formed the great ephemeral drift of girl and woman advertising in the new media: advertising billboards, hot-air balloons, blimps, auto shows, slip-in ads to weeklies, the margin space in real estate handbooks, and virtually anywhere a print space could be sold for a profit.

By the 1930s, beautiful compositions like the FLIT ad were commonplace, and emotional advertising had become the industry-wide theory and practice. The media-saturating Ford car ads of Ling's agency followed

4.15 A sophisticated ad comparing an emotionally taxing and unhygienic old method of fighting bedbugs with the emotionally uplifting modern FLIT brand DDT. *Funü zazhi* 17, no. 4 (April 1931).

4.16 Ford ad set on the Bund. *Dagongbao*, September 4, 1931.

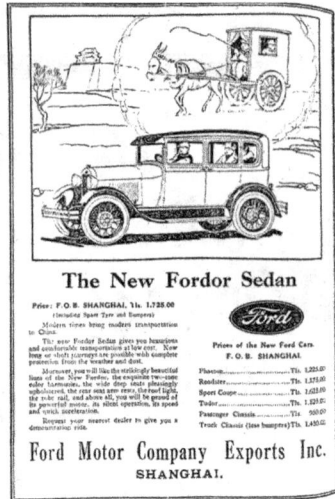

4.17 Ford and drayage animals. *Millards*. May 28, 1921.

the outline laid down in Scott's 1908 *The Psychology of Advertising*. Ford ads all featured the script logo to tantalize viewers as well as cartoon scenes lifted out of modern Shanghai housing estates and associated lifestyle elements like banks, trips down the Bund, and chauffeured Ford sedans delivering lovely women to their shopping spots. Ling and Ford cars targeted two demographics. For the first, a female figure—a modern wife, concubine, mistress, or daughter fulfilling the role assigned in the modern family—drives or is driven to do commodity consumption (figure 4.16). Second, the business buyer got ads that stoked feeling of joy in the ability to haul astoundingly heavy loads, outcompeting donkey- and horse-drawn drayage, to truck in materials to building sites, courtesy of the Ford Motor Company (figure 4.17). Class aspirations, never far from the psychology of advertising, are at the forefront in lifestyle advertising, but here the spotlight shines on emotional drawings and the desires they sought to unleash.

VARIATION IN SOCIAL SCIENCE AND BODY MORPHOLOGY

Whether they were selling racialized-blood imperialism, as some Japanese brands did, or natural-rights imperialism, advertisers preferred anatomically *female* icons, as did commodity consumers. How is this possible to know? First, where active figures appeared in advertisements, the majority were not male; second, female icon drawings became more sophisticated aesthetically than others; third, commodities targeting male users (we can never know who actually bought commodities), like watches, "Brill Crème," masculinity-enhancing hormones, flashlights, batteries, or cigars (figure 4.18) often have no human figure in them at all; and, finally, the majority of ads feature male figures fetishized professional accomplishments like putting in a day at the office (figure 4.19) or studying the new national language (figure 4.20) over objects.

In at least one case, the decision to focus on the procreative female body emerged out of brand testing results. The ad in figure 4.21 ran only once in the Japanese-owned *Shengjing shibao*, a Chinese-language newspaper located in Japanese-occupied Manchuria. The ad copy reads something like: The classiness of Two Gorgeous Girls adornment material! *If everyone, young and old, male and female,* uses this adornment material every day, it will absolutely improve your skin . . . and absolutely improve your natural beauty.[28] This bulky, primitive ad copy listed commodities like scented powder, perfume, jade oil, hair-anointing cream, and tooth powder. It is a text-heavy photorealist advertisement, using key terms like *civilization*. The katakana, or Japanese alphabetic inscription, for the Chinese characters *shuang meiren pai* (Two Gorgeous Girls brand) is the Japanized word for "club," given as クラブ, flagging the brand's alternate names, the Club Cosmetics Company, or CCC. Two features are key. First, the copy literally invites women and men to use the same, sexually undifferentiated products, and, second, the ad image features two Chinese opera stars, at least one of whom, an anatomically male performer, Mei Lanfang, was a nationalist Chinese theater arts performer who played the ultrafeminine characters in opera repertoire.[29] Why did the ad appear at all, and why did it disappear?

Nakayama Taiichi founded a retail network near Osaka to sell CCC or Nakayama Taiyodo products, including branded soaps, hygiene items, and chemical products. In 1911 the CCC began advertising its "China" brand of products, Two Gorgeous Girls. Like the Morishita Jintan Company, the CCC built corporate imperialism into its business plan, so it strategized lines of products specifically tailored to Chinese social conditions, such as new markets created around the Sinicized Japanese-designed products. The company field-tested its brand name and gradually translated Japanese visuals, rhetoric, a sense of girlness, the emotion of excitement, and an incitement to modernity into a local consumer-friendly package.[30] Given that the Japanese-dominated commodity

4.18 Three Alhambra cigars. *Dongfang zazhi* 22, no. 20 (October 25, 1925).

4.19 Inchcape Shanghai Shipping Office. *Dongfang zazhi* 20, no. 9 (May 10, 1923).

4.20 Study materials for learning national language. *Dongfang zazhi* 22, no. 23 (December 10, 1925).

advertising also relied on the social theory that sexual difference drives human evolution, it seems that designers were also embroiled in a problem of feminine performance.[31] As Maki Isaka has shown, Japanese "women in society" or urban, anatomically female subjects confronted an established theatrical preference for drag femininity.[32] Just as drag queens project stylized femininity, anatomically male Kabuki actors had long, creative histories of feminine public expression since women were banned from public performance. In the event of women, acts to force social acceptance of physiological women acting publicly or in society proved contentious. Kabuki remained a theatrical domain of artifice, just as Chinese opera did for decades. Particularly well documented in the Japanese case, during the rise of commodity society, sociological arguments attached performative femininity to physiologically female bodies, insisting that femininity and physiology occurred together in one body *by nature*. Theories about the natural femininity of women prevailed, perhaps consequent to mass cinema, and the cliché about male performers giving femininity its purest expression declined.

When Japanese ad strategists tried linking Mei Lanfang to soaps and cosmetics, they were calling attention to established conventions in Chinese theater at the very moment when strictures against the performance of femininity by physiological females were under attack. Moreover, the ad copy did not disaggregate consumers into male and female; there was nothing gendered about soap powder. What made the ad anomalous, even retrograde, was the surge in advertising theory and vernacular sociology toward aggregating commodities into sexualized categories, fixing them in hormonal bodies and presuming femininity is exclusive to women. A century later, we know there is no sexual essence and no reason to believe that femininity arises out of physiologically "female" bodies exclusively, just as we know that morphology is partly a psychic projection, and the qualities of masculinity and femininity may override physiology. I speculate that in both Chinese and Japanese variations, modernist disputes over morphology shaped themselves around preexisting popular arts. Alternatively, although the long history of Kabuki and Chinese opera may have conditioned the debates over essence and sexuality, consumers preferred the sexualized girl image.[33]

And CCC advertising speedily resurged with sexually differentiated commodity advertising. Its 1912 CCC "This! This! It's THIS!" campaign created a cute girly girl icon to kick off its women in society icon.[34] A "Who" campaign starring the same icon followed in 1916; Nakayama's branding practices immediately stamped universalized cartoon drawings of physiological women onto the company's mass-market commodities.[35] The girl-icon line drawings universalized and particularized specific human social characteristics.[36] Nakayama planned and executed the strategies himself: testing the drag woman, inventing girl figures and a brisk, one-character slogan style, using multiple corporate names for the same company, drawing "product maps," and associating his product with Japanese trains crisscrossing Manchuria. Like C. P. Ling, Nakayama was a creative advertiser in a moment of tremendous change.

On February 11, 1893, the Osaka entrepreneur, capitalist, and civilized, Mencius-style humanitarian Morishita Hiroshi (1860–1934) founded Morishita Nanyōdō and debuted Jintan miracle pills first in China and then around the world. Today the company markets the same recipe Morishita cooked up in the mid-1890s, but 130 years later, it cannot make any medical claims because it has no active ingredients. It recently resurfaced in Thai markets as a legacy breath mint. Morishita was also a political progressive who wanted to establish a superior-quality herbal tonic medicine, amass capital, and "make the world a better place through advertising."[37] He accomplished the latter by marketing Jintan magic pills from South America to Thailand, from Singapore and the Philippines to Abyssinia and Uganda.[38]

Like Nakayama, Morishita was a Taylorist industrialist, a cultural innovator, an advertising entrepreneur, and a small player in Japan's statist corporate imperialism. Both belonged to a medium-sized corporate group from Osaka that was forging print advertising on the Chinese mainland.[39] When the Japanese imperial state established the yen zone in its Asian empire (1868–1947), including a fictive legal entity, Manchuria, Nakayama, the scion of right-wing Buddhist sectarians, set up his cosmetics and soap factories in Shenyang, Tianjin, and Shanghai and also in Pusan, Korea, which Japan annexed in 1910.[40] Corporations often contracted with Dentsu Advertising Company, founded in 1901 by Osaka native and former journalist Mitsunaga Hoshiro. Dentsu agents bought space in local media and newspapers owned by the British, Americans, Chinese, and Japanese in China, including *Shengjing shibao*.[41] Like AMCO, Brunner Mond, BAT, GE, SOCONY, and so on, the Osakans streamlined corporate colonization in Asia. They rationalized labor practices and suppressed worker discontent, created surplus value, stabilized the business-firm plan, accumulated capital, forged consumer markets

4.21 Mei Lanfang. *Shengjing shibao* 23 (December 5, 1911).

4.22 Jintan ad showing a modern liberated woman writing at desk. *Shenjing shibao* 30 (February 26, 1916).

at home and in its colonies, and made capital efficient; they established domestic commodity markets while limiting political expression.[42]

Thus, Morishita Jintan's colonial modernist marketing activities situated horizons of thought and their campaigns imagined sexual difference. The image shown in figure 4.22 appeared regularly during the 1920s and 1930s in *Shengjing shibao* and elsewhere. The top right corner of the advertisement shows the Jintan diplomat icon and the slogan, "Jintan brings you back from the dead and is second to none in the entire world; use this miraculous medicine regularly." The lower left-hand corner box announces "Osaka, Morishita Apothecary." In literary Chinese, between two banner headlines announcing "Enjoying fortune is the most important key" and "Passes the test for highest quality and given full-throated praise," is a statement in smaller font that reads, "Those who support the Jintan life are those who conquer fate. One dose is like a first starlight [falling] on the wet soil. Invalids, to become healthy, to become strong, do it with the Jintan medical efficacy, and you will without doubt startle heaven and rock the earth." Above the box of the Jintan product, near the electric light, a slogan reads: "Jintan medicine is packaged in a book-like shape; here is an illustration of the actual medicine box."

The drawing shows an intensely focused female figure caught inscribing the English words "Jintan book" as she peers into an open package of product. The slogan intimates that the package is a mirror dispenser-compact where she can see herself reflected back in relation to the "silver pills," which are actually the size of BB shot, yet rendered many times larger. What is historically legible here? A girl positioned in poetic, faux high-class ad copy sits with the tools of modern civilization around her—electric light, books, English, modern dress, scientific medicine, exhortations to national fitness, and references to advanced hygiene, with a scientific but national-sounding or "Chinese" brand—advertising her physical stamina, internationalism, and selfhood in relation to a commodity.[43]

The Jintan girl's cosmopolitanism (electricity, unbound feet, commodification, grace, and taste) and healthy eugenic body are half the story; she has a male partner, a weakened, sickly boy (figure 4.23). They are pictured individually but form a pair. The trope of the enlightened girl reflected in the electric lamp is reproduced in the visual speculum of the boy, who has just found the life-giving tonic tablets he needs to turn the corner, transforming from the clichéd, racially degraded,

4.23 Jintan ad showing a sick boy. *Shengjing shibao* 30 (January 13, 1915).

4.24 Ajinomoto social-scientizes MSG. *Shengjing shibao* 93 (March 10, 1925).

opium-addicted "sick man of Asia" into a healthy, sexually attractive man. The copy reads:

> From in the darkness I see a flash of light, a lucky star opening on a longevity sphere. I basically did an about-face after these past few years of illness, as I had been getting weaker and having headaches, belly fire, wheezing lungs, heart skipping beats, and so on. The sickness developed slowly, but once it was at full strength, I had so much pain that I could not do much. I heard about people who took medicine or had treatments and still have not recovered just as I had. I was losing confidence in recovery. Wow, today how fortunate and lucky that when reading the new newspaper, I saw about JINTAN medicine and how effective it is in controlling disease. Luckily, I had no idea how effective this medicine would be and how comfortable I would feel after taking this medicine that I read about in the newspaper.[44]

The Jintan ads pair a productive and healthy girl with a weak and depleted boy, perhaps to emphasize Chinese racial degeneration and the emasculation of Chinese male figures.[45]

Two moments of high activity characterize Japanese brands' takeoff. First, in 1895, immediately after the Russo-Japanese War, the farsighted entrepreneurs Nakayama, Morishita, Mitsunaga, and Nakajima Masao (a newspaper magnate) plunged into advertising and founded their companies.[46] At this point, the social sciences of selling began to be offered in the newly established Japanese university systems, just as they were at Columbia, Barnard, and New York Universities. Nakagawa Shizuka (1866–1935), for instance, made advertising theory a social science during seminars at what later became Waseda University and founded the first Japanese-language advertising research journal; he wanted multidisciplinary approaches (economics as well as psychology) in advertising media to expose social issues.[47] Nakagawa is the founder of advertising science at Japanese universities.

Second, in the 1910s advertising research and the translation of U.S. models into Japanese accelerated.[48] Iseki Jujirō (1872–1932), an architect of this surge, studied in the United States and translated into Japanese Norris Arthur Brisco's oeuvre on retail selling, retail credit, telephone selling, and the pedagogy of selling, including *Economics of Efficiency*. Iseki, like C. P. Ling, introduced and activated key advertising and retail philosophies. Iseki also used Walter Dill Scott's 1908 *The Psychology of Advertising* as well as works by Harry L. Hollingworth and Albert T. Poffenberger.[49] There is no evidence yet in Japanese sources that Iseki knew the Shanghai advertising industry's favorite, Tipper, the Texaco artist whose *Principles of Advertising* swayed China-based advertisers. But as early as the 1910s modernist advertising was so well established that Iseki could, in 1915, restate Hamada Shirō's 1902 query, "Is advertising a science? Or is it a technique? In other words, is advertising worthy of study as an academic discipline, or does it warrant nothing more than acquisition as a technical craft?"[50] Hamada argued that advertising theory was oversubscribing to the discipline of psychology and needed to reestablish its social and political credibility.

A consensus emerged that advertising *is* a social science, notwithstanding its appeal to emotions, and that commodities require social scientific attention.[51] Keep in mind what this meant in that moment. Claims about advertising social science unfolded while mainstream Japanese vernacular sociological speculation focused on nativist theories of ethnicity and blood. Japanese colonial imperialism would collapse in 1945, but its intellectual roots lay in racist blood theory. Early advertising scholar Tsuboi Shōgorō (1863–1913) had been Edward S. Morse's (1838–1925) junior partner when the two men established the cryptosciences of ethnic racial identity underpinning Japanese anthropology, ethnology, and folklore studies. Morse later taught at Tokyo Imperial University and became an apologist for Japanese imperialism's *dosoron*, the theory of common descent arguing that Japan was a multiethnic country originally settled by Koreans and that since the Japanese emperor had once ruled Korea, Japan had every reason to annex Korea back to itself.[52] Thus, Tsuboi's racist social theory and his advertising interests coincided with Japanese social scientific claims to common racial descent, all expressed in sexually differentiated images. And this overlap surfaces in imperialist, corporatized, branded, theoretically sophisticated advertising images, including the Ajinomoto ad in figure 4.24, which shows a Japanized figure, Mrs. Pan, a member of the Manchurian Family Reform Committee, who spends her days lecturing about law and who just read about the most famous MSG brand in the world, Ajinomoto, which her maid, pictured in the cartoon, has most certainly sprinkled into the meal.

The most common large-scale selling strategy in the 1920s and 1930s was the comparative story ad campaign. Story campaigns explicitly communicated vernacular scientific truths about species and social evolution in two different ways. First, we saw in figure 4.17 how individual Ford Motor Cars cells compared an onerous past to a bright future, as trucks replaced mules. In the early 1920s, AMCO-GE campaigns in the business-targeted periodical *Eastern Miscellany* (Dongfang zazhi) illustrated a future when Chinese commodity consumption would reach "Western" levels. Second, and more cleverly, advertisers created a long story by linking numbered cartoon cells, each flexible enough to stand alone but more exciting when linked together to form continuous narratives about China's archaic feudalism and its evolution toward present and future moments.

This ploy's best example is the decades-long Cutex campaign premised on how science supplants old, natural, or outmoded skin-care products. The Cutex story recapitulated a diorama-like Chinese dynastic history through the Shu Han period (221–263 CE). Each cell adroitly pointed out that while archaic tradition had virtue, beauty culture in the past was not always safe. Natural herbs and dyes harbored dangerous side effects, and those selfish, premodern beauties hoarded their secrets, taking them to the grave. As we see in this series of images, Li Zhuang, Han Wudi emperor's lady-in-waiting, whose alabaster jade skin is the issue, and Wang Magu, a Daoist immortal who hoarded an elixir of life, should be condemned because in social evolutionary terms self-grooming products must be shared. Any consumer with money should have the right buy them, because all societies have to evolve and move from traditional practices (good then, obsolete now) to universally available scientific products, found in all department stores.[53] The Cutex campaign showcased how Chinese society is on the forward evolutionary track, which individual consumers can expedite using science. In figure 4.27, a girl and boy appear in a drawing with text reading: "Coeducation of men and women and public intercourse involves shaking hands in greeting since this is now the fashion in society." In a colonial ballroom (figure 4.28) where girls are dancing with boys, the copy explains how fashion is evolutionary: the ad slogan in this image reads, "In the field of social intercourse, if your hands are coarse and your skin is flawed, people will laugh at you."

I have written a lot about the Cutex campaign and the question of why the past is depicted as not that bad, just not as good as the future. The ads are not participating in a New Culture Movement style effort to invent a soul-destroying "tradition" out of the past as He-Yin Zhen had. Quite to the contrary, the dioramic sequences showcased gradualist, naturalized, historical transformation and hygienic possibilities within every consumer's reach in a progressive society. Mostly, though, the women using the products are pleased. Their future looks good. They can handle the new anxiety of public scrutiny. Their bodies are good for pleasure. The life of modern times opens before them.[54]

DEVOLUTIONARY SOCIAL FORCES

It took advertisers time to get things right. For example, BAT flogged a short-lived, devolutionary New York brand only once in the Tianjin-based national newspaper *Dagongbao* (*L'impartial*). Its thirty or so ads are superbly drawn, droll, and full of verbal and visual puns, and each cell encourages readers to anticipate the next. The sophisticated ad layout puts a headline on top and a slogan in couplet form on the left side, providing a contrasting or reinforcing idea. The smaller-font bloc of text describes the product or gives information about it (it comes in a famous blue tin container, for instance) and extols its taste and value to smokers. The repeating slogan alongside the box of cigarettes says British American Cigarette Company, and above the box in the ellipse is the statement that the price is worth it or that this is a good price for this product. This product series ran only once.

The New York ad campaign images depict men with other men in the exact ontology modernists attacked starting with anarchists and gathering steam in the New Culture and May Fourth movements. Clever, wordy ad copy references the hierarchical Five Bonds: monarch to minister, father to son, husband to wife, age relations among brothers, and friends stacked hierarchically by birth order. In life as in philosophy, these lopsided dyads bound everyone together in dynamic, naturalized, unequal relationships in cells 4.25–4.28. This is the world that society displaced after unfrocking or denaturalizing these "feudal" ideas. Each cell refers to filiality, ritual propriety, and fraternity and links smoking to dependability and reciprocity (the qualities a gentleman host would show his male

4.25 Cutex ad featuring Empress Gan of the Shu Han. *Funü zazhi* 11 (February 2, 1925).

4.26 Cutex ad explaining why brand-named products are better than herbal potions. *Funü zazhi* 10 (October 10, 1924).

4.27 Cutex ad arguing that modern coeducation means touching men in society and that good skin there saves you from humiliation. *Funü zazhi* 11 (May 5, 1925).

4.28 Cutex ad about dancing in a nightclub where you need to present your modern best to society. *Funü zazhi* 11 (July 7, 1925).

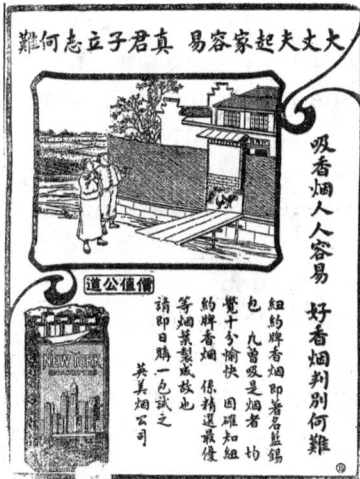

4.29 One cell in an ad story arc campaign for New York brand cigarettes drawing an analogy between how well-bred gentlemen manage the patriarchal household and how they choose the best commodity. *Dagongbao*, May 26, 1919.

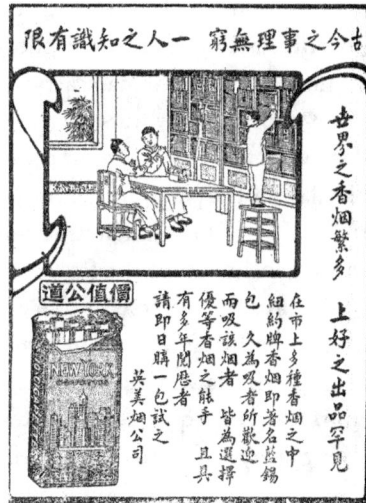

4.30 One cell in an ad story arc campaign for New York brand cigarettes showing gentlemen in their home library. *Dagongbao*, May 24, 1919

guests). Campaign polemics explicitly drew attention to skills gentlemen already had and could apply to choosing a brand appropriate to every occasion. Smoking in all of these images is like the other skills the elite man masters in his stable, hierarchical, fraternal, predictable lifetime. They analogize from a patriarch's obligation to naturally establish a patriline, to the gentleman (*junzi*) easily and naturally selecting a superior brand product. Underlying all of the cells is that since the patriarch comfortably establishes a household, defends against intrusion, and lives a peaceful life with chickens in the yard, he achieves the good life *with no effort*. This entire campaign plays on the logic that the manly man moves effortlessly in a man's world to choose the best accessories—including industrially produced and branded cigarettes—to intuitively fulfill the role of the family head.

Except for the cigarette and the Manhattan skyline, no manufactured commodities are manifest: no cars, fans, electric bulbs, reading lights, sofa chairs, glass windowpanes, sofas, mirrors, or anatomically female icons. In figure 4.31 the patriarchs are attending a meeting yet the drawing has no commercial or domestic commodities. And figure 4.32 meditates on labor, analogizes physical effort to rolling your own smoke: two gentlemen watch a third man carrying a load under a banner reading, "Why roll it yourself, why not buy a machine-rolled cigarette and enjoy good taste with no effort on your own part?" Encapsulated in this jokey but banal style, the panorama of the Manhattan skyline strains to suture over the reality of how a machine-made cigarette came to be available to these gentlemen in the first place. New York and Cutex brand campaigns are the inverse of one another. The former reified a logic of male sodality, as we saw in figure 4.31, while the latter accentuated a singular figuration, the sexed female's job of forwarding social evolution. Read in sequence, the Cutex campaign ads show planners creating a long story arc of numbered cells that ram home the social evolutionary argument for why commodity use transforms society and, as in figure 4.32, nature.

In other words, the social life of ephemera proves to be as philosophical as Li Da's discourse on exchange value or Yan Fu's empiricist theories of the struggle of the fittest. Perhaps New York brand disappeared

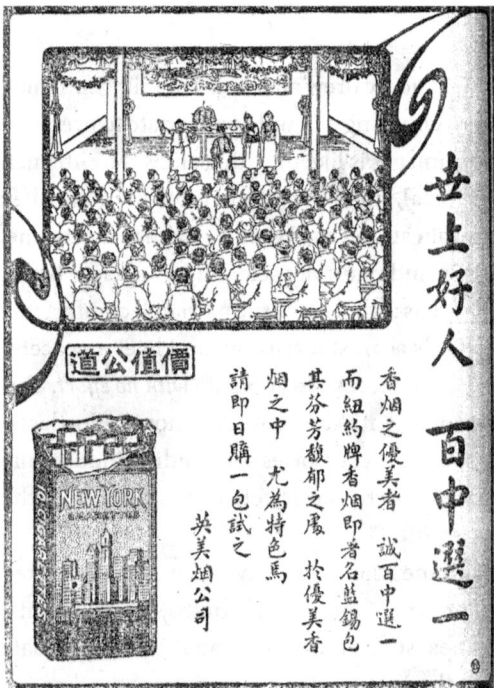

世上好人 百中選一

儂值公道

香烟之優美者　誠百中選一
而紐約牌香烟即著名藍錫包
其芬芳馥郁之屬　於優美香
烟之中　尤為特色焉
請即日購一包試之
英美烟公司

4.31 One cell in an ad story arc campaign for New York brand cigarettes showing a group of gentlemen together. Dagongbao, June 6, 1919.

4.32 One cell in an ad story arc campaign for New York brand cigarettes arguing that since gentlemen do no physical labor, they should not roll their own cigarettes. *Dagongbao*, May 24, 1919.

because buyers found incremental stories about engrained hierarchies funny but boring. After all, if you are buying an expensive machine-rolled cigarette, why associate it with a series of historical clichés? Local gentry-class men in multigenerational compounds; men in the study, managing their estates, hosting, examining each other's art collections, maturing into solid, manly men; but absolutely no men glancing at sexy modern women with love in their tiny cartoon eyes.

SURPLUS DESIRE, CHEMISTRY, AND CARNALITY

Some ad campaigns directly insert carnal male and female figures into the mise-en-scène. The routine Daqianmen brand cigarette image in figure 4.33 communicates sexuality in a complex tableau, seemingly the interior of a modern domestic space.[55] This ad ran over many decades and repeats the truth of women, although nothing of the sort appears in the copy. The slogan says that smoking Daqianmen brand makes a happy family. Yet the image is peculiarly carnal because it is ambiguous. Exactly what social distinctions govern the relation of the young man, the old man, and the nubile, anatomically correct woman? Is this a procreative couple looking over the head of a wizened and diminished father, happy to see that all is well in their newly nuclearized family? Are they doing filial duty by having dad over but sharing with his now-redundant generation the same brand of excellent tobacco that they smoke? Or is the nubile girl the older man's concubine and the son is looking over his father's head to clarify that in nature he should be her mate? Or does the boy belong to the old man erotically, but the boy prefers the girl, who is perhaps the man's daughter? Once a nubile female figure enters the scene, possibilities accelerate. The drawing pulls historians into an encrypted advocacy where freely chosen heterosexual congress is, by definition, a eugenic surplus: come hell or high water, age-appropriate heterosexual coupling must take place. No matter how erotically muddy the trivial Daqianmen image is under scrutiny, it advances "the now of its recognizability."[56]

Constellations of ambiguously eroticized people appeared routinely in a many ads for 4711 brand German body products. In figure 4.34, two men, one in a Sun Yat-sen suit and the other in a tuxedo, sit at a banquet

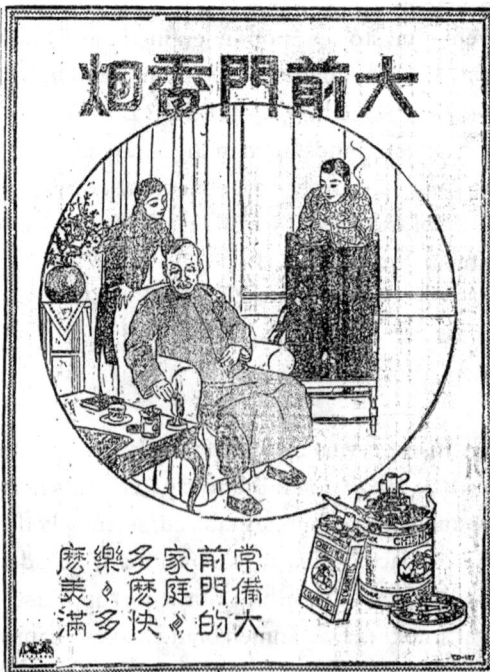

4.33 An ambiguously erotic Daqianmen brand cigarette ad. *Dagongbao*, April 17, 1930.

4.34 4711 brand genuine eau de cologne ad uses a formulaic erotic triangle to sexualize commodity. *Dagongbao*, October 3, 1931.

table while the procreative couple flirts. Is the figure in neotraditional clothing her father? Is she choosing between an old husband and a young erotic object? What carnal relationship is the threesome, a constant fixture in all ad culture, indicating? In fact, the association of women's eugenic choice, individual will, commodity desire, and desire for sex became so casual in advertising culture that national, international, and local brands came to associate increasingly vulgar depictions of the agile, independent, and eroticized girl with modern society.

Surplus erotic desire highlights why New York brand is asocial and retrograde, while Daqianmen smokes or Kotex ads are progressive; society is predicated on women and men having sex. Given that vernacular sociology particularly presumed that eugenic procreation accelerates social and national evolution, Kotex, Tampax, and an apparently China-based brand, Sanitary, were advertising in the mid-1920s and placing menstruation, hygiene, and commodity together in the mise-en-scène. All brands promised to replace allegedly unhealthful, self-fashioned menstrual products with scientific, disposable, absorbent sanitary pads since, according to the ad, homemade, recycled products are harmful to female reproductive health. But multinational sanitary pads are not surprising. Socially expressed desire, drawing on Freudian pop theories, is a graph or indicator and encodes time. These ephemera are Benjaminian dialectical images at a standstill, harboring the "nucleus of time lying hidden within the knower and the known alike."[57]

Drug products that have no active agents, like Doan's and Jintan, have been studied. But as the physiology of sperm and eggs became open knowledge, and a broad swath of new commodities with known chemical properties flooded into advertising culture, fidelity to the event of women got further encoded into advertising culture. Medicinal commodities become "vectors of modernization and medicalization," because hormones and pharmaceuticals reinforce sexual difference and offer upwardly mobile consumers a chance at physical modernity never before imaginable.[58] Various products were marketed as relieving menstrual pains and gynecological conditions: narcotics like the Schering German line, which belonged to Bayer and marketed a barbiturate called Veramon; hormones under the name Satyrin; steroids that the Swiss CIBA brand named Agomensin/Sistomensin (figure 4.35); a Japanese brand, Vagitoran (figure 4.36); a German Hemogen Musculosine; and the French Cryogenin-Lumiere and Hemogene Tailleur, an anti-inflammatory steroid.[59] Giving chemical-sounding names to commodities led to products like the Hemogen drugs, a solution of aluminum chloride hemostatic to treat gingivitis, and products that relieved neurasthenia, tuberculosis, gonorrhea, and many other maladies.

In much advertising graphesis women's contribution to social progress lay in personal hygiene. A hygienic modern woman actively bathes herself or showers regularly. Unlike her mother and grandmother, she bases her life practices on clinical scientific truths about female sexual maturation, hormonal menstrual cycles, egg-sperm conception, pregnancy, and antiseptic, postdelivery, self-care.[60] The repetitive invocation of the sanitary and healthful qualities of machine-made, brand-identified, antiseptic menstrual and medical products found explicit scientific reinforcement in articles appearing alongside the ads in journals of opinion like the *Ladies' Journal*. The linking of menstruation and hygiene could not be more explicit, for instance, in Wei Xin's 1923 translation of Wil-

4.35 CIBA ad for a hormonal menstrual regulator with the pseudoscientific name of Agomensin/Sistomensin. *Funü zazhi*, September 1, 1931.

4.36 Vagitoran brand chloride, salicylic acid, acetate, and glucose compound for vaginal relief. *Shengjing shihbao*, December 3, 1918.

liam Robinson's work on eugenic improvement.[61] In this environment the menstrual pad is an ideological entity linking social improvement to a woman's sexed body.[62] Vaginal bleeding is physiology, and Kotex a brand; physiological fact and industrial commodity combine in the commercial ephemera that flowed through everyday life in cheap newsprint and magazine images.

THE SOCIAL LIVES OF SEXUALLY SELECTING ADVERTISING GIRLS

Christopher Norris has argued that a "truth event" is "the discovery of hitherto unthought or unsuspected ontological resource."[63] The truth here is sex-difference sociology, and it subsumed Chinese intellectual life in the late nineteenth and twentieth centuries. Inside the ontological resource are social theory, sexual instinct theory, advertising social science, and hormonal pharmaceuticals, all publicized in everyday newspaper and magazine ephemera. In vernacular sociology's foundational categories and in young intellectuals' explosive personal statements, praxis, too, was often conscientiously individualized. The material gathered in this chapter is commercial graphesis that opened ways to establish that "women" is a novel set of commands authorizing a modern being, different yet as central to social and natural evolution as human men. Ads themselves are not generative. They do not make things happen. But they facilitate, solemnize, or ratify that commercial capitalism worked in Chinese treaty ports to open up a novel fealty to an imminent future where the true humanity of biological, procreative, hormonal women will finally be recognized. As the Cutex and the New York branding comparison showed, commercial ephemera form dialectic images and thus make ontological claims. Images communicate a departure from the comfortable (or not, depending on your sex assignment) gentry life celebrated in the failed New York brand campaign and indicate readers' and gazers' willingness to be pulled into being modern.

Omnipresent commercial art bound commodity capitalism to the truth of women because it made claims: if you buy and use Vagitoran you are a physiological woman living large in a changing society. The next chapter more fully analyzes what kind of thinking was going on in the artistic commercial ephemera. Here it is enough to underline the actions taken among new commercial capitalists who were dynamically linking iconic females, machine-made commodities, and women's modern life in society. Electric lights and advanced women, all-purpose family cars with females driving, these present high-anxiety indications that a capitalist modernity is around the corner. Nonetheless, commercial claims are not politically inert; Carl Crow sold Colgate toothpaste but his laisse-faire political beliefs did not establish airless hegemony. As Li Da, He-Yin Zhen, Ding Ling, Lu Xun, and Marxist and anarchist thinkers all insisted, even if the truth of women had revealed itself within an industrial and commercial capitalist revolution, capitalist culture could not be allowed to define or limit the truth of women. Struggle over truth and women's violated natural rights far exceeded the peculiar cul-de-sac of treaty port consumption culture, which I argued, conflated women with brand commodities. Advertising creatively generates imaginary use values, the other scenes of use value, so while there is no doubt that capitalism and corporate imperialism upset older ideologies and made the case for women as social beings, this is only the beginning of the story. In the event of women, militants step forward to declare what woman is. This discussion has suggested only how the truth of the generic procedure of commercial ephemera, immanent and singular, could launch colonial modernity in treaty ports. Women's presence in society guaranteed a plausible future for the Chinese nation-state. After 1919 theories about society were inextricable from commercial drawings of society in pictographic ads, lithographs, photographs, and illustrations.[64] Any advertising drawing of a female character with a commodity in the same frame is a cryptograph for women in society.

CHAPTER FIVE

Nakedness and Interiority

Conscious life activity, Karl Marx observed, regulates humanity's estrangement from nature. Evolutionists were correct that "the animal is immediately one with its life activity" but wrong about humans because we live by social praxis. Social evolutionary theory struggles to explain how humans, particularly women, manifest consciousness at all, given women's reproductive burdens. So, Marx noted that while only humans possess strategic, cumulative self-awareness, we continue struggling to grasp what self-awareness is.[1] Among Chinese social theorists, women's interiority, women's desires, and qualities distinguishing women from men posed problems that also become apparent in visual art. A generation later than He-Yin Zhen, the modernist painter Pan Yuliang (1895–1977) addressed the pleasure principle as she painted naked women's erotic gaze. In commercial art, females gaze at commodities, at consumers, or at themselves. Modern high art, however, featured the nude. And in this moment theorists stepped forward to suggest that Sigmund Freud's theory grasped the conditions of women's abjection.

Why seize on Chinese modern art and philosophy to make visible and intelligible a truth about these women's self-awareness? Because visual art elucidates a general crisis. Suddenly May Fourth intellectuals found it easier to declare *what art was not* than what art was.[2] Part of the trouble was that modernist high and low art shared a mise-en-scène of naked and seminaked female figures. The mise-en-scène of the self-gazing or the out-gazing, self-accepting erotic woman, from Édouard Manet's *Olympia* and *Luncheon on the Grass* to classics like Titian's *Venus of Urbino*, shocked everyone. Pan painted orientalist female nudes that directly referenced Jean Auguste Dominique Ingres's *La Grande Odalisque*.[3] But she lived a marginal existence in Paris because she, a female painter of female nudes, could not live in Shanghai.[4] A former concubine from the demimonde, she promoted a truth about women's erotic pleasure in being gazed at, at a time when Chinese critics and viewers generally had trouble countenancing pictures of naked women at all, not to mention images who stared back at them.[5]

ART, COMMERCIAL ART, AND AWARENESS

In January 1919 Lu Cheng engaged the famous philosopher Chen Duxiu in a discussion about commercial art, which both the younger and the older man hated. Cultural figures from Feng Zikai, Ding Ling, and Lu Xun to Shi Zhecun piled on, excoriating commercial culture for sexualizing the female form. Although these critics had a tough time identifying what exactly modern Chinese art was, they repudiated eroticized commercial drawings, declaring them *not art*.[6] A lesser known contemporary, Lang Shu, however, insisted that industrial art and advertising presented something genuinely new, a perspective I adopt in this chapter. Lang proposed a new category he called *commercial art (shangye yishu)*, bundling together industrial arts, store-window displays, signboard ads, advertising icons, and commodity packaging. Commercial art, he argued, had a short life, which ratcheted up its charisma since advertising and other ephemeral arts had to maximize sensory impact. Lang made advertising's ephemerality an attribute of alluring commercial arts generally.[7]

Lang Jingshan (1892–1995) began life as an advertising agent.[8] His Jingshan Advertising Agency (Jingshan guanggao she) supported his multiple wives, children, and extended family.[9] While relatively little concrete evidence regarding his business operation survives, Lang's main commercial account was Tiger Balm. He drew the images, and his third wife, Yang Huiya, also a former advertising agent, handled the business end.[10] He is significant because he began in commercial advertising and ended as a Chinese modern high-arts pioneer in pictorialist art photography. Like Ulrich F. Keller and Peter C. Bunnell, Lang wanted photography to borrow "concepts, styles, subjects, motifs, artists and works of art" from bourgeois oil painting; to achieve that end, he pioneered "composite" photo images.[11] Using different negatives, he imposed foreground, middle-ground, and background dimensions photographically.[12] This created a Sino-European landscape, and from there he reworked modernist *Chinese* canonical aesthetic theories, touting aesthetic formulas that painters had used for millennia to position rocks, trees, and water but in a European style three-dimensional frame.[13]

Lang did this alongside Peking University president Cai Yuanpei (1868–1940), who also attempted to synthesize Chinese and Western essences in neo-Kantian philosophy. Cai popularized semiphilosophical ideas in modern Chinese thought and had an oversized impact on trends, but as many have pointed out, he put his own spin on interpretation. Along with Kantian aesthetics, Cai promoted a version of Hegelian philosophy that transformed dialectics into a theory of national evolution: "a world process, not a process of thought."[14] And Cai, who studied under Wilhelm Wundt in Germany and acquired German psychology and psychoanalytic sociology, taught Wundt's sociological philosophy of emotion.[15] Consequently, Lang adapted Cai's nativist aesthetic art philosophy.[16] "We must," Lang wrote, "fully express our own characteristics, and the unique interests and literary *qu* [taste or intrinsic fascination] of *we Chinese* through the camera."[17]

Lang was part of complex contemporary discussions about technology, genre painting, and national essence involving an entire cohort, including Cai and Liu Bannong (1891–1934), an activist who had organized experimental photo artists and was the group's aesthetic guru. Liu taught that since modern philosophy and technologies aspired to be universal, artists had to know what Liu called the "'me' involved," meaning to him the artists' cultural essence. This aesthetic debate authorized Lang Jingshan's composites to be art but also gave cover to pinup girls that Lang also published under the rubric of art, just like Hu Boxiang, another member of Liu's circle, who drew BAT ads to support his photographic art, including pinups.[18] As an artistic photographer, Lang Jingshan took formal studio portraits of the painter Pan Yuliang; her contemporary Tang Yunyu, a female oil painter; and the male modernist Xu Beihong. Significantly and unlike such studio portraits of painters and artists, Lang's naked-girl images rarely reciprocated; they tend to gaze away into the consumer's gaze.[19] He often photographed nubile girls in states of sexual arousal; some draped with transparent scarves, appearing like deer in a forest landscape or holding musical instruments, and most are situated along

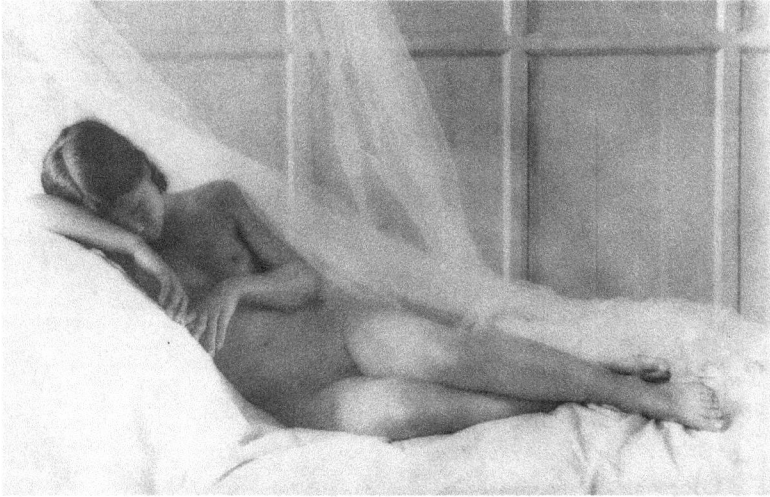

5.1 Lang Jinshan's art image *Meditation*. Professional-quality portrait said to be the first surviving Chinese art nude photograph, 1928.

the fuzzy border separating masturbatory image and formal modernist nude in figure 5.1.[20]

Lang was distributing nudies, images in which women appear disinterested in the viewer yet are not gazing in a mirror or painting themselves. Compare the nude to the Five Continents spermicide girl in figure 5.2. Locking onto the viewer, the ad woman is merry, and the advertisement has a silly side because her tiny, cartoon-like face looks outward to summon potential consumers. Five Continents was a successful Chinese-owned medical pharmaceutical company, and it placed ads in all media, although the ads usually presented lower-voltage female images than this one. In contrast to Lang's naturalized female animal, this happy, naked, pedagogic ad figure is nakedly transforming the social world. Not only does the ad copy reference the physiological or menstruating woman, the girl is in on the joke; in the mise-en-scène, she appears to be an aware social actor. Holding the advertising signboard across her breasts, she integrates her own image into the message as she informs readers about Mussolini, fascism, sexual health, sanitation, eugenics, and mindful breeding.[21]

The Five Continents ad is social because it is incomprehensible outside the conditions that made it legible to contemporaries: the viewer

had to know a lot to fully get the point. Sperm, eggs, ovarian tubes, female sexual selection, the avoidance of conception during each ejaculation, industrially produced condoms, Margaret Sanger's 1922 visit to Shanghai, medical sequencing of births for the sake of the race, and so on: while these are biomedical commonplace now, they were novel in the 1920s. The same holds for nakedness. The female figure in the contraceptive ad is naked but not in the same way Lang's images are. Lang stripped consciousness away from the models in his photo-representation of actual human bodies. The ad girl showcases human racial perfection. While the drawing may strike the viewer as sexy or not sexy, funny or vulgar, the girl has long legs, a nice hair bob, a merry smiling visage, and a seductively dancing character. You might reproduce happily with this naked person. It also seems a particularly domestic carnality compared to Lang's masturbatory images. In figure 5.3, the dilemma that Lang confronted us with takes the shape of a caustic joke. In this cartoon an editor is asking

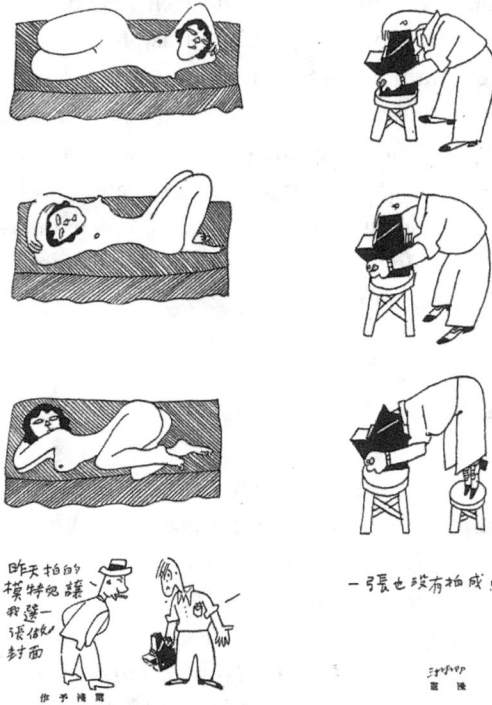

5.3 Cartoon satire drawn by Fei Ying showing an "art" photographer shooting a nude. *Manhua* 7 (n.d).

whether the photographer has finished shooting the model for the cover image; the photographer answers that he has not shot a single image.

Whether art or commerce, all these images convey fantastic scenes. Particularly in the case of the contraceptive drawing, the ad graphically conveys a situated "material reality," in Teresa Brennan's terms, because we know that chemicals really do prevent conception. That fact is a material and yet not a natural reality: knowing about chemistry does not change how elements interact. And yet aware adults, male and female, can buy chemical products and interrupt the most archaic and primeval mammalian activity there is, procreation. Contrary to social scientism's truisms, the material world is infused with human consciousness and emotion or, in psychoanalytic terms, libido. The truth of the Five Continents commodity and its ad image are the "concretization of fantasy;" actual in both a material sense and also a psychic one.[22] In a social world where the Five Continents girl looks right at the consumer, self-awareness of species-being means that any consumer can buy protection. The ad girl offers an improved, maybe even an evolved, sociological and historical future. Lang's image, in contrast, foreclosed female self-awareness and left out the role that nakedness plays in individual self-consciousness. Nakedness in his figuration is mechanical since the object of a gaze, the female model, is unaware of herself and cannot meet the gaze of the viewer, cannot engage, even erotically. So while high and low art share a common mise-en-scène—the naked, mammalian, anatomically correct human female—how these images operated was historically significant and different.

WHAT WAS ART THINKING?

In his discussion about how art expresses truth, Alain Badiou announced that he would abandon the question "What does this mean?" Aesthetics provides a conventional answer to the question of what an image or object means, he argued, which makes art not only context dependent but also inconsequential. It is hard to answer the question "What does this image mean?" Lang Jingshan's work "means" that he reworked a Kantian, archaic Confucian, modernist theory and shot pictures and photo-paintings of naked girls to demonstrate his Chineseness. If, however, the question is about what art does and how images or graphs, photos or calligraphy, reach into social life, then "art is itself a producer of truth, [and we ourselves should] make no claim to turn art into" an illustration of the past or an adjunct to a Kantian aesthetics.[23] *Inaesthetic* theory, to the contrary, insists that art is active out in the world. It has its own truths, and that eventually forces historians to accept art's active, insistent, irreplaceable truth.

Approaching art inaesthetically means figuring out how "to think what happens in [art]": what truth the "art" or art presents; what is singular about that truth that could not be put into words, science, or music; how it changes the social world; and so on.[24] Here Lang Shu's category of commercial art comes back into play. Commercial advertising art, being itself a real (i.e., it does not reflect a real outside itself and is neither a representation nor an effect), activates truths that are irreducible. Commercial ephemera have powerful ways of communicating social truths, and they (at least in the form of advertising images) can also be approached as generic commercial art.

PEPSODENT, PSYCHOANALYSIS, AND THE SELF-GAZING WOMAN

In figure 5.4 an anonymous commercial artist has drawn a woman at her mirror, toothpaste in one hand and a brush in her other, her robe casually falling off her shoulder and exposing her breast. Pepsodent Company (an LLC founded in 1915 and guided to international profitability by the advertising genius Claude C. Hopkins) began advertising in developing Chinese markets immediately after the company's founding and, just like BAT, did research directed at domestic and offshore marketing.[25] Pepsodent turned a profit and along with others saturated the Chinese advertising environment. The image in this ad may have been redrawn from the pages of the *New York Times* or other U.S. papers, available in Shanghai at many offices and still held at the Jesuit archive in the Xujiahui district of Shanghai. The motif of the self-gazing girl at her mirror or vanity table appeared in many product ads for many branded commodities, so that is not the point of comparison here. Here the question is Lang Shu's argument that commercial art is art. The Pepsodent image illustrates the point about genre and ambiguity: one image is art, but the other usually is not considered artful or as belonging under the rubric art (which is why Lang Shu's claims are so significant). One represents within itself a commodity, toothpaste, an internally referenced brand logo, and situates the iconic girl and commodity in a dynamic relation, a mise en abyme, where the girl gazes at herself gazing at or using a commercially branded commodity.

The high-art equivalent, depicted in figure 5.5, is a painting by Wen Yiduo (1899–1946) of a dissipated, full-lipped young woman gazing into a French mirror in a private bedroom suffused in blue light.[26] It is the modernist poet's only extant painting, the others having perished in the war, but he had trained at the Chicago Art Institute before turning his attention to reinventing Chinese poetry. He was assassinated in 1946. Wen's image is suprageneric, in the sense that when it is viewed alongside banal Pepsodent advertising ephemera, high and commercial art blur the line distinguishing the high and low arts. *Fundamentally, each image has the same content*, which I call a *mise-en-scène*, though the phrase is often associated with film critic Andrew Sarris, who adapted it to refer to how movie sets are dressed and to the way auteur cinema inhabits filmic conventions and fuses authorial vision to visual frame.[27] Considered cinematically, particularly in the numbered story arcs discussed in the

5.4 Pepsodent ad showing a woman at her vanity table. *Dongfang zazhi*. April 1925.

5.5 Black and white photograph of Wen Yiduo's only surviving oil painting.

对镜　　《冯小青》初版篇首插图
闻·多先生手笔（闻立雕提供）

previous chapter, the ad cell becomes a freeze-frame.[28] Wen's image allegedly depicts an eighteenth-century girl poet, Feng Xiaoqing. Wen drew it for his friend Pan Guangdan (1899–1967) to illustrate Pan's famous set of publications that culminated in a widely read book, a Freudian case study of Chinese femininity.[29] Actually, Wen painted a generic, morphologically Europeanized erotic body, so although the figure purports to be an eighteenth-century Chinese woman, there are no period signifiers in the painting: no tiny feet, painted face, jewels, cloistered bedchamber or drawing studio, or maidservant.

PAN GUANGDAN, FREUD, AND FEMALE NARCISSISM

"Freud quietly asserts," Gayatri Chakravorty Spivak once noted, "that at the origin of the hypothesis of separate ego and sexual drives *there is no grounding unity but only a riddle . . . of biology*."[30] The riddle of biology—instincts, physiology, basic mammalian biology—does not resolve the question of human self-awareness in Freud any more easily than in Marx. Freud accepted, as all moderns have, that we are mammals and have instincts to manage, so he posed a dilemma he could not resolve. Sexual energy might be inherent in humanity, as in every mammal, but psychic development, the "hypothesis of [the] separate ego," and separation (What does ego separate from? Does it remain separate? How do anxieties and contradictions afflict it?) remain problematic. The European-educated intellectual polymath Pan Guangdan (or Quentin Pan) directly addressed Freud's riddle using Narcissus and Echo to argue that Chinese women suffered from educated narcissism.

This move opens the general problem of female self-awareness and secondary narcissism. A chronic Freudian dilemma is whether narcissisms in women are a helpful restaging of psychic energy, a maladaptation, a banal condition, an enabling condition, a disabling fixation, a fundamentally distinguishing mark of the feminine, or something else. Freudians promise that males and females experience existence differently: although their internal lives consist of the same collection of drives, urges, and blockages, they are acquired in different order and in different relation to primary caregivers, mothers and fathers. This is among the many reasons to take Pan seriously. He insisted that physiological women had a singular psychic life: yes, they were perverts, but they possessed a separate ego and consequently a genuine self.[31] Just as we are human because we have species-being, in the event of women, theorists like Pan addressed theoretically and philosophically the question of subjectivity (ren'ge). While Spivak has a lot more to say about this type of phantasmagoria, as do I, Pan was making female narcissism into a cultural issue.[32]

In 1924 Pan published a short article, originally drafted in 1922, in *Funü zazhi* (the *Ladies' Journal*) under the title "Research on Feng Xiaoqing" (Feng Xiaoqing kao). In part 1, "Historical Xiaoqing," he listed known facts about the poet: a fateful meeting with a nun who warned Xiaoqing's mother to keep the girl illiterate; her marriage as a child concubine into the Feng family; Feng's first wife's vendetta against Xiaoqing; her close relationship to a girlfriend, Yang; Xiaoqing's death at seventeen and the jealous wife's destruction of Xiaoqing's poetic legacy; the girl poet's eventual entombment; and the enshrining of her few remaining poems in a male literary cult.[33] In part 2, "Xiaoqing in Literature and Sexual Psychology," Pan drew on Freudian psychoanalytic technique to diagnose female narcissism.

"Sex is the origin of religion, literature and art," Pan argued; indeed, he continued, psychoanalytic psychologists go so far as to say that "sexual desire explains everything about human behavior."[34] Yet, among the varieties of abnormal psychology that Freudian analysis has identified is narcissism (yinglian), which in Xiaoqing's case meant that she had declined heterosexual and homosexual intimacy in favor of self-gazing activities, particularly writing poetry, and had directed her libido into a pattern typical of many educated Chinese women. In an homage to Freud's speculative biographies, Pan highlighted Xiaoqing's importance as an iconic example of "Chinese society's attitude toward women."[35] And this is where things got particularly interesting. In Pan's theorization, the Chinese big or feudal family system blocked Xiaoqing's natural avenues of erotic expression. As He-Yin Zhen had anticipated in her philosophical anarchist feminism two decades earlier (see chapter 1), the old-fashioned family warped all human sexual expression but women's sexuality particularly grotesquely. In Pan's hands, Xiaoqing became not just a case study of a sexual perversion but a critical autopsy of China's sick culture. Declining to blame the victim, Pan sought to use modern psychiatry to diagnose culturally perverse developmental norms in Chinese literature and art. In two subsequent longer versions of his study, the 1927 "An Analysis of Xiaoqing" and the 1929 Feng Xiaoqing: A Study in Narcissism, as well as a number of smaller afterthoughts published in the 1930s, Pan further developed his insights.[36]

It is unsurprising that the consolidation of the event of women in modernist theory involved a psychoanalytic appreciation of women's collective, internal personhood. Psychoanalysis made its appearance in Chinese treaty ports at the same time as European-style art nudes and commercial design. As earlier chapters have noted, Qu Qiubai and others were relentlessly attacking the same putrid feudal culture and took similar positions regarding how feudalism stifled women's personhood. The mirror, the commodity, and the woman figure exhibited the endless spiral of self-referential gazing, clearly on display in the fetishized images of the Jintan pill girl and the GE bulb girl.[37] But the human sciences in the 1920s and 1930s frequently attributed narcissism to Chinese women's interior reality, their consciousness. Women's interiority appeared to consist of psychopathy, an inability to flourish, and eventually a death drive. Commercial ephemera are sticky in this way: categorical narcissism attaches itself to naked female figures in high art (if Lang Jingshan's composites qualify, if you accept Wen Yiduo's art nude as art) and commercial art in the endless mise en abyme.

But there is more to Pan's theory of Chinese female narcissism. Literary critic Jingyuan Zhang has pointed out that Pan believed that Xiaoqing's death was brought on by self-mourning, seeing as how she *"mourned for her lover—her Self, considered as the Other*—and wished her image, not herself, to live forever."[38] In Brennan's terms, this is the precise definition of secondary narcissism in which the "ego drives and the sexual drives are on the same side" and narcissism is "self-preservative precisely because [it] preserve[s] identity."[39] In this stream Xiaoqing preserves her sense of self only in her refusal to become something other than herself: she is not a wife, consort, daughter, lover, or child. In Brennan's argument, subjectivity supersedes life: her logic rings true here because we do remember Xiaoqing although she died young and left little behind. Jingyuan Zhang considered this, instead of secondary narcissism, "a displaced master-slave dynamic in which Xiaoqing as a slave submits to the law that she is to satisfy the desire and enjoyment of the Other," meaning she is trapped because the Other *is* the self.[40] That is why, according to Pan, when Xiaoqing opened herself to systemic abuse, she is said to have exercised perverse will. Pan does say that Xiaoqing *chose* to ignore all the other conventional possibilities open to unhappy concubines. She chose not to remarry, not to become a nun, not to follow Buddhist self-renunciation, not to take a female lover, not to fight for her husband's attentions, but instead to open her own twisted pathway to death. She suffered from "abnormal psychology"; that is, she exhibited in a tortured way the natural germs of a normative human, female, emotional interiority. She was a self, just not one that should be further countenanced. Xiaoqing's obdurate erotic drives created a singular agency even under these most difficult conditions. Martyr to a perverse family romance, she still possessed a core inner drive, a female personality. In effect, Pan used this case history to publicize his view that evolutionary eros worked as forcefully in women as he believed it worked in men.

Wen Yiduo painted the portrait of Xiaoqing to illustrate Pan's sophisticated ideas about femininity and consciousness. Both men speculated about self-awareness, or interior consciousness, in females of the human species-being. I phrase it awkwardly here because it is important to keep in mind the larger agon all artists confronted in the 1920s and 1930s. In all these cases, the question revolves around how femininity works, and if there are problems (the bad Confucian tradition, the big-family system, patriarchy, sexual misbehavior, the social problem, individual hateful men, capitalism, and so forth), then a diagnosis and a cure could be laid out. The problem is that Wen's drawing is absurdly commercial. It could be construed as lewd, even lewder than the Five Continents contraception ad. And while the Pepsodent ad is not technically brilliant, there are dozens of gazing-women ads far more artful than it, ads that are as artful as Wen's painting. Boudoir ads for Lever Brothers' Sunlight Soap, Colgate dentifrice, Ding Song's drawings of nationalist women, and the scene presented in a FLIT insecticide ad are all artful commercial images replete with mirrors, self-gazing women, and libidinized commodity objects.[41] The conventional commercial rendition in the Colgate ad calls into question Wen's claim to high-art mastery and suggests, to the contrary, the omnipresence of a commercialized mise-en-scène. In the event of women, women's interiority and its pathologization happened all at once. Pan went on to be twentieth-century China's preeminent eugenic philosopher and a specialist in sexuality and family relations.[42] Nationalist Party "secret agents" assassinated Wen in 1946 just after he eulogized his comrade Li Gongpu, a Communist, who had been killed in exactly the same way.

COLGATE TOOTH POWDER AND FEMALE SECONDARY NARCISSISM

The mise-en-scène of the woman in her boudoir has high-art precedents. But a precedent does not determine what images mean in the now. Pulling precedents out of the long Chinese history of visual art helps to underscore differences, in fact, because what is being thought here, the twentieth-century female nude and particularly the commercial advertising images, is not the same as what was being thought in an image during the Song (960–1279), Ming (1368–1644), or Qing (1644–1911) dynasties. Figure 5.6 shows another toothpaste advertisement, this time for Colgate, which appeared in elite magazines like *Dongfang zazhi* (Eastern miscellany) in the late 1920s. The image of a young woman using a European palette and easel has Song-dynasty (and other Chinese) precedents. Art historians will notice these precedents almost immediately. A paper image rubbed off a bronze mirror depicting a learned a female artist in her boudoir shows femininity split into painter and child minder, each vividly depicted in a well-appointed study (figure 5.7).

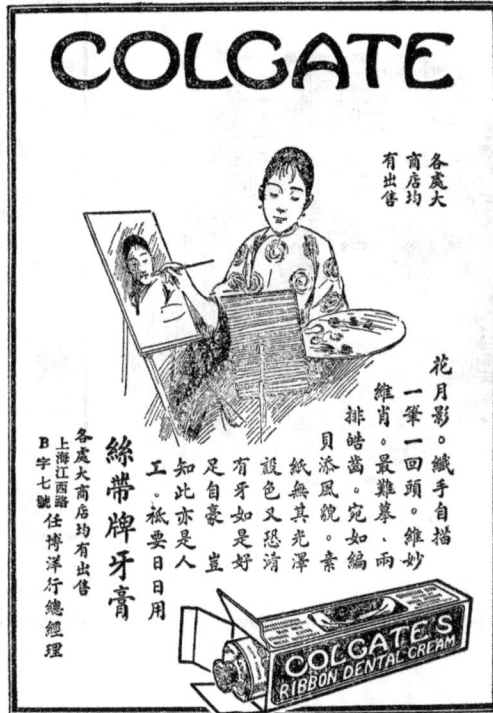

Women in a Pavilion and Children Playing by a Lotus Pond shows the woman amid her scholarly paraphernalia, changing the baby's diapers before returning, one imagines, to her books, calligraphy, or painting.[43] Next is the familiar mise-en-scène of the learned, scholarly woman in her boudoir. Figure 5.8 is a portrait of Xichun, it comes from an 1839 strike of *Hongloumeng* (The dream of the red chamber), still circulating in collotype form as late as 1921.

The Colgate ad's visual singularity also nods to Ding Song's contemporary female figures. In a 1917 *Min'guo ribao* (*Republican China*) image (figure 5.9), the woman is wearing distinctive pants and a high-collared smock and confronts an easel holding a square canvas; to her right is a vase of brushes, palette knives, and trowels. But in the ad the self-painting painter is depicting a learned female artist with her head oriented toward the viewer, her gaze cast downward toward her reflection in the mirror as she paints herself.[44] This suggests the immediate precedent is Du Liniang painting her own image while gazing in a mirror (figure 5.10).[45]

5.7 Song dynasty mirror rubbing. From the collection of Martin Powers.

5.8 Collotype of Xichun painting in her studio, taken from 1839 block print. From the collection of Martin Powers.

Many observers have pointed out that in the drawing Du, the heroine of the beloved opera *The Peony Pavilion*, glances away from the viewer per literati convention.[46] The image has a virginal bed, a mirror, painting implements, the maid Chunxiang, and the artist herself. As Chunxiang looks out at the scene from behind her mistress, her perspective catches the gaze of the self-portrait, as well as Du's reflection in the mirror, setting up a four-point gaze among the women and the images, while closing them off from the viewer. While no literal wall exists, the drawing has sealed the interior space from scrutiny using a systematic geometry of interfemale gazing.

The twentieth-century Colgate ad brings this drawing to mind, but the commercial art image is organized differently. Its lyric does not animate an actual opera scene, though it nods to operatic precedent, and it absolutely does not replicate the issue lying squarely at the center of *The Peony Pavilion*, which is a meme: Is this portrait of my body wasting from desire my perfect corpse or my resurrected ghost?[47] Like Xiaoqing, Du died for love (in Xiaoqing's case her lover was herself), and on her way out, Du created a self-portrait intended to guide her ghost back into the world, should her lover return. Here a crucial break occurs. Far removed from the dilemma confronting Du with regard to sixteenth-century dynastic conventions regarding coordinate axes, or three-dimensional ontology, the commercial lyric reads:

[To the tune "Yue hua ying."]

A delicate hand paints a self-portrait,
The head looks back and forth.
So marvelous and slender!
Hardest of all to capture: the two rows of shining teeth.
Just like two rows of strung cowries, they add to her attractive appearance.
The white paper lacks the splendor to depict their glow;
Rare it is to have teeth like these,
A reason for pride.
Whoever knew that they were produced by human effort,
By the daily use of COLGATE'S RIBBON TOOTHPASTE![48]

The young woman's mimeses of her own bioself (natural teeth, scientifically enhanced) and her process of self-capture in a square—silver backed with a tain—European-style mirror, using a three-legged easel and thumbhole palette, indicate she is painting herself in a European perspective.[49] The metaphysics of the advertising image play on the alleged relation of nature and scientific representation. Moreover, while the horizon for Du is death, and her self-portrait is for her resurrection, the commercial image's horizon is the box of product just outside the girl's framework, the mirror. This self-portrait offers not death and resurrection but immediate physiological self-enhancement. The preponderance of a girl, a mirror, and a commodity in commercial artworks, though maybe not always as conceptually sophisticated as in this ad for Ribbon Dental Cream, repeats the dynamic of the continuous future moment and structures a situation where animal life and not death, flesh and not spirit, European (or even Bergsonian) vitalism and not a death drive, breath and not resurrection, is at stake. Moreover, taken together, the images form a situation, a "presented multiple," where the real of art proposes a truthful accounting of a situation.[50]

And what about secondary narcissism? In most Freudian philosophical traditions, all subjects have the experience of realizing they are a self unto themselves, so primary narcissism must occur for human individuation to take place. In Lacanian philosophy, this is called the *mirror stage*.

漢圖春山此畫
笑人龐眉瞋
恐畫圖知
楊柳似雾
調青美黛憮
尋憑莫教粉墨
腰雲又弱
否多頻
脂此情
疑眷
無奇顗
調青沒汲少
無奇顗

Reencountering oneself as a projection for the second time occurs (as in the Five Continents ad) but can be deadly. Pan fixed on the phenomenon of female will and narcissism but placed Xiaoqing inside a drama in which the female subject could exercise only negative will and in the end preserve herself only by killing herself. In this regard, Pan echoed Freudian lessons about individual self-awareness but never blamed Chinese women for their compulsive, secondary, deathly narcissism. Rather, Pan made the case that the society around them was so claustrophobic that death was a form of rational self-preservation.

5.10 Tragic heroine Du Liniang painting her death image. Tang Xianzu, "Mu dan ting hai hun ji," 1617. Ming Wanli 45, Taiwan National Museum, Taipei, Taiwan.

Courtesy of the C. V. Starr East Asian Library, University of California, Berkeley.

Like Xiaoqing, Du chose death over life, but to my current knowledge, Pan did not reference the opera. Du was a celebrated cultural figure in an established poetic and musical history, and she died for love. The iconic "girl poet" in a long, though peripheral tradition of artistic adolescent girl deaths, Xiaoqing died over surplus self-knowledge: she read too much. All the girl-gazing and mirror-gazing images are narcissistic. But the advertising Colgate girl celebrates her identity or self-consciousness and her will to life, her knowledge that we are social animals and that using domestic commodities can improve one's natural, organic, anatomical body. The primary social relation in play in all of these girl and women images is that of self to self. Freud's question of how psychic life is related to animal instinct can be resolved many ways, and in the Colgate ad, the psychic or interior experience is self-possessed, life-affirming power. It was impossible to be in society (the truth a century ago in contemporary Chinese treaty-port commercial culture) unless a woman grasped herself to be under her own command.

THE PSYCHIC LIFE OF COMMODIFIED WOMEN

These self-gazing women images suggest that it is the mise-en-scène of the self-regarding girl itself that warrants interpretation as art. The mise-en-scène is not a representation, and it is not a context. Alain Badiou's insight about what art does opens avenues for interpretation, even beyond the already noted formal consistency linking Pan Guangdan's psychoanalytic philosophy, Wen Yiduo's illustration of that philosophy, and the generic, coextensive self-gazing girl. Some might argue that Pan's interest in the self-gazing or narcissistic woman reinscribed older, conventional Chinese brothel literature, moving it out of the demi-monde and into the nuclear family.[51] These scholars have a point; there are always precedents.[52] Just as twentieth-century advertising images sometimes referenced eighteenth-century classical poetry, they also alluded to eighteenth-century prints and nineteenth-century lithographs, not to mention drawings and photographs of, and news reports about, the late Qing public courtesans. Pan inserted learned discussion about Euro-American psychoanalytic theory into his article and expanded on his points in later publications to account for a native tradition of poetics and criticism that had accreted around the poet and her admirers.[53] They all have precedents.

Precedent aside, what is being thought here is that the commodity makes normal or normative femininity possible. In the relation of a commodity (toothpaste) and female cloistering (here Pan agrees with He-Yin Zhen: patriarchy kills!), life in public view using commodities is liberating and enlivening. Our species-being is singular because in the social relations of production we make things and extend our lives into more and more sophisticated arrangements. Hence, putting a commodity in the scene allows the image to open out onto a common plane of visibility where the viewer—and *not the maid*—completes the circuit of meaning. The nineteenth-century image depicted a static scene that referred back, not to a reality, but to an opera, a theatrical performance whose temporality would become clear only once the artists took the stage. Wen Yiduo's picture makes sense in a situated moment of thinking where the mise-en-scène of a half-clothed woman cuddling a commodity references biological female narcissism. But Wen's woman and the Colgate woman are thinking about a future in which their natural teeth will shine forth brightly and female seclusion and sexual repression will end forever.

The Colgate girl is thinking about her ability and will to extend her self socially in an age of mechanical reproduction, commodification, and fetishization. She literally draws a new self, applying chemicals to her teeth and brushing linseed oil and mineral pigment onto canvas. This association of the commodity and the girl subsisted in the new media for several reasons. Xu Junjie and I have both argued that product advertisers actively created new markets and drew on new clichés to power sales.[54] In the ads showing mirror-gazing girls, not only did prosthesis (the extension of the body using means neither cultural nor natural) put women's teeth onto the public stage, but chemical toothpaste improved on the natural order. Finally, mirror-gazing ads starring women promised a future in which technical implements were intelligible, available, applicable, and affordable. The presented multiple of the seventeenth- to twentieth-century mise-en-scène gives the appearance of a kind of universality to ubiquitous, banal recitations, and not representations, because they did not represent anything in particular or, better said, not anything in the material historical world. The subject's apparent universality (Are not all women the same? Is not a Chinese woman just a woman?) is heightened because a citation has occurred. But the citation is not to be confused with a representation. That is how the truth of the generic procedure of commercial art, understood here as a commodity cartoon, can be immanent both to an imagined past and to an explosively emergent event.

Many have noted that Walter Benjamin's sense of the historical promoted an act of "awaken[ing] congealed life in petrified objects" or blasting the real stakes out of ephemeral remains.[55] In his oeuvre this is known as *immanent critique*, or the theory of the dialectical image. To grasp how things make sense, Benjamin forwarded a complex idea that the criteria of critical judgment in art should be generated out of the work itself and that the critic should reveal these in a landscape that is neither formalist nor rooted in some imagined past. It should roll out a sense of formal and experiential excitement, a now that art embeds in itself—a bit similar to Badiou's inaesthethic. And by the dialectical image Benjamin imagined a graphic, material fragment emblematized with its own political contradictions.

THE GRAPHIC ARTS AND THE EVENT OF WOMEN

The generic conventions separating high and low art collapsed toward the end of China's imperial period. The conventional advertisement and the precedent art image demonstrated confusion about generic boundaries but at the same time offered a common mise-en-scène.[56] A bit strangely, these ads forward Qu Qiubai's dream of a mimetic world of scientific representation. The presence of anatomically correct female figures in vapid commercial art reminded viewers day and night about human physiology. Moreover, these ads secured, as noted before, a common plane of visibility or a mise-en-scène inviting public recognition. Any literate person could see how advertising and women consumers would make China stronger and better able to compete against imperialists.

The late Qing reformist philosopher and activist Tan Sitong (1865–1898) wrote, "Man and woman . . . differ only in those few inches where their reproductive organs are placed."[57] That turned out to be a minority opinion. Tan was executed as a consequence of his political and intellectual work in the late Qing reforms. The few inches of difference become, with psychoanalytic attention, magnetically formidable. The issue of sexual difference and efforts to syncretize physiology to think truthfully had engaged Chinese thinkers from Kang Youwei, Tan Sitong, Zhang Taiyan, and Liang Qichao to the foundational sociologists Qu Qiubai and Li Da and the vernacularists whose media speculation ratified theories about consumer society. An image where a modern woman extols branded toothpaste is legible under the conditions of corporate imperialism, in the ruins of an older philosophical order. The generic ad thinks about the commodity and the woman together. It fuses them. Pan's psychoanalytic narcissist case study fused the real of Chinese women to the universalizing claims then being made internationally, that women are human subjects and have rich (if perverted) internal or intimate lives.

An event consists of agonistic, politically inspired acts to install a newly discovered truth. In the event of women, the truth at stake was the evolutionary mammal, physiological female's humanity. Popular social science always risked a default into instinct theory and the ever-fascinating realization that humans are mammals. Yan Fu avoided the question of human consciousness altogether to stress the evolutionary instinct for lebensraum and complex theories about human consciousness as twentieth-century thinking confronted riddle after riddle. While it is a cliché that Freud introduced theories of human consciousness in relation to the discovery of the unconscious, in fact he never resolved the modernist question of human self-awareness, and neither did Pan, except in the political sense of "What is to be done?"[58] Thus, while Freudian theory posed this question but could not provide an analytic solution, Pan's theory of Chinese women's narcissism argued that only one option remained, and that was to change the terrible cultural conditions in which sensitive women read themselves to death. Pan thrived under Mao socialism until 1957, when he lost high offices in the Anti-Rightist Campaign. Persecuted during the Great Proletarian Cultural Revolution (1966–1976), he died in 1967. In 1967 a struggle broke out over a version of this same question, which was not resolved then, either. I think it has not been resolved anywhere yet.

POLITICAL ACTION IN THE EVENT OF WOMEN

The now-banal modernist truth is that the biogenetic, hormonal, expressive female body changes in social relations of production and the *longue durée* of evolutionary time. Everyone in the struggle analyzed so far concurred on another part of the truth of women: that women are categorically "victims of oppression" who "declare" and are "part of a tentative search for an autonomous politics of the oppressed."[59] Marxist and vernacular sociologists, legal reformists, and Marxist and bourgeois nationalists shared the expectation that modern Chinese women had a right to life, liberty, autonomy, and self-awareness in service to the state.

There was no way around this. One could conceivably double down on inequality and argue that it has value, but you could not ignore modernist facts about the power of the patriarchy any more than you could question humanity's mammal origins or physiological sexual difference. May Fourth vernacular sociology called inequality a "social problem" and promoted an orthodox view that inequality proliferated in the Chinese feudal family, patriarchy, painful body modification, the marriage market, infanticide, polygyny and the hoarding of women, and unhygienic conditions for sexual reproduction. Perversely strict codes for gentry women's respectability crushed and sublimated female sexual expression, as He-Yin Zhen had anticipated and Pan Guangdan declared. Women's victimization was the cumulative result of feudal social problems. And as social science vocabulary expanded, so did critics' ability to excavate and describe oppression in sociological terms. Moreover, when reformers imported effective technologies for fighting women's victimization in the 1920s, they directly addressed the physical body. Fixes included industrially produced technologies like contraceptive pessaries, chemical spermicides, the rubber contraceptive cap, and gynecological surgeries for birth canal emergencies. Practical tools against the Chinese feudal family reinforced the truth that human bodies are irreducibly corporeal and that modern hygiene can improve and resolve social problems.

When people declare a new order, they are acting to rescind an older order. The event of women does not rest just on the revolutionary assertion that women are part of species-being, central to the struggle of the fittest (in national terms); it also breaks a hole in the old order. Historians know that precedents to the event of women existed, but a precedent does not cause a new truth. For instance, Francesca Bray has written extensively about taking control of sexual reproduction. *Gynotechnics,* or everyday knowledge about social relations, sexual reproduction, and social practices, was widespread in the millennia from 1000 to 1900 CE. People had an arsenal of medicines, practices, and procedures to address all gynecological problems from abortion to pregnancy and childbirth. Historians also know about elite, dynastic women's scholarly networks, gentry women's extensive reach outside the domestic sphere, and their interventions in ethical theory and literate culture over the millennia. Susan Mann, voicing a consensus among her scholarly generation, notes that premodern elite Chinese women often lived comfortable, engaged, rich emotional and intellectual lives; although they were barred from government service and could not take the civil service exams, they learned with boys and found among their kin and class talented men and women to instruct, teach, and play with them. Mann also focused attention on debates over the subject of women in Confucius scholarship, particularly historiographer Zhang Xuecheng's (1738–1801). Male elites, Mann showed, recognized kinswomen's ethics, abilities, and limitations and knew their traditions in poetic, dramatic, and ethical expression as well as in calligraphy and scholarship; sometimes these creative literate women were these men's own kin or wives.[60]

But the appearance in a Song-dynasty bronze mirror of a mirror-gazing woman did not cause anyone to draw a Colgate tooth-powder ad. At best, the mirror-gazing woman was a citation; precedent and causation are not the same thing. Although seventeenth-century scientists Robert Hooke and Antonie van Leeuwenhoek found microbes when they used their microscopes, no one, including themselves, realized that some microbes are infectious pathogens. That discovery occurred two centuries later, in the 1890s, when Louis Pasteur and Robert Koch discovered how infectious disease works and chemists began applied experiment to commodify, brand and market chemical products. Analogously, while Chinese men's sympathy for the discomfort their mothers, wives, sisters, and daughters suffered is recorded, that sympathy did not cause modernists to discover women to be *socially* victimized: precedent does not create new things or cause people to adopt new truths.[61] New truths are declared and installed politically. At issue here is how the new truth got installed, declared, or simply realized as being incontestably true.

The truth of Chinese women's social victimization and potential eugenic power was established in the late Qing dynasty and the Republican period, when people began to act on natural science and to accept social facts. Old social expectations (foot binding, for example) rapidly shifted from being a banal fashion to being singular to the Chinese race and disgraceful in comparison with other countries. Modernists, socialists, capitalists, fascists, missionaries, and colonial subjects all believed that society and its problems caused Chinese women's victimization.[62] In the journal *Funü shibao* (The women's eastern times), for instance, educated and privileged Republican women instrumentalized themselves. They presented their exemplary selves and made the case that victimized Chinese women should participate in the new commercial, medicalized, scientized, pro-woman modern society. These forerunners had a lens or way of seeing a reformist role. In other words, the event of women was always about social justice, the physiological body, and the demand that women were entitled to autonomous social lives.[63]

The search for self-actualization among educated, middle-class female reformers began in the final quarter of the nineteenth century and by the mid-1920s included well-studied figures like Lü Yunzhang (1891–1974), an activist and political liberal. These are the "new women." Lü's critical policy theory divided Chinese women into two populations, the traditional and the modern; among the traditional were the rural, undereducated, illiterate, and uncivilized masses. She accused them among other things of self-abnegation, which she argued would retard Chinese social evolution.[64] To vanquish traditional restraints, Lü fought for women's education, civil rights under new laws, and a national effort to create more modern women to take active roles in the national community and shoulder civic and national responsibility. Unlike the figure of the modern girl, new women seemed less engaged in consumer culture because they appeared in the decades before World War I and had fewer consumption options. They largely focused on the national problem, which is why historians used to refer to them as nationalist feminists.

Historian Shaoqian Zhang has floated the idea that this new way of thinking about women might be called body engineering (*shenti gongcheng*). As intellectuals and patriots encountered vernacular sociological ideas about race and society, they started arguing that Chinese people should engineer a population with stronger bodies and minds. The word *shenti* is a modern calque (so is the term *engineer*, for that matter) meaning the biobody. Modern Chinese brings into usage a social-scientized calque, *shenti*, to replace an older, inescapably haunted and philosophically charged term, *shen*. *Shen* had many meanings and played a metaphysical role in premodern philosophy and medicine, because it was believed to mediate between the earth and the heavens. We saw this classical triadic construction in the opera *The Peony Pavilion* and its suicidal heroine, Du Liniang. Unlike *shen*, however, the shenti was "the object of knowledge," or "a vessel for objective knowledge amid the construction of a politically-desired social order."[65] And in modern Chinese it meant human or species beings. Social engineering and feminist social engineers acted on the shenti and, as Shaoqian Zhang points out, sought to "establish a new relationship between the nation and the individual" and "reshape each citizen in line with the requirements of the nation."[66] Part and parcel of the consensus about women's central social and physiological importance to political revolution, parallel to the changes traced in this book, the category of the physiological body became the solid base for social reform and revolution.

Anarchist feminist women in the late Qing and early Republican eras acted on their truth, but there is no chronological, political sequence to show for it. The generation of new women and later the modern girls reached historical legibility acting on truth. While they, too, shared the general consensus that society victimized women and that women needed to take responsibility in the new civil order, activism split organizationally into social reformists and social revolutionaries. The largely middle-class women's movement under the Chiang Kai-shek regime brought individual elite women into the medical, legal, and teaching professions; ushered them into modern secondary education; and modernized a hybrid legal system to regulate women's marriage relations. The Guomindang legal code reform of 1929–1930 particularly addressed property, marriage, and divorce laws. Under the changing regulations, women arguably lost some of the protections of the old-school patriarchy, but they could expect to exercise new powers in marriages of choice and legally enforced monogamy because the new laws banned concubines and second wives. Being a wife was professionalized, so, as in many movements of this kind, child management shifted onto the new woman's shoulders.[67]

The Chinese Communist Party (CCP) acknowledged women's social oppression, too, of course, but it targeted proletarian women and factory workers and experimented with strategies to organize them. The party fostered a movement-based, female activist subculture where educated women thrived. While targeting female industrial workers was somewhat successful, the Northern Expedition (1926–1927) shocked everyone because it showed how effective mass organization of ordinary—that is, rural—women could be. The Northern Expedition took place under the auspices of the First United Front, which meant that the Communists and Nationalists held a truce long enough to form a national army, under Chiang Kai-shek's leadership, and march north from southern most China to Shanghai, disabling local warlords and attempting to centralize a national state. The "bloc within" focused on mobilizing and educating rural people about sovereignty and their own status as citizens. Communist strategists Wang Huiwu (1898–1993; Li Da's wife) and Xiang Jingyu (1895–1928; wife of rural Communist leader Cai Hesheng) played roles at this national level. Provincial-level women Communists, according to historian Christina Kelley Gilmartin, mobbed the route that the Expeditionary Army took, organizing effective ways to agitate for women's revolutionary participation, including mass popular celebrations of March 8, International Women's Day. In village after village, CCP female activists worked to raise women's social awareness and to educate them about their natural and social rights.[68]

In 1927 the Guomindang carried out a coup d'état against the Communist bloc. The iconic short-haired, educated Communist girl became a particular target for rape and well-publicized mutilation and extermination campaigns. In the immediate post–White Terror (1929–1931) period, the CCP's surviving leadership began its famous improvisations. Mao Zedong, working with the collective leadership of the CCP, started figuring out how Marxism could lend itself to a rural strategy and formed a Red Army made up of poor peasants. As they fled extermination in the cities, these remnants established the first rural "soviet" state, and in 1931 the CCP laid down basic laws and political mobilization strategies for future Communist soviets. Over the next two decades (1927–1947), the CCP would establish many of these social laboratories. In 1934 the Nationalists' effort to annihilate the Communist movement once and for all drove the CCP army out of its Jiangxi stronghold and onto the Long March. Fleeing north into the border provinces of Ningxia, Shaanxi, Shanxi, and outer Hebei at first, the Red Armies and political operatives settled into a long period of New Democracy, headquartered in the northern Shaanxi town of Yan'an. Here the policies that came to characterize Maoism waxed and waned.

Maoism is a variant of Marxism and included a set of practices called the "mass line," which amounted to a feedback loop in which the Central Committee set tasks for local organizers with a finite time frame and then evaluated the results. Some policies demanded labor mobilization (the spinning and weaving campaign, or pulling women out of the domestic space and into fieldwork, for instance), while others raised or lowered land taxes according to how the government was using landholders to boost grain production or to stabilize small commodity markets. The overall goal was to reorganize social relations of production, provide mass livelihood, open markets for food and domestic supplies, and steady an economy on a war footing that could support both the standing army and village-based guerrilla forces.

This general policy paid more attention to the women's movement at the village level than any other political party in the country ever had. In fact, the backbone of the Maoist New Democracy economy and policies was the Marriage Law. First propagated at the founding of the Jiangxi Soviet, over the decades the Marriage Law has been rewritten around changing circumstances but never altering its core focus on monogamy, divorce, parity, children, and property. To this day, the Marriage Law guarantees Chinese women the right to self-determination in marriage, family, and social life. To defeat Japanese aggression and, in the long term, win the eventual civil war against the Nationalists, the CCP drafted guerrilla-style People's War strategies resting on support for soldiers' dependents. To constantly adjust its tactical purchase on long-term goals, the government used social surveys to focus on family and marriage relations and adjust around wartime exigencies. Fusing liberation language with economic realities and the social problems of the family and prosecuting a resistance war, Mao policies moved village women into structured, compulsory social participation.

Strategically, income from women's spinning and weaving on the village level helped to stabilize the rural economy and provided, using wage labor, the clothing needed by soldiers in the standing army. Social labor policy also sought to change personal life because spinning women earned a salary, increasing their power within the family. Complex strategies with multiple aims drew women into social experiments with civil equality, basic sanitation, self-awareness, health campaigns, and in some degree an armed militia. Through literacy, self-respect, communal work outside the immediate family, wage labor, and political praxis, the CCP and its adherents sought to reinvent and revolutionize the so-called social problem. The CCP correctly anticipated that women's liberation, in ideological, practical, and material forms, had to lie at the heart of social revolution. A practical feminist consensus remained intact throughout the War of Resistance: modern Chinese women would be, by this definition, liberated. Which groups and social classes were legitimately included in the rising political subject, Chinese women, changed during the years of revolutionary war. But in this regard, the CCP never lost its connection to the 1920s.[69]

People expressed new conditions in commercial art and ephemera and theorized them in international Marxism and sociology, social evolutionary ideas, and the early twentieth-century consolidation of the human sciences in Europe, the United States, and Japan and their colonial holdings. When commercial artists and advertisers recruited these images, cited them, and reinterpreted them, this may have resonated with readers' conventional expectations, but it fed that trope back in the shape of something new.

THE EVENT REDEFINED

So far I have defined the political loosely. The question has never been whether women were victims but rather how emancipation should be engineered. Yet while political figures accepted that the truth of women rested on social factors, there was never a Pauline figure, a single individual whom feminists and modernists could point to, in the way that Christians did to St. Paul, who allegedly grasped the living God of Christ and declared his being universal. This suggests that fidelity to a discovery does not need to be mysterious or uncanny. On the contrary, while Chinese modernists concurred on the fact of mammalian procreation, they took various paths to explore how sexuality, perversion, race, eugenic development, the problem of will in female subjects, and so on worked socially in society, and they strategically planned flexible tactics that, in the future anterior, would structure policies in villages and whole provinces living in Communist territories.

The struggle to disentangle women and the commodity, however, has an overt political history. This book's final argument highlights the life-threatening political stakes that a struggle over the institutionalization of the truth of women ended up having. Actors struggled over the relation of women and the commodity culture where women had emerged onto the horizon of history. The organized Maoist movement relied on the promise of justice to women. But, as it turned out, powerful individuals disagreed over what kind of truth political action should reify. A political act may or may not have a sequence or clear chronology pitting known enemies against each other. In chapter 6, the struggle to separate women's truth from commodity culture and to invent another way to liberate victims of patriarchy can be witnessed playing itself out within the Communist movement.

CHAPTER SIX

Wang Guangmei's *Qipao*

At 6:30 a.m. on April 10, 1967, the Red Guard Jinggangshan Regiment, established on September 24, 1966, opened the first of its "struggle sessions" against Wang Guangmei (1921–2006) to prepare for her public trial "in front of the masses."[1] By the late 1960s, the Chinese Communist movement had spent half a century throwing off feudal constraints. Political castigation of semicolonial cultural forms skyrocketed during the Cultural Revolution (1966–1976). Convinced that China should end "semifeudal, semicolonial" cultural residues, revolutionary students sought to dramatize bourgeois femininity and rework class relations and the capitalist commodity form itself. Wang became exhibit A for the evils of commodity fetishism.[2] A brutal, ugly, and extreme conflict over political practice in Maoist women's liberation, the trials resonated globally from Peru to India, the United States to France, the Philippines to Myanmar. The Red Guard's bob-haired, makeup-free young woman, wearing de-commodified clothing (usually army gear), sometimes armed, abruptly materialized to become a hallmark of women's liberation movements globally. A life-and-death struggle, an immanently structured, ideologically delimited environment of mass youth mobilization set the larger stage for rationalities that are horrifying in retrospect, yet seemed absolutely thinkable and completely actionable in that moment. Moreover, in the wake of the Global 1960s, a Thermidorian revulsion to Maoist physical and rhetorical violence and an ex post facto repudiation of it erupted, on the grounds that revolutionary politics had violated women's natural sexual difference. Today, fifty-five years after the struggle over Wang's dress and pearls, the truths put at stake in the event of women remain unresolved.[3]

Woman is a political subject in Maoist language. By the 1960s, morphologically or biologically delineated female persons had long since come to define Chinese women's political visibility. Chinese Marxist sociology before Maoism had originated with the truth that social and species evolution originated in mammal reproduction. But visibility invoked a problematic truth: only political subjects can act on truth voluntarily to declare themselves to be women, which is how Maoist liberation theory empowered political subjects to inflict physical violence on female "feudal elements" and perhaps a reason why crowds of enthusiastic witnesses attended the public struggle against Wang. A decade following the events analyzed here, Wang's chief accuser, Comrade Jiang Qing, received the death sentence for her role in these politics, and the official policy of the People's Republic of China repudiated the sexual injustice waged during the now largely discredited Cultural Revolution.[4]

After liberation, the CCP's victory in the civil war (1947–1949), it completed national land reforms and installed two battle-tested laws (the Labor Law and Marriage Law) and a court system and cadre corps that reached, for the first time in China's long history, down into rural villages. The struggle over development, or "national reconstruction," among the collective leadership was intricate and will not concern us here except for two issues. First, the origins of the Cultural Revolution lay in high-level struggles over political direction and thus economic planning. Second, a triumphalism underlies the political theater analyzed here because so many citizens supported the government's achievements, including the end of a century of war. In the two high-tide years between 1966 (the political declaration of Cultural Revolution) and 1968 (when the Maoists disarmed the student movement and "sent down" urban, educated youth to learn from the revolutionary peasants), the Red Guard seized on and retooled the revolutionary political arsenal. The struggle performance scripts, the trial presessions to rehearse charges against the accused, the choreographing of stage settings, the belittling costumes that "struggle objects" were forced to wear, and the stoking of mass emotions to the breaking point all had revolutionary precedents reaching back into the 1920s and 1930s. These cultural policies proved so effective that they still characterize global Maoist revolutionary theory and praxis. The Red Guard called on this heritage to instigate their revolutionary action.[5]

Although Wang's purge reverberated with struggles begun in the late nineteenth century they are anything but over. Just in the past decade, Marxist feminists have sought to evaluate what trials like this one squandered. Nicola Spakowski has regularly evaluated the new Chinese Socialist Feminist movement of Dong Limin, Song Shaopeng, Yan Hairong, Pun Ngai, Zhong Xueping, Bai Di, Lü Xinyu, He Guimei, Wang Lingzhen, Zuo Jiping, and many other scholars and researchers in the People's Republic of China and abroad.[6] Post-Thermidorian scholars form a loose movement seeking to reconsider the socialist heritage, including the painful stakes that remain at the center of feminist politics, as Wang's case shows. An event is a politically inspired action undertaken to install a discovered truth. Yes, but historically events are long, long struggles to resolve how truth will be worked out and how political actors will voluntaristically resolve truth's social, economic, and emotional implications.

MISPERFORMING THE TRUTH OF WOMAN

The Jinggangshan Regiment consisted of mobilized college students acting under the direction of Chairman Mao Zedong, and, in this case, Mao's life partner and wife, Comrade Jiang Qing (1914–1991). Kuai Dafu (b. 1945), a twenty-one-year-old chemical engineering major at Qinghua University, headed up the regiment and dramatically expounded on the revolutionary processes for subjecting class enemies to mass criticism. The pedagogical readying sessions against Wang Guangmei and Wang's final, compulsory public performance showed bodily poses, visual clichés, rhetorical language, ideas, motivations, and options for attacking "objects" (a criminal who misrepresented women and personified the capitalist road, in the rhetoric of the time) and "struggling" them (and their bourgeois feudal society) to death.

For the 1967 public trial, Kuai and his regiment outfitted Wang, their "struggle object," with a necklace of gilded Ping-Pong balls and a "Muslim" head covering seen in figure 6.1. In other graphesis, she appears in a 1930s-style straw garden-party hat and a tailor-made *qipao* (the national dress of modern Chinese women from the 1920s to the late 1960s), accessorized with a little purse or an umbrella and a string of pearls. The grossly

6.1 Wang Guangmei and Ping-Pong ball necklace. From Yang Kelin, *Wenhua dageming bowuguan*. 1967

large necklace of Ping-Pong balls during the trial denoted the pearls Wang had allegedly worn, against direct orders, during a diplomatic mission to Indonesia. The qipao, also called the *China dress*, or *cheongsam*, became the central signifier in the revolutionary actions taken against Wang. This was not the first time Wang had been indicted, but it was the most elaborately staged and was a direct consequence of Wang's role in criminalizing the actions of Kuai, the key Qinghua rebel student leader.

On June 9, 1966, Wang, an elite-level cadre in the Communist Party's Central Committee General Office, together with five hundred members of a work team sent by the Politburo Standing Committee, had arrived at Qinghua University, China's second most important university after Peking (or Beijing) University, to resolve a student uprising. The ad hoc work team was also a venerable political tool of Chinese Communist Party governance. The only singular thing about this one was the work team's composition: its ranks consisted overwhelmingly of high-level party members. Nonetheless, high-ranking federal officials intervening in a revolt of undergraduate students was not surprising given the key role universities played in party governance. The work team suppressed the "radicals," students who would burgeon into the Red Guard movement, and Wang, the work team leader, reported back to Liu Shaoqi, then China's president and her husband, that the episode was over.

In late June, Kuai would publicly attack Wang, calling her work team's intervention a "White Terror." He intended the term to invoke General Chiang Kai-shek's order in 1927 to massacre an estimated 300,000 Chinese leftists, Communist operatives, sympathizers, and suspected sympathizers. Kuai posted his accusatory *dazibao*—or "great character poster," the signature graph of the Chinese Great Proletarian Cultural Revolution— exposing Wang's so-called backstage or "black hand" activities. The result? Kuai was locked down in his dormitory and "hatted" with the dunce cap, meaning that he and his supporters were now under indictment as counterrevolutionaries. No picture exists of the hatting of Kuai, but had a public hatting occurred, it might have resembled the image in figure 6.2.

6.2 Photograph of a class enemy being hatted. Taken by Li Zhensheng. Harbin, August 25, 1966. Courtesy of Contact Press Images.

In mid-July 1966, Mao Zedong returned to Beijing and pulled the high-level work team out of Qinghua University. At that point, Wang had to deliver a pro forma self-criticism to acknowledge her political error and that she had overdisciplined the student; in ritual penance, she did a bit of symbolic labor, cooking in the student dorm kitchen, and left the campus. Over the next year, as the Maoist Red Guard political movement spread, satiric renditions of Wang's actions appeared in cartoon format and commentaries in Red Guard media proliferated, including the prominent broadsheet *Jinggangshan News* Kuai's group put out. These commentaries specialized in mocking Wang, as in figure 6.3, where Mao's avatar, the monkey king Sun Wukong, dispatches evildoers, and figure 6.4, where Wang is an evil grabbing hand.[7]

Yet Wang had every reason to assume her actions were legitimate. Chinese Communist circles had targeted women's emancipation since 1927, and elite politics and political policies encouraged all women with political standing to express their natural rights. Precedent suggested that she had acted normatively, an expectation to which all ranked party members laid claim in a hierarchical order. Unexpectedly, however, while it became increasingly clear, that the major conflict pitted Chairman Mao

6.3 Cartoon of Wang Guangmei being defeated by Sun Wukong (Mao Zedong). Jinggangshan News, reproduced in Zhou Yuan, *Xinbian Hongweibing zilaio*, 1.

6.4 "The Grabbing Hand." *Jinggangshan News*, January 1, 1967.

6.5 Red Guard women dance. Red Guard stock image, API/Gamma-Rapho via Getty Images.

against President Liu, the mounting criminalization of Wang raised an important and long-standing riddle that theorists had confronted: how is sexual difference physiological yet at the same time social? The immediate problem Wang confronted, the strategy that Kuai and Jiang Qing developed, put her feminine performance on trial; it raised questions about the appropriate performance of Chinese womanhood on a global stage. In the end, Wang stood accused because she had incorrectly performed the truth of women. In the end it turned out that correct performance for high-ranking female comrades notwithstanding, girls would also be transformed into joyful, smiling, air-gun-armed fighting performers, as figure 6.5 shows.

RETHINKING THE TRUTH OF WOMEN

Jinggangshan Regiment's newspaper richly documented Kuai's campaign to hold Wang to account.[8] Of course, the primary target of all the Red Guard publications was Wang's husband, Liu Shaoqi.[9] However, *Jinggangshan News* ran even more broadside satiric poems, cartoon histories of Wang's work-team activity (claiming she used her stepdaughter Liu Tao to manipulate meetings, purge radical students, peddle potatoes at the student dorm kitchen, and so on), and general polemics against

Wang than other Red Guard publications did, perhaps owing to Kuai-Wang and Jiang Qing–Wang relations over personalized quality. Selling the cartoon histories as earlier graphesis sold Cutex hand-care products or New York brand cigarettes in the 1920s, repetition established the key accusations that Kuai's team martialed to interrogate Wang. Political cartoons were adapting story arc advertising widely current when Jiang Qing, a cinema actress, joined the left-wing cultural world and migrated to the Border Regions during the Anti-Japanese War, where she met and married Mao.

Like advertising cells in the first half of the twentieth century, Cultural Revolution cartoons can be understood graphically, although in this case accessibility to illiterates was a mere conceit, since the images, published in Red Guard papers, circulated primarily through radical student media. "The Grabbing Hand" (see figure 6.4), efficiently lays out the sequence of Wang's crimes in what became a monotonously familiar Cultural Revolution meme. But the advertising element is only one part of the leftist political culture's heritage. The campaign strategy included so-called research, which largely consisted of written accusations, transcriptions, satiric visual attacks on Wang's revisionism, and photographs of her in demeaning poses, all of it feels bizarre in hindsight but held truths about women in the moment.

GLOBAL COLD WAR AND CHINA'S WOMEN'S LIBERATION

The events took place at three levels. The first level involves actors in a political struggle for power: Kuai Dafu, the Qinghua chemical engineering major; Zhou Enlai, China's premier and arguably the second-most-powerful Communist Party figure in the country during the Maoist period; Liu Shaoqi, the main target in the Cultural Revolution, accused of "taking the capitalist road" and being "China's Khrushchev"; Liu Tao, Liu Shaoqi's daughter; Jiang Qing, Mao's wife; Nikita Khrushchev (1894–1971), the leader of the Union of Soviet Socialist Republics (USSR) during the Cold War, who was responsible for "de-Stalinization"; Sukarno (1901–1970), Indonesia's first president, an office he held from 1945 to 1967; and one of Sukarno's wives, Hardini. In 1956 Khrushchev had publicized the extent and violence of Stalin's policies, which in the minds of many called the Communist heritage into question. This heightened tensions between the People's Republic of China and the

USSR over ideological hegemony. Eventually, the CCP accused Khrushchev of heterodox thinking, thereby initiating the first Sino-Soviet split. Indeed, the term *Khrushchev* became an imprecation against any CCP member who "took the capitalist road" during the Cultural Revolution.

Second, demonizing Khrushchev and Liu Shaoqi gave Kuai and Jiang Qing a political ground to attack Wang for her allegedly inappropriate attire and political disloyalty not simply to the nation but, since the Cultural Revolution was perceived in China to be a global struggle to the death over truth, disloyalty to the global event of women, the truth of women's personhood, women's political standing in the Communist movement, and history itself.[10] When Khrushchev decided to withdraw nuclear missiles from Cuba in 1962 during the standoff between the USSR and the United States, the Chinese again accused him of betraying Communism, and the two countries severed diplomatic relations. Consequently, as the Chinese-government-sponsored, global, sporadically violent Maoist Cultural Revolution began to unfold, acts that in retrospect appear trivial or absurd seemed reasonable, even necessary, to defend truth. Politically, this parallax truth implicated a U.S.-supported massacre of the Indonesian Communist Party—killing an estimated one million—in the struggle over Wang's dress.

At a third level, conflicts arose over ideas. Wang and Jiang took polar-opposite points of view on what female liberation looked like in a revolutionary future. Jiang's supporters criticized Wang's presumptuousness and her belief that she embodied the iconic liberated Communist woman subject. They committed to media graphesis their visionary biofemale model: a strong, sometimes violent, hefty young worker or peasant looking to Jiang Qing for a proletarian self-sacrificing, maternal figurehead. The event of women resurged integrally in Red Guard research and their "evidence" of Wang Guangmei's duplicity: while declaring herself a Communist, she had held fast to the commodity form, betraying the truth of women. Wang seems never to have foreseen that working-class or rural village women revolutionary heroes (or women modeling themselves after them) might one day trump her own revolutionary credentials or supersede her demonstrated level of commitment, becoming themselves the barometers of redness. An accomplished, sophisticated, highly educated party official up until the Cultural Revolution, Wang had little reason to second-guess her own stature or historical value.

On January 6, 1967, Zhou Enlai permitted Kuai to capture Wang using Liu Shaoqi's daughter, Liu Tao, as bait. Kuai failed to make charges against Wang stick due to lack of evidence and insufficient preparation.[11] Over the subsequent months, radical student researchers all over the country gathered dossiers on Wang and Liu Shaoqi. In April 1967, four months after the initial January capture, the Central Committee recaptured and remanded Wang back to the Qinghua students. Eventually, a formal struggle session would be performed before the vast crowd that Kuai and his group assembled to make certain that this time their charge that Wang was a counterrevolutionary would prevail. In three presessions, the Kuai forces prepared their witness for interrogation. In the verbatim transcript of these pretrial sessions, which are reminiscent of lawyers prepping a hostile witness, Wang confronted outraged students whose raw passions are moving and absurd because the question of inappropriate feminine performance in a diplomatic setting is central and inflammatory. The materials allegedly documented a series of courtesy calls that Liu and Wang had made in Indonesia in 1963 and 1966 and judged the content of the relationship between "China's Khrushchev" (Liu) and Indonesia's nationalist hero, Sukarno, who had in their view suddenly turned anti-Communist. The presession transcript and other evidence in the anti-Wang dossier suggest that the students sought to use the emerging Cultural Revolution line against the "privileged bureaucratic capitalist class" and particularly the Maoist critique of the USSR's "social imperialism," which, they believed, Wang injected into China's inter-Asian diplomacy.[12] This allegation connected China's Indonesia policy and the battle over the subject of women. The students prevailed. In early 1967 Wang gave her self-criticisms and was jailed.[13]

Wang went to prison for the following crimes: the Liu family had managed to ideologically poison Qinghua University; Wang, wearing her iconic qipao, had aristocratically hectored the masses; Wang had played the backstage boss to condemn Kuai; Wang had hatted legitimate Red Guard students, including Kuai, putting them at risk of being executed; Wang had done perfunctory service and apologized, but it was a cynical performance; and so Wang's black hand had manipulated the situation until, in cell 10 of figure 6.4 (with the pen mightier than the sword and used for cartoon graphesis), the mighty, gender-balanced forces of the Jinggang-shan Regiment knocked out Liu and Wang with flexed, muscular fists!

Another ritual visual castigation is a graph where Liu is painting a picture of his wife in the false guise of a revolutionary, while he stares (and we follow his cartoon gaze) at the actual cartoon Wang, who is wearing the bourgeois qipao (figure 6.6) captured in a contemporary photograph in figure 6.7. The feudal fan in Wang's hand reads, "In form it is left, but in fact it is right," and in a speech bubble, Liu is congratulating himself on his art's capacity to alter reality. Liu's fake painting has Wang dressed in the military clothing of Jiang Qing. This supercharged environment and visual iconization of political stances—namely, the lovely, maternal Jiang Qing figure and her painted image reflecting her revolutionary devotion—reads as clearly as the points of Wang's prominent stiletto heels and her sexualized ankles (or the bourgeois modern-girl consumers of imported Cutex hand-care products in 1930).[14]

In its first year, the Cultural Revolution was carnivalesque, because the known political world had suddenly turned upside down to reveal that royalty like Liu and Wang were in fact fakes. Student activists believed that the pedagogical mass arts of plays, cartoons, graphic books, movies, and model operas fulfilled the mandate Mao Zedong had set out—namely, a cultural revolution to reset the consciousness of, as Mao had put it, the poor and blank Chinese. Like so many other graphs, images, and texts, the cartoons were intended to educate the masses and reveal political realities. Although Red Guard publications provide important

6.6 Anti–Wang Guangmei cartoon, "In form it is left, but in fact it is right," 1967. Red Guard Publication, 1967.

15. 改头换面巧打扮，派遣夫人去上场·
"错误人人有，关口人人过"，形"左"实右臭名扬·

6.7 Wang Guangmaei wearing the qipao and sitting between Hardini and Liu Shaoqi. *Jinggang-shan News*, 1967.

details and information about the case against Wang, most historically provocative is the verbatim transcript of the Jinggangshan Regiment's interrogation of Wang at 6:30 a.m. and 1:30 p.m. on April 9, 1967, just before her appearance at the mass rally, and again at 5:30 p.m., after the session had ended. A small group calling itself the "'South Sea Great Wall' Fighting Detachment of the Jinggangshan Regiment of Qinghua University" (apparently a coalition that Kuai formed in a series of Red Guard group congresses) claimed responsibility for circulating the transcript, urging that this trial be used as a negative case to educate the masses.[15]

Wang emerges vividly in the transcript, a wily and intelligent antagonist and an aristocratic woman with a strong sense of personal entitlement. Her retrospectively celebrated vulnerability to the student interrogation is clear, but so is her commitment to Liu Shaoqi's positions, which Kuai, the leading student Maoist, was framing and attacking as revisionism. Her debate strategy seems clear. She confesses mistakes to protect her overall domestic political record, the standard ruse of "veteran revolutionaries confronting a new situation" (lao geming yudao xinwenti), who may misunderstand the immediate struggle but are still educable.[16] In the afternoon presession, for instance, she refused to admit that she had behaved autocratically in relation to the masses during her earlier service on a work team in Taoyuan during the Socialist Education Movement. But she abjectly confessed that she had made significant errors during the Qinghua work team's process when she quashed student revolutionaries and targeted them as rightists. Though willing to concede that Liu had misunderstood the objectives of the Cultural Revolution, she refused the students' charges that Liu had taken the capitalist road or had reversed the verdict on Stalin and was thus "China's Khrushchev" (that is, a "veteran rightist"), as Liu was known in the Red Guard media and later the national Communist Party organs. Wang refused to indict Liu but volubly agreed that Liu should be overthrown. That way, the revolution could proceed in the direction that Chairman Mao and the Cultural Revolution Group (aka the Gang of Four: Jiang Qing, Zhang Chunqiao, Yao Wenyuan, and Wang Hongwen) had marked out. In this regard, Wang echoed Liu's offer to Mao that Liu be allowed to retire into the peasantry. In Wang's final, poststruggle evening session, it is hard not to hear a mixture of pride and resignation as she once again recounts her family's elevated class background and debates the fine points about her girlhood, her pathbreaking academic achievements, her work as an underground Communist operative and high-level CCP translator from English and French, her companionate marriage to the much-married Liu, and her official life as the first lady of the country.[17]

In the first presession, the student interrogator also compelled Wang to put on a dress that had been provided for her. Wang refused many times. In general histories of the incident, the question of Wang's dress is generally the only entry found under her name in the index. The transcript shows that the students were intransigent: Wang was to wear exactly the same dress she had worn during her visit with Liu to Indonesia in 1963. Wang declined again and again, saying that it was cold out and offering to wear something else, a garment that was "a gift from Afghanistan," which the Afghanis had given her because they knew she was "fashion minded." In fact, she offered to wear a spring dress, a fur coat, anything, it would appear, except the dress the Jinggangshan militants had presented for her. The interrogator repeats, "We want you to put on the dress that you wore in Indonesia."[18] According to the transcript, after she had been physically forced into the too-small silk dress, sheer silk stockings, and pointed, heeled shoes, Wang was photographed and then removed to the mass struggle site.

Reading and understanding struggle session transcripts is not easy. The interrogators and Wang herself express themselves elliptically in the patois of the time. Because so much rides on extracting details and forcing or resisting certain interpretations of what these tiny factors will mean, the larger context of the struggle recedes. In publications like the Red Congress Propaganda Group's May 1967 volume, *Liushi fufu milan de shenghuo chou'e de linghun* (The Lius' decadent life and despicable souls) and the Jinggangshan Regiment's *Sikai Wangguangmei de huapi* (Rip off Wang Guangmei's evil disguise), the case against Wang is clear-cut.[19] Liu had defamed what, in deference to Marxism and Leninism, modestly came to be called "Mao Zedong Thought," and Wang had "lost face" for the Chinese revolutionary nation by coddling class enemies and international rightists like Sukarno, shown in figure 6.8 resting his arm on a bloody club.

The evidence suggests that, from the point of view of the Red Guard faction, the Indonesian case was only one diplomatic incident in Liu's sleeper-cell revisionism. An alleged journalist, Zhu Lie shows in *Decadent Life* that, for instance, at a 1958 meeting between Liu Shaoqi and "a party representative from an Eastern European country," Liu resolutely took the Khrushchevian revisionist standpoint. This alleged fact suggested that Liu's revisionist pragmatism had poisoned the entire Chinese diplomatic cause and compromised world revolution ever since the founding of the People's Republic of China. The lead chapter of *Decadent Life*, "Look! China's Khrushchev—Liu Shaoqi's Despicable Ugly Face" (Kan! Zhongguo de helu xiaofu Liu Shaoqi de beibi choulou miankong), addresses this question of China's external, antirevisionist foreign policy.[20] The chapter accuses Liu of undermining Mao's entire *anti*revisionist foreign policy when he questioned the CCP's enduring commitment to Stalinist policies. The immediate charge was that Liu had somehow played a role in the October 1, 1965, murder of six Indonesian army generals, which triggered a six-month-long liquidation purge of the Indonesian Communist Party, its leader Aidit, alleged followers and village- and factory-level cadres.[21]

Thus, dress or no dress, Kuai's political stance rested on understanding Liu and Wang's diplomatic work. This was not simply a matter of opportunism or callow adolescent savagery. The book's editorial

6.8 Satire of Wang Guangmei wearing the qipao alongside Liu Shaoqi and Sukarno as he holds a bloody club. *Jinggangshan News*, March 8, 1967.

committee accuses Sukarno of being a "bourgeois political hack [and] anti-Communist, anti-Chinese old hand." They cite as their source an unnamed journalist who traveled with the Liu party in 1963 and 1966 during its tours of Southeast Asia and substantiated the authors' charge that the Indonesia trips were, in fact, "Khrushchevian junkets":

> Chairman Mao has taught us that it is impossible to fundamentally change imperialists and reactionaries. . . . Chairman Mao also taught us that "power grows out of the barrel of a gun." But Liu Shaoqi on the contrary takes Chairman Mao's directives and runs in the opposite direction, singing a countermelody while strongly flattering Sukarno's NASAKOM, saying: "We are so happy to see President Sukarno's initiative, to use NASAKOM to create and strengthen a new Indonesian peoples' collectivity. . . ." Using these completely Khrushchevian reactionary ideologies of "taking the parliamentary road" [*yihui daolu*], "peaceful coexistence" [*heping gongchu*], and "peaceful transition" [*heping*

guodu] [Liu Shaoqi] deracinated the revolutionary vigilance of the Indonesian people. [These wrong policies continued] right down to September 1965, when the reactionary Indonesians overthrew the political authority and bathed the nation of a thousand islands in blood. Untold numbers of party members and revolutionary masses were cruelly exterminated, which caused the Indonesian national democratic people's revolution to sustain great damage.[22]

Liu not only swore friendship in diplomatic terms with Sukarno, dubbing him an anticolonial hero, the report continued, but also promoted a reactionary and U.S. imperialist "third road" policy, and in 1965 it was the Liu-Khrushchev-Sukarno policy that had failed.[23]

That students launched this accusation suggests they had compiled their dossier to bolster the strategy and avoid embarrassing themselves a second time, insuring that the second interrogation and mass struggle concluded well. Wang would be directly confronted and judged for her role in the allegedly problematic diplomacy and for taking the wrong position in a two-line struggle. In fact, Wang did answer the accusation directly. "At the time [in 1963]," she sharply rebuked the students, "Soekarno was quite progressive . . . in diplomacy."[24] Given Soekarno's documented friendliness to the CCP, she was right. But that was not the issue. Wang's interrogators linked the question of a revisionist line in inter-Asian diplomacy to the charge that Liu had engaged in "wife diplomacy." During the 1963 trip, they alleged, Liu had her use her charms to flirt with reactionaries. Not only had she ignored the masses of Indonesians (a standard accusation), but also her behavior had lost face for China by disclosing the casual common-law element of her marriage to Liu, a problem compounded by the fact that on her trip she took personnel and implements in order to boost her star power. These included a personal hairdresser and a qipao that she had had made in Hong Kong— the very qipao that the Jinggangshan Regiment insisted Wang put on before she was taken to the struggle session. So not only did Wang behave like a feudal empress in the course of her duties, but through the lens of allegations about her marital impropriety, she had also allowed Sukarno to use her like a sexual toy. (And Liu had worn a Khrushchev-style hat!)

In the 2006 publication *Wang Guangmei fangtanlu* (Interviews with Wang Guangmei), interviewer-editor Huang Zheng devoted a full chapter to Wang's recollections of the 1963 visit.[25] Wang took the opportunity to refute each of the points that the Jinggangshan interrogators had used against her forty years earlier. Sukarno visited Beijing regularly in the early 1960s, she explains, so that is why she and Liu knew him, and her relations with him were relatively warm. When they arrived at the Jakarta airport, Mrs. Sukarno was not there because Sukarno had many wives, as is customary in Islam (and Indonesia is an Islamic country), and none of them accompanied him on state greeting occasions. In other words, Liu did not use Wang's beauty to attract Sukarno, but rather Indonesian habits differed from Chinese official expectations, and so Sukarno's daughter had acted as the official host in place of her mother. However, Wang continued, later in the visit she did indeed travel with one of Sukarno's wives, Hardini, who before her marriage to Sukarno had been the wife of a powerful regional official. Indeed, Hardini had visited China in 1962, when Mao and Jiang Qing met her at official functions.

Analyzing a political sequence that unfolded during a global world war helps to distinguish the national from the women as such. In this political sequence, two female Chinese politicians are fighting to the death over what a liberated female performance will be. The circumstances are a dispute over the state performance of femininity at the highest diplomatic levels during an anti-Communist purge, a single Cold War conflict. Wang stated for the record that she knew very well that Sukarno was a skilled politician who used his relationship to China and the United States to his advantage whenever possible. This is what diplomatic relations are all about. Wang herself had informally gathered information for Liu on the Cold War balance of power from a French reporter, because Charles de Gaulle's government remained relatively independent from the United States and had its own unilateral Franco-Chinese relationship. That was the substance of her routine diplomatic work in Jakarta in 1963. The Lius visited Bali and returned home. And she stated again for the record that neither she nor Liu could have pursued a revisionist diplomatic line, because they were simply forwarding established Central Committee objectives: "In that period, Sukarno was from our perspective more progressive. He had studied Sun Yat-sen, worked with the Communist Party, and employed a slogan called NASAKOM, which meant that all the political forces, including the Indonesian Communist Party, were all together. What this meant is that at the airport the welcoming leaders included Aidit, the secretary of the Indonesian Communist Party. But because on this occasion [Liu] Shaoqi was traveling with the status of chairman of the nation, we did not see much of Aidit."[26] In other words, it was not for lack of interest, or lack of prior relations with

Aidit, but for reasons of state protocol that she and Liu did not spend their time with Communist revolutionary movement leaders.[27]

Each point emerging out of this claustrophobic, intensely motivated struggle between Kuai and Wang places the truth of women at stake. The Qinghua struggle was consequently not just domestic politics, nor simply a personal dispute between the wives of Mao Zedong and Liu Shaoqi. Wang's trial involved high-stakes geopolitics played out among scientifically demonstrable, biogenetic, physiologically living women who both demanded a political end to their social oppression, including the defendant herself, who insisted on exercising her natural rights to shape communitarian and normative behaviors.

In fact, there is no way to extricate the event of women from geopolitics, here the 1950 Chinese participation in the Korean War and the 1960 Sino-Soviet split. The more these great political earthquakes are studied, the clearer it is that political events and population-mobilization campaigns throughout the Cold War drove policy on women and family formation, whether in an emancipatory social revolution as in China or Cuba or in what some call the most constricted and hyperdomesticized world ever in the United States immediately after the world war and throughout the Cold War. Widening the circumstances where the event of women is undertaken from the nation to international politics clarifies how historically visible women's liberation struggles become. But it also shows why, once the humanity of women is accepted, the way out of injustice and the way into parity cannot be simply national citizenship, suffrage, or property rights. Obversely, contest over truth in the event of women is a modern politics. Wang's appearance on the world stage as China's first lady was a political act. She and Jiang Qing were in the room, so to speak, from 1963 to 1965, when Liu and Wang made regular diplomatic visits to Jakarta.[28] As unequal as these marriages were, high-ranking women participated in a Chinese-Indonesian relationship that would accelerate U.S. involvement in bloody massacres to overthrow Sukarno's coalition government.[29]

FIDELITY IN THE EVENT OF WOMEN

Why is this microbial, intensely ideologized conflict over the modern woman so important in an intricate, ever-proliferating geopolitical story about global Communism in the Cold War era? The Wang Guangmei affair was part of the larger event of women that suffused and shaped modernity as such. An event is possible when people apprehend a new truth and invoke that truth in an effort to transform their political lives. Here, immanent, lost in the material gestalt of dresses, shoes, and pearl necklaces, yet unequivocally present in assertions made by Kuai Dafu, Wang Guangmei, Jiang Qing, and many others, is the revolutionary claim that women not only have a scientifically demonstrable, biogenetic body emerging over evolutionary time but also demand revolutionary legitimation. Everyone involved in the small-scale struggle agreed that women were categorically "victims of oppression" who "declare" themselves oppressed and are "part of a tentative search for an autonomous politics of the oppressed."[30] The world of the Red Guard rebellions qualifies as an autonomous politics of the oppressed; it arose in the heat of battle over how the political superstructure of the country would be constructed. When the subject of women is at stake, the battle over women's truths cannot but take a political form. Femininity itself takes on a revolutionary stylishness.

Wang, Jiang Qing, and their adherents struggled to define what a woman is and in so doing displayed an agonistic distress about the truth of womanhood, a feminine performance determined to be appropriate given women's innate rights, physiological responsibilities to the society, and personal volition to break out of narcissistic attachment to pearls, hats, dresses, brooches, and shoes. Women achieved historical political visibility at the end of the nineteenth century, and earlier chapters of this book have shown how this discernibility accreted, petrified in evidence spewed from corporate imperialism and canonized in vernacular sociology, compacted into the social amber of commercial ephemera and advertising images, visual graphs, to nonetheless insist on the truth of women. Living the truth of women in social existence proved difficult, however. Increasingly, politically progressive women and men saw proof of the truth about sperm, ovaries, ova, and hormones in procreation and knit this into a platform where they voluntaristically acted in fidelity to the event of women.[31]

If modern womanhood is an event rather than a new representation of an always already known anatomical body, then people were acting out a new historical reality. They were affirming that women are half of humanity because humanity is actually composed of evolutionary mammals: volition sweeps us beyond questions of the real and its representations. The real itself changed, and so did the political struggle that sought to establish actual rights-bearing subjects correctly performing the truth of women. Scrutinizing this small-scale struggle over a dress and a necklace drags a socialist-era conflict back into focus.[32] Also, sometimes it is forgotten that the Cultural Revolution assumed a radical and hostile distance from the Chinese state. The geopolitical drama Wang and Jiang Qing played out was an extreme form of egalitarianism. Overthrowing Wang Guangmei, criminalizing her female performance, supplanting what the Jiang Qing Red Guard charged was commodified femininity has had implications for Communist feminisms and their distinctive vision of the human truth. What felt demure and natural to Wang Guangmei was revealed in this struggle to be a dangerous portal back into the commodity fetishization of women.

The intellectual vitality of that long-gone world, in which a dress could have such overwhelming political consequences, needs to be acknowledged. Feminism throughout the Communist bloc of Bulgaria, China, Korea, Romania, and the Soviet Union displayed a remarkable commitment to education and women's liberation that significantly impacted social reproduction. One strategy for acknowledging Communist politics of women is to follow Jiang Qing's preoccupation with women and feminine performance. From her adolescence to her ultimate arrest and suicide, she remained committed to dramatically acting out female characters. According to her *Collected Work* [Jiang Qing wen lu] she began writing about Henrik Ibsen's Nora character from *A Doll's House* in 1934, when she played for the first time the role she would later reprise.[33] In a short published comment, "The Soliloquy of the Performer," Jiang Qing celebrated Ibsen's assertion that a liberated woman should "be a true person" but also noted how difficult it was for young women in her situation in early 1930s China to live this creed. Though no option open to Jiang at the time seemed palatable, she states, becoming an actress was her choice.[34] Throughout the late 1930s, Jiang Qing's publications returned repeatedly to how she resolved her artistic and personal contradictions, performing alternative versions of womanhood onstage. So although the real historical conditions limited new women's ability to achieve economic and social independence, Jiang Qing's spirit of innovation and revolution compelled her to try to forge a Communist political strategy that acted out new possibilities while she remained immured to semifeudal, semicolonial conditions. Although the advertising ephemera analyzed in chapter 4 offered no Communist or anarchist pathway, they normalized women's physicality. We see in Cultural Revolutionary graphesis that draws on advertising stories and cartoon methods muscular, vital bodies that repurposed the older forms to establish astonishing new points.

Within the entire Communist bloc, intellectual, social, ideological, policy, and economic transnational flows were rich and constant. Jiang Qing, for instance, knew a great deal about Russian experimental theater; North Korean artists used Maxim Gorki's *The Mother* (1906), and their own work found millions of fans in the People's Republic of China. The struggle among leftist artists over how the actual truth of women should be enacted theatrically was a staple in leftist art circles through the late 1920s and the 1930s. In literary terms, writers dealt with the theme of "love and revolution," showing female revolutionaries' struggle to balance sexual expression against social discipline, commodified femininity against the graceless physiological chastity that, it was claimed, the revolution demanded. Literary founders Ding Ling, Lu Xun, and Mao Dun celebrated the tension between the modern girl and the revolutionary woman in their pathbreaking work. In film culture, Ruan Lingyu made this tension iconic. In *New Women* (Xin nüxing) (1935), her despairing petit bourgeois heroine dies with a silent scream "I want to live! I want to live!" pouring out her desperation as she dies, torn between the revolution of her flesh and the political challenge that independent life imposed on free women. Scholars in the United States and the People's Republic of China have put critical energy into interpreting and analyzing the emotional and political double binds that independent women experienced. But in this study the stakes are philosophical. And that is where "Jiang Qing's Thought" is relevant.

In an early, strikingly banal story, Jiang Qing analogized the contradiction that set her physiologically material body against the lack of social supports required to live free, using a pathetic childhood story about a sparrow she had "rescued." The bird's spirit of independence outstripped the care that the little girl gave it. In "saving" the bird, she accidently killed it by breaking its spirit. Jiang Qing's tedious point was that liberated women, like wounded sparrows, must be given the opportunity to fly, even when or if their path leads ultimately to death. She embraced, even reinforced and banalized, the theory of women's necessary secondary narcissism that Pan Guangdan had forwarded in his Xiaoqing case study. Moreover, her related essays posited that to know one's true self or spirit, every woman would need to act—to literally act out herself. Jiang Qing was proposing that literally acting out one's personhood in public dramatic art enabled her and by extension all women to understand their future lives. In 1936 she had begun writing about her life as an actress in left-wing theater groups. She fictionalized her own process of entering the life (*shenru shenghuo*) of the rural poor to soak up knowledge about their lives and prepare herself to be a dramaturge, to dramatize and crystallize their experience and vision. At the same time, she sought to puncture the rural masses' provincialism without alienating them, developing a thoughtful process for indigenizing avant-garde Russian and European theatrical experiments. Even here, however, Jiang Qing threads issues through her own needle to underscore rural people's problematic sex roles. Gender trouble in rural areas included peasants' belief that in the absence of long hair and bound feet, it was impossible to tell whether revolutionary youths were male or female. This local feudalism forced Communist drama troupes to balance local customs against the liberatory potential of short hair, natural bodies, mass revolution, and anti-Japanese resistance.

Jiang Qing's 1937 "Our Lives" explains her consciousness of herself in relation to world theater. She not only embraced Ibsen's character Nora but *became* "a Nora," she explained, a woman indistinguishable from the stage role and its agonistic script of liberation. In my terms, she became an autonomous self in relation to her socially violated natural rights. Jiang had absorbed dramaturge Richard Boleslavsky's technique after reading his 1933 book *Acting: The First Six Lessons*.[35] She went on to play other Nora-like roles, particularly Katarina in Aleksandr Ostrovsky's melodrama of women's oppression, *The Storm*.[36] These experiences led Jiang Qing to speculate about performers' lives, their offstage or personal lives, and to consider how the performing arts might be enabling political thinking, particularly the question of individual will.[37] These are familiar literary tropes in many strains of the Chinese national traditions of feminism. A case might be made that Jiang Qing's juvenilia is distinctive because she loosely connected questions of personality or temperament in women (*ren'ge*), the sociological trope of the sex role (*xing de juese*) and stage advice born out of her own experience as both a woman and a performer. The importance of her 1937 article "Our Lives" is that women are like actors, in the sense of having to consider political liberation as an intellectual problem at the same time as they must discipline their bodies, use reason judiciously, and, as all performers must, exercise spiritual control.[38]

In the early 1960s, Jiang Qing began organizing scripts, performers, performance groups, and stage directions to innovate what became her model operas during the Cultural Revolution. Six of the eight scripts have female protagonists and plots involving a heroine's valiant efforts to seek self-liberation, the liberation of women as a collectivity, and the triumph of the revolutionary nation. Though Jiang Qing could have continued to employ expressive short stories and autobiographical essays, she turned away from literature to release sets of what appear to be basically stage notes and later transcripts of her "chats" when she met experimental theater troops. Her notes and commentaries focus exclusively on Peking opera (*jingju*). Throughout, she focuses on operatic procedures, as in her essay "On Instructions Regarding the Creation of 'Great Wall of the Southern Sea' and Shooting the Film."[39] Jiang Qing did not analogize to other dramatic art forms, and her remarks remind the reader that performance enables the actor to rise beyond poor life conditions into a realm where they can spell out alternatives futuristically in a disciplined, routinized, choreographed, and schematized graphic theatricality.[40]

COMMODITY IN REVOLUTION

In the concentrated brief against Wang Guangmei, *Rip Off Wang Guangmei's Evil Disguise*, the Beijing Assembly of Red Guards, Beijing Engineering Institute of Chemical Fibers, opened with a charge that Wang was evil because she was literally a "modern woman" (*modeng funü*).[41] The pathos of the transcripts is obscuring. Jiang Qing had indeed, the student interrogators reminded Wang, complained that in 1963, on a trip to Jakarta, Wang had worn a pearl necklace in defiance of Jiang Qing's advice. Wang responded that in fact, Jiang Qing had forbidden her to wear a brooch, not a necklace, but that obviously it is all the same. This plot element explains why the Indonesian costume struggle usually gets interpreted as a catfight between two powerful wives. No doubt it was, in part. Yet the scandal of the jewelry is only a small part of the charges the militants leveled against Wang related to her ill-performed Indonesian trip. Once the prosecutors turned to the specific charges against Wang, the case documented her lack of seriousness or Communist Party "attitude" (*qiwei*).[42] Specifically, the haute bourgeoisie, the "modern woman," had drawn on all her social capital and physical advantages to such a degree that she had *mis*performed the truth of women. In Maoist revolutionary struggle, adherents must seek the truth, and Wang's characterization of womanhood did a disservice or injustice to the truth. Jiang Qing, by contrast, swore fidelity to the agonistic difficulties that being or performing female entailed. She and her adherents claimed they would turn away from the qipao and its bourgeois origins, the jewelry, the entire mise-en-scène of the commodified femininity of Shanghai circa the 1930s appearing in the Red Guard press and of course in documentary photographs starring the glamorous Wang Guangmei.

The strongest evidence against Wang concerned her performance on the world stage. During the 1963 diplomatic mission, she wore a Shanghai designer dress and a hat that had been specially fabricated for her in a bourgeois marketplace in Hong Kong; in 1966 she wore a Hong Kong tailored qipao while embodying the highest-ranking Communist Party wife in the People's Republic of China. Moreover, given her bourgeois family training, she knew how to light Sukarno's cigarettes and to present herself in "modern woman" guise to flatter him like a serving girl. Her class background and her high position blinded her so she literally could not see why the wife of a Chinese leader of the world Communist revolution should not dress like a commercial advertisement, costuming herself like a modern woman.[43] In other words, the most chargeable offense against her was Wang's depoliticization of women; worse, Kuai and Jiang Qing took the position that each of her private actions showed her to be *anti*political. She went to Indonesia and spent no time with Comrade Aidit; she was supposed to forward the Chairman Mao line on Asian solidarity against U.S. imperialism and USSR revisionism but flirted with Sukarno instead; she took her hairdresser with her; she wore jewelry in defiance of the codes of behavior; and so on.

It is hard not to imagine shock in the transcribed testimony as Wang realized that she was being criticized, not for her role in the Qinghua work team in 1965, but for her leading role in the alleged depoliticization of the subject "women." When Wang finally staked everything on her gender, as in her statement to the interrogators "I am a Communist, a woman, and a Chinese," she had already been strategically outmaneuvered. (This claim on the subject of women comes up only once in the transcript and only in this context.) By that time, revolutionary girl students seeking to politicize themselves and rethink the event of women already occupied the high ground.[44]

In the dossier that Jiang Qing had probably helped create, the Red Guard Congress built a strong case against Wang over the truth of women. Accompanying the constant presentation of information about

6.9 Photograph of Wang Guang-mei wearing her white qipao and sunhat, 1966.

Wang's clothing and accoutrements are the charges that in Pakistan, Burma, Indonesia, and so on, she poisoned diplomacy with, of course, China's Khrushchev, Liu Shaoqi. The uncomfortable point is that the students were right. Wang's performance style and her garb were iconic and were not oriented toward a political future. This book has shown in great detail how in advertising images of the 1920s and 1930s, so-called modern-girl (*modeng nülang*) fashion drew attention to the modernity of a physiological profile and put the internal reproductive organs out into the public media sphere (figure 6.9).

The history of the qipao is well studied although no one has conclusively proved how it originated. It was either a modified version of the Manchu men's long jacket or a synthetic design that intended to mix European waistcoats and Chinese outerwear. With origins in Guangzhou, Shanghai, and the Manchu communities of the north, the dress ended up hugging breasts, waist, and legs and, depending on the wearer's taste or status, could be split up the sides to let silk stockings or pants show through. The qipao's ambiguous origins and the fact that it became the modern "Chinese" dress rendered its significance equivocal. No matter where it derived or how many kinds of people wore it—from schoolgirls and young married women, to movie stars and streetwalkers, to Nationalist Party women worthies and brand models—the dress could indicate femininity, out-of-bounds sexuality, consumer nationalism, the Chinese version of a flapper culture, and enthusiastic desire for a modern commodity life. From this perspective, Wang wore a fetish dress on her state tours as seen in figure 6.9.[45]

The accusations and trial against Wang put her on the defensive, particularly the graphic images flaunting her bourgeois class origin and linking her qipao and branded commodities to commercial advertising ephemera during her youth. Feminine behavior is difficult to parse. Is it biological and therefore instinctual? Is femininity provisional because women's natural rights have historically been negated, so her behaviors will always reflect oppression? Or, as the Maoists argued, does it arise voluntarily, a necessary political behavior inventing more truthful ways of living, both different from men and equal to them in "the equality of men and women"? As the Communist movement grew and loyalists to the event of women invented new rituals, women stepped forward to be counted as individuals, as natural rights–bearing persons, whether or not their rights were honored in the breach.[46] The political scenario analyzed here had deep roots in various domains, including the problem of women's political subjectivity. That events that are recognized ex post facto are actually rooted in new truths helps illuminate what the Kuai Dafu and the Jinggangshan Regiment's assault against Wang means historically in the event of women.[47]

Turning back to confirm that the truth of women is something they can claim for themselves, people transfigure themselves. In philosophical language, if the truth of an event is constructed "bit by bit, *from the void*," and subjects are "always in literal excess of their situation," then "a subject is an individual transfigured by the truth she proclaims."[48] One does not qualify as a woman by virtue of anatomy (that would be an identitarian claim, not a truth claim) but rather in the act of seizing personhood. That is where Wang's defense disintegrated. A political subject, woman, is evaluated by her degree of political awareness and egalitarian devotion. The verifiability of the event of women and its subject has caused no end of troubles, and in one respect what we see in this Cultural Revolution scenario is not so much the politicization of women to the detriment of gender as a vivid charge that the Liu-ist party state had *depoliticized* and *commodified* what by all rights of interpretation was foundationally a Maoist subject.

There is no point in arguing the relative merits of the Red Guard position. The stylized presentations of Wang's qipao open a central problem in political life regarding the veracity of "woman": How are female political subjects stabilized? During the struggle, posters and demonstrations attacking bourgeois revisionism were commonplace:

> [A] poster of a female student from the Department of Mechanics who posted on egalitarianism in relation to gender wrote in criticism of gender-based work rules: "Regardless of her financial circumstances, [the female worker] gets 1.5 yuan . . . extra for food. . . . If she's on the factory floor . . . if she has her period, she only has to work a maximum of four hours/day and no night shift. If she has to operate a lathe or welding equipment, she gets an extra two or three days off. She doesn't have to do any heavy labor at all, not even bend her back washing vegetables. *This is nothing more than nurturing revisionism!*[49]

Like all of us, the Red Guard had trouble articulating female difference, which they maliciously called "nurturing revisionism." The Red Guard did not simply invert femininity or masculinize it into so-called gender neutrality. While more research remains to be done, Hung-Yok Ip, Tina Mai Chen, and Rosemary Roberts have all shown that in body movement and performance styles, femininity, sexuality, and expression of female difference from masculine performance never "disappeared" in the Great Proletarian Cultural Revolution. They were rerouted.[50]

If the depoliticization of women's liberation was congruent with the statist policies that Wang Guangmei, Liu Shaoqi, and most Chinese Communists promoted, then the battle between Wang and Kuai Dafu must be considered epochal. Maoist feminism is being rethought these days, and its disavowal reconsidered. The U.S. political feminist thinking of the 1960s was deeply influenced by the Cultural Revolution's emphasis on the political female subject through the device of speaking bitterness, or, in the 1960s U.S. argot, "consciousness raising." Alice Echols made brilliantly clear years ago that the notion of the political in so-called U.S. second-wave feminism derived from the shock of learning about Third World struggles and the anti-imperialist nationalisms of

China, Cuba, and Africa.[51] Perhaps as U.S. liberation thinking realizes its self-isolation, this abandoned project of Communist feminism will be taken up again in the United States. But the great revulsion against the political subject of women has not subsided. At Wang's death, websites filled with postings noting that she was the flower of Chinese femininity and rebuking the horrid politics of the 1960s. This was given as a major reason to celebrate her life.

Conclusion

Historians blast or grab truth out of the past in order to demonstrate how new things came into a previous world. The actress, socialite, and businesswoman pictured in figure C.1 had herself photographed in the likeness of silent film star Lillian Gish. The image of Miss Ing Tang (Tang Ying) approximated a modern, commodified, biological, physiological, universal new woman. She and the thousands of other players we have encountered in commercial art, cinema, political theory, ephemera, vernacular sociology, and countless other areas confirm women's truth. Eyes upcast, Ing proffers a generic self to the public, secure in the conditions of its own possibility. Her posture and open publicity show her fidelity to an event. Commercial publications like *Beiyang huabao* (Beiyang pictorial, 1926–1937), where figure C.1 appeared, used beauty portraits to brand themselves. Every issue featured a female model on the front page just above a mélange of commodity ads, cartoons, drawings, jottings, essays, sexual gossip, and photos of social life, military life, and nudes.[1] A typical page might have a nudie picture, a movie pinup, and cartoons, ads typical of the generic *huabao* (pictorial). Figure C.2 is typical *Beiyang huabao* fare. Surrounding this image are the troubling photographs in figures C.3–C.5. These images show executions and sexual mutilation of women Communists; a bystander claiming to be a photojournalist took them. My point in exposing these degrading images is to note that by this time, even torture and mutilation of women's bodies had become

C.1 Ms. Ing Tang dressed as Lillian Gish. *Beiyang huabao*, September 21, 1926.

Female commandants of Canton Communists executed by Anti-Red army.

C.2 A typical page of the Beiyang pictorial, including a nudie pin-up. *Beiyang huabao*, May 16, 1928.

C.3 *Beiyang huabao*, January 18, 1928.

tabloid fodder. White Terror extermination campaign images made their way into a commercial pictorial alongside beauty queens, pinups, socialites, and educated mothers, all of this in technical fidelity to the event of women. Almost ludicrously, on the same page an ad image showcases movie star singer Gu Meijun assuring us in the commodity ad copy that morphology and sensibility line up perfectly because women have a female instinct (*benneng*) for beauty.

Miss Ing Tang's voluntarist act of self-reproduction in the event of women authorized and confirmed the inchoate forces that made her photograph historically intelligible. As I have shown throughout this book, the conditions of thought—the territory where a truth appeared to be declared—included activists carrying out capital financialization and marketization of industrially produced commodities, commodity fetishism, petrochemicals, and significant social change. Miss Ing Tang stands in for the thousands and thousands of woman images that made good on corporate imperialism's dreams of mass consumption. *Beiyang huabao* sprinkled media with Chinese bourgeois girl images like her, ephemera left behind to connote epistemological and sociological transformation. The Chinese Lillian Gish is a reminder that acting on the new regime, biophysicality, is to reassert an incontestable truth, which makes physiology an integral element of colonial, capitalist modernity. Likewise, the modern story is always about the woman in the same way ephemera are part of the oceanic number of leftover old newspapers, ad posters, movie magazines, popular sociologies, and poster fragments that, in Walter Benjamin's terms, demonstrate how "the relation of what-has-been to the now is dialectical . . . not progression but image, *suddenly emergent*."[2] This ripped-out or suddenly recognized-to-be-emergent dialectical image means that Miss Ing Tang and Comrade Jiang Qing were each in their own way loyalists to the truth of women and militants in the event of women.

What about the usual cast of characters in histories of Chinese modernity? This study has aspired to loosen the grip on our histories of abstract categories like nationalism, culture, sovereignty, gender, identity, and so on. Benjamin A. Elman's decades-old polemic condemned mainstream writing in Chinese intellectual historiography and showed how abstractions and teleologies wrecked histories of thinking.[3] He castigated its airy disregard for its own conditions and, rejecting "reductionism," he provided a situated case study showing how to raise and resolve questions in thought and political situations *without* invoking abstract players like

前之鋪店之怒羣所其行經時次相場刑赴押(△)黨產共女州廣
A woman Communist just going to be executed, Canton.

c.4 *Beiyang huabao*, January 18, 1928.

The bared body of a woman Communist after being executed, Canton.

c.5 *Beiyang huabao*, January 18, 1928.

modernization or *transitional*. Undoing reductionist histories of civilization is also possible when we reconfigure the questions we ask around jumbled, compromised, conditional, irregularly shaped, and multiform physical evidence. Old sociology books and dictionaries, ephemeral advertising images, high modernist art, etymological crises in language revolutions, sales technologies geared at circulating commodities, propaganda, Cultural Revolution posters, and theories of consciousness and the physiological body merge to become an immanent critique addressing a historical conscious; all clarify what abstractions like *nationalism* or *women* may have meant in everyday life and where in the world of sensation and psychic life such abstractions resided.

This is not to say that nationalism is unimportant. It is just not always the immediate stake, and evidence does not readily support or betray the agonistic issue of the national teleology. To the contrary, publications like *Beiyang huabao* show how ephemera make social forces and events evident even in situations where the nationalist harangue is significant. Putting aside the sad old historiographic stories about a forced marriage of male chauvinist nationalists and female feminist activists or about how liberal and anarchist theorists lost their social purchase to a vengeful, amoral Communist Party, this book notes that in fact conflicts do not revolve around polar opposites. The core point and the basic stake in this study is how to communicate the eventual quality of women's truth, a truth put into actions that set off social evolutionary theoretical studies and commercial culture. The event of women was, in conventionally Althusserian language, "overdetermined."[4]

Loyalists to the event of women, its militants or "agents," seized on the reality that human animals evolve anatomically, and at least in the Marxist camp they added that humanity also evolved ethically toward a better society. Social science ideology shaped everyday social life. That is why a broadsheet published in North China and reflecting the interests of a resistant Beiyang military political clique stitched together photo images of society, cartoons, a repeating Renault brand car ad, reports about Nanyang boy scouts in Tokyo, and Garage Central auto repair ads into an inviting society of plenty. *Beiyang huabao* is not a context. Nor can we interpret *Beiyang huabao* inside another, larger context, like nationalism or sovereignty. Rather, in part and as a whole, it is an endlessly iterative rendition of a revolutionary new society. Printed illustrated magazines were unprecedentedly modern in their content, and repetitiveness was part of their attraction. Endlessly repeating girl and women images in advertising cartoons and the clichéd photographs of movie stars, flappers, corpses, educated women, housewives, and cosmopolitan prostitutes: the more banal these images become, the more universal they appear. This psychosocial world of reiterative dissolution and visual ephemera reinforces Jing Tsu's counterintuitive argument that Chinese intellectual men's sense of self was "based not on [loss of] sovereignty but on the embrace of failure."[5]

HISTORY

Buried in media mash-ups like *Beiyang huabao* are two final historical points: first, that something as indisputable as physiology and sexual reproduction could ever have formed the conditions for an event; and, second, that an event of women rests on that fifth condition of generic truth, history, which opens as contingency until someone seizes it. A new truth is never self-evident, and it is never stable. Truths are contests, as the political struggle between Wang Guangmei and Jiang Qing's proxies has shown. Battling over femininity meant seizing political control over the truth of the event of women under international eyes. Analogously, ephemeral incidents contesting what the subject "women" would be in the twentieth century are too numerous to count. In 1919, famously, a bride, Zhao Wuzhen, slashed her throat with a knife and died on her way to the marital family's house. Zhao Hailou, her father, had sold her to a rich family over her religious and ethical objections.[6] No matter what motived Zhao Wuzhen, this suicide sparked an intellectual rebellion in Changsha, where the young Mao Zedong lived. He and other intellectuals claimed it as proof that all women had inner, natural, subjective, voluntarist drives and should be liberated to pursue their natural rights and sexual imperatives to forward social and biological evolution. Women should be free to choose their mates. When they all published essays, they politicized a suicide that may have been until that moment just another bridal suicide. Here again intellectuals like Li Da and Qu Qiubai, analyzed in chapter 2, claimed that like the peasantry, the proletariat, and the people, women were subjects defined to some degree by their oppression.[7]

It has been a hundred years since Zhao's death. Over time, philosophers and revolutionaries like the anarchist He-Yin Zhen, the nationalist Qiu Jin, the feminist agronomist Wu Juenong (aka Y.D.), the revolutionaries Mao Zedong, and countless others have vociferously claimed that women's sexual difference is a site for revolutionary innovation and political invention.[8] In a sophisticated, tumultuous philosophical world, Zhao's suicide opened to women and men a singularity in the body of a categorical, physiological, philosophical female subject and helped to initiate a struggle over this truth. If an event and its truths can, as I hope to have shown in this study, restructure historians' understanding of the past, then historians' accounts also rattle the foundations of Alain Badiou's philosophy. This was Alenka Zupančič's point when she noted the fifth generic requisite, history.[9] Philosophy (Elman calls it theory) according to Badiou "seizes truths, shows them, exposes them, announces that they exist."[10] Inescapably, modern philosophy begins from "our times."[11] There is no way around the historicity and the sociological facts of our times, because it is precisely the social science notion of society and the rise of philosophy of history that demark modern times as such.

Helpfully, Badiou acknowledges that contemporary philosophy "grasps the disposition of undefined terms."[12] Undefined terms are most frequently encountered in poetic work, according to him, since that is a condition of poetics as a truth procedure. But increasingly historians and philosophers of history are arguing that grasping the disposition of undefined terms is central to intellectual history. The term *modern girl* is a neologism, as most sexually taxonomic terms are in modern twentieth-century Chinese. Modern-girl studies broke the ground for studying how girl-branded commodities were globalized. Prescient scholars also have speculated about whether "real modern girls," or girls who embodied the brand, actually existed. The problem until recently has been that neologisms are not all necessarily even measly epistemic events. An ambiguous and underdefined phrase, *modern girl* makes sense in relation to a categorical, *women*. And, it turns out, women is a modernist category that has been historically established in enormous, monotonous detail because it is a subject declared in theoretical, philosophical, anatomical, physiological, and political terms. This is the value of Badiou's position to me; when contemporary philosophical thinking encounters a term such as *women*, for instance, "it is not in the sense of *a naming whose referent would need to be represented*, but rather in the sense of being laid out in a series wherein the term subsists only through the ordered play of its founding connections."[13]

Yet when Badiou himself treats women at all, he forbids the possibility of there being a historical female subject, women or a truth of women "there"—in other words, "of there being a historical female subject, women, or a truth of women" at all. Why? Because "truth depends on a bar imposed on sex."[14] Badiou's Lacanian Freud comes down decisively on the side of sexuation and against what Badiou disparages as the "gynaecologist." Untangled, this just means that medical scrutiny of sexed bodies colludes with the scientization of the real and the drive to slice life into mechanical parts and feed them into the machine. "Should he," Badiou argues on Freud's behalf, "adopt the model of medical objectivity, which has always registered both body and sex? Or is it a question of the subversive subjectivation, bearing on the sexual narrative and its effects, from which nothing—not femininity as it is ordinarily understood . . . will come out unscathed."[15]

This is a weak argument on its face. There is no either-or here. Actually, the gynecologists were themselves revolutionaries, and the mystery of organic sexual difference has, as argued in chapter 2, never fully been resolved. Not only is there nothing to be gained by demonizing the rise of the anatomical body, newly discovered in the past century, but the drive for sexuation is intimately connected to the gynecological order, whatever one calls it. There is a difference between sexuation and sexual pleasure and sexed subjects and surplus sexual desire, but the point at stake here is the political emergence of the split, physiologically describable, sexed woman in her struggle to assert a natural right to be human. Badiou, himself a Maoist, ignores the drama playing out in Maoism and the Cultural Revolution over the question of the event of women.

Badiou's failure is astounding. Badiou's philosophy of the event has proved valuable in rethinking historical method. Historical work now returns the favor to uncover what is, even measured by the rules of philosophy, a scholarly blunder: Badiou cannot discern a term, *women*, even during "the century," in a book he wrote that is self-importantly entitled *The Century*. Badiou's philosophy of the event is complex, and it is a philosophy, as he himself defined it in his own enormous body of work. Yet he knows that he cannot avoid an essentially historical problematic, what he terms "the mistress of the moment: History." And that is because, even he must admit, History is "the unshakeable support for any politics whatsoever." Philosophy cannot avoid sociological reasoning.[16] There is no other place to hang the generic procedures. Still he struggles. Badiou's history of "the century," for instance, renames biology the bestial question. In the chapter "What Is Life?" he argues, "Knowledge must become the intuition of the organic value of things."[17] Now, logically, the discovery of organic, physiological processes should make it impossible to ignore the central role biowomen play in the organic value of everything—particularly in sexual reproduction. Yet Badiou's reference to the organic value of anatomical sexual difference comes in a toss-away parenthesis regarding Paul Claudel, who defines woman as "a promise that cannot be kept."[18]

Or let us take Badiou's second thought characterizing the twentieth century, the "passion for the real," which requires a fundamental restructuring of a bellicose new man, possessed by the will to power, and his third thought, via Bertolt Brecht, regarding the theatrical power of war in the making of the new man. We could take the fourth characteristic, the preeminence of ideology and theories of ideology, which is the power of the real conveyed by misrecognition but is also montage—such as the montage of the *Beiyang huabao*, which makes a colonial modernity out of images of nudes, cars, flags, advertising icons, generals, and corpses. In Badiou's complicated language, "semblance is the true situating principle of the real," meaning that the artistic arrangement presents in its graphesis an ontology of which philosophy cannot speak.[19] Even then, despite enormous, ephemeral reasoning and analytic evidence to the contrary, in Badiou's complex investigations there are no women, no truth of woman, no female subject, no event of women, no physiological or "organic" or "gynecological" discovery leading to the subject women in evolutionary terms. There is nothing.

My earlier work asked how the event of women, an integral element of what defines the modern as such, could be absent in world-scale analysis both in precapitalist or capitalist takeoff studies and in their inverted form, the Eurasian paradigm. I was preoccupied with how the new globalist or regional histories might accommodate the event of women. If "great divide" neoglobalists rest their case on contingency, as seems to be the case, then how could the question of women or proletarianized female labor power become so utterly epiphenomenal? How could world-systems theory exclude the sexual division of labor as a cause or an indicator of modernity? But how could it include it?[20] Inclusion, one might think, is the responsibility of gender historians. And yet Slavoj Žižek's question about the "infinite multiple" of women in feminism has drawn attention to the fact that while gender scholars may claim that there is no woman as such, it supplies as proof of its own assertion a reference to infinite numbers of specific or "historical" women.[21] In this study I have argued that women is not an impossible category and is not asserted through infinite multiples but rather is an event inherent in modernity; that is, the evental quality of women cannot be registered or written about or even acknowledged merely by changing the "scale" or "units" of analysis in play. Badiou claims that the proletarian in Marxist thought forms "the central void of early bourgeois society."[22] It is just as likely, my evidence suggests, that *women* is the name that twentieth-century thinkers—sociologists, philosophers, demographers, census takers, poets, and biologists—gave to the "central void" of modern citizenship and consequently of the nation and nationalism. The central antagonism of modern middle-class men and women was precisely the deficient ground of the Enlightenment refusal to grant citizenship and thus subjective fullness to women as women.[23]

And if we seriously consider Badiou's claim that the twentieth century is marked with anabasis, or the desire to return and reclaim community, then we cannot rest, for the subjects recaptured or made anew are always, in Jacques Nancy's words, the "fraternal order"—a masculine community poised to build the revolutionary future.[24] And there is no real debate. Badiou is correct when he insists that in this century, historically, "the real is not represented, it is presented."[25] Many scholars, including historians, argue the same point, that the real may be encountered, manifested, fought over, attacked, or constructed, but it is not represented. Qu Qiubai's terrible discovery of the powers of realist representation immured him in the still-ongoing event of women so the struggle is by no means over.[26]

In the Event of Women has built a case that the truth of women transformed the thinkable in philosophy and historiography, and not just in Europe. The shared ground of theoretical translation and competitive mass marketing meant that the event of women occurred in the alleged periphery, even in an acephalous nation colonized, divided, and commercially restructured by imperialist, commercial capital, and again in a revolutionary state formation and its undoing, and continues, as this matter continues in China and elsewhere. Badiou's attempts to make love to history fall apart here. Historically, the most enduring event of the late nineteenth and twentieth centuries—the event of women— is illegible in his *philosophy* of the century. Even granting that philosophers "meditate philosophically" on historical questions, when Badiou says, "The question is not what took place in the century, but what was thought in it," his conclusion admits defeat.[27] In the immanent process of locating categories and reading historical catachreses, finding the disposition of as yet undefined terms in the sociological foundations of the modern Chinese order and in the ephemera that blanketed its modern environment, the immanency of the scientific is incontestably modern and highly saturated. There is no historical distinction among the gynecologist, the anatomist, the advertising agent, the commercial capitalist, and the corporate imperialist: there is no difference among the socialite, the flapper, the girl student, the professional woman, the factory worker, the murdered underground Communist girl, or the prostituted movie star. They all show the anatomical nakedness of the new woman, women's truth, and the montage or fantastic commercial arts that deliver her to the viewer as a subject or, as we have seen in chapter 6, as a struggle object. And each takes up the political struggle over the truth of women, in the event of women.

But history cannot be just an imprecation against philosophy. As Badiou's disciple Alberto Toscano argues in his addendum to *The Century*, speaking in the words of Frantz Fanon, "Come then, comrades, the European game has finally ended; we must find something different."[28] We will see. I do not fathom a way to square the circle yet. As my work suggests, the surfeit theorization in the modes of popular and philosophical sociology saturating ephemera, mass images, and the physical and social environment; images of females in advertising campaigns for foreign-branded commodities; and Communist women with muscles show how an event of women is a constituent part of modernity. This is no longer debatable or avoidable. Massive, revolutionary conditions provided means for thinking a new truth of women; the new category, society, laid out in social science terms, established an ontology that has yet to be dislodged. Historians should not ignore the modernity of the event of women. If the biological body of a woman is alleged to be *ahistorical*, then historians will pursue the idea that anatomy is a naive puppet, that culture or psychic drives clothe subjectivities that change over time but merely "historically." Only when women's historians and historians as such recognize *a political event of women* in modern times will the mystery of gender be resolved. The global phenomenon of women as a category of modernity was constructed precisely with world-scale ambitions—in the moment of commercial capital and the release of domestic commodities into new markets savagely carved out of older distribution networks. At the same time, women had to acknowledge (if not submit to) the protocols of the global to even be articulated. That is why the event of women in Chinese trading ports can be generalized as a universal. Women's articulation was a singular launched from the multiple. Perhaps the better solution for Badiou's dilemma is to reapproach philosophically the ambiguities of Mistress History.[29]

Notes

Introduction to the Event

1 Kuai Dafu (1945–) put Wang on trial with the cooperation of the Central Committee and the Beijing People's Liberation Army PLA Garrison, according to Tang Shaojie. See Tang Shaojie, *Yi ye zhi qiu*, 51–53.

2 J. Chen, *Mao's China and the Cold War*, 242–43.

3 My use of the transcribed struggle against Wang draws inspiration from Russo, "'Probable Defeat.'"

4 Coward et al., "Phospholipase Cζ." The issue at stake is how, chemically speaking, sperm "induce" activity in eggs. The team finds that they do not yet know precisely how it happens, but they know this same inducement can be found in chickens.

5 Cobb, "Amazing 10 Years"; Briggs and Wessel, "In the Beginning . . ."; Hodge, *Human Genetics*; Hayden, *Evolutionary Rhetoric*. Wendy Hayden's work particularly reinforces my argument. When laboratory scientist Johannes Friedrich Miescher (1844–1895) isolated nucleic acid and showed it played a role in inheritance and, in the mid-twentieth century, this got the name of DNA, social evolutionist theory claimed its definitive truth.

6 Judge, *Republican Lens*.

7 See Barlow, "'What Is a Poem?'" for Ernesto Laclau's concept of context dependency and conditions of visibility.

8 Benjamin, *Illuminations*, ch. 16, "Theses on the Philosophy of History."

9 Foucault, "Impossible Prison" (1980), in *Foucault Live*; White, *Metahistory*; Foucault, *Discipline and Punish*; Bove, *Critical Ontology*.

10 Patton, "World Seen from Within," 6.

11 Patton, "World Seen from Within."

12 Chakrabarty, *Provincializing Europe*, but particularly China historian Prasenjit Duara's *Rescuing History from the Nation*. These historians disavow history that is credible and true.

13 Bensaïd, "Alain Badiou," 94–105.

14 Russo's scholarly impact is important here. See Day, "Interpreting the Cultural Revolution Politically," for an overview. Jacques Rancière and Fredrick Cooper have also raised the salience of the political event. See Rancière, *Althusser's Lesson* and *The Names of History*; and Cooper, *Colonialism in Question*.

15 Zupančič, "Fifth Condition."

16 In Badiou's philosophy the political sequence is so rare that truths cannot be considered continuous, structural, or subterranean (as per the Annales school or Foucault or even Badiou's own in-house critic, Sylvain Lazarus) but are always in Badiou's system truth in a fitful, absolute, ontological disruption. Only those who make revolutions—logician Paul Cohen, poets William Shakespeare and Paul Celan, political theorist/actor Mao Zedong, philosopher of love Sigmund Freud—make *history*. Others exist under conditions neither of their own making nor in any zone of awareness that would merit the term *history* or *historical subject*. We vegetate or, in fealty, militate for already existing truth.

17 I do not evaluate Badiou's efforts to dispute charges of ahistoricism and philosophical authoritarianism. Between *The Century* (2005), essays written in the 1990s allegedly to produce a "history" of how the century thought itself, and in the 2009 volume *Logics of Worlds: Being and Event II*, Badiou attempted to address the issues I am raising here. Two essays in *The Century* ("Sex in Crisis" and "Anabasis") can be usefully read for his continuing philosophical and historical weakness. In the first case, Badiou is forced to argue that the real of sex has no relation to historical physiology discoveries. See Myung Mi Kim's "Anna O Addendum" for a clever grasp of how Freud dealt with the "real of sex" by making the woman an addendum. In "Anabasis," Badiou again balks at the implications of his own analysis. In the same book, *The Century,* he speculates that historical modernism/modernity "is witness to a profound mutation of the question of the 'we,'" and still ends investigation denying any possibility of a we that includes women: "How are we to move from the fraternal 'we' of the epic to the disparate 'we' of togetherness, of the set, without ever giving up on the demand that there be a 'we'?" 97. I can think of many ways to resolve this rhetorical question. But as in most discussions of coming community, Badiou makes no effort to comprehend a "we" that includes evental historical woman because the real of sex (Jacques Lacan) can never be the real of the social, the social sex, the woman, even the fantastic phallic woman. It appears that when he decided recently to reengage the dialectic, Badiou has taken the criticism more seriously. His formula of "democratic materialism" is forwarded in *Logics of Worlds* and in "Affirmative Dialectics: From Logic to Anthropology."

18 Lam, *Passion for Facts.* I regret that I am unable to integrate Arunabh Ghosh's 2020 monograph, *Making It Count,* into this discussion. See Ping Zhu, *Gender and Subjectivities,* for the "anamorphic feminine," meaning an inescapable feminine assumed as an element of modernity that Chinese intellectuals sought for China.

19 Timothy Brook and Bob Tadashi Wakabayashi's *Opium Regimes: China, Britain, and Japan, 1839–1952* demonstrates the transformative impact of financial capital's tools and methods (bookkeeping, branding, franchising, distribution, commercialization, etc.) using commodified opium as its focus.

20 In her article "The Fifth Condition," Zupančič sketches out her view that to unravel the double bind Badiou should return to a psychoanalytic reconsideration of the politics of representation, or psychoanalytic semiotics. Zupančič would

no doubt find my argument hard to swallow. Unfortunately, there is no way to follow her further here without going completely off track, but Zupančič's rebuke is to return Badiou back to what is potentially a feminist position. Citing Badiou "La Scène du Deux," Zupančič reiterates Badiou's own Lacanian point that Two "would be counted for two in an immanent way . . . , where Two is neither fusion nor a sum; and where Two is thus in excess over that what constitutes it, without there being a Third [term] to join it.'" Zupančič, *Shortest Shadow*, 147. The impression Zupančič leaves is that were one to follow out her statement and Lacan's insight through Badiou, one would encounter a "pure disjunction," and this pure disjunction might be borrowed into the conceptualization of the woman subject. This would put Lacan in the midst of the Chinese theorization of sexual difference in the 1920s and 1930s, according to Howard Chiang in *After Eunuchs: Science, Medicine, and the Transformation of Sex in Modern China*.

21 Bensaïd, "Alain Badiou," 94–105

22 Bensaïd, "Alain Badiou," 101; my emphasis.

23 Drucker, "Graphesis," 19. "To conceptualize graphesis as visual epistemology," she argues, means pictorial graphs are a way of presenting meaning. There is a debate over how Drucker defined her term in a later major publication, *Graphesis: Visual Forms of Knowledge Production*. I use the 2011 paper because I like the term visual epistemology.

24 Drucker, *Graphesis*, 15–16: "Most information visualizations are acts of interpretation masquerading as presentation . . . arguments made in graphical form."

25 W. Yeh, *Becoming Chinese*.

26 Two major monographs on the technology transfer of biology and "the view of modern life," that is, a conjuncture of Kantianism and popular biopsychology, have established that elite and popular science or scientism tremendously affected how literate people understood their lives. These are Gad C. Issy's *The Philosophy of the View of Life in Modern Chinese Thought* and Laurence Schneider's *Biology and Revolution in Twentieth-Century China*. Both reworked Danny Wynn Ye Kwok's 1965 classic *Scientism in Chinese Thought, 1900–1950*. Scientism—in Kwok's words, "the attitude that science, in its function as an accurate natural discipline, as a total system of nature [was] capable of informing physical existence and of categorizing human life and society"—and science proper have captivated the historiography of China since the 1960s, just as they did Chinese cultural critics and science journalists in China during the 1920s and 1930s. Historians in the Modern Girl around the World Research Group have established the generic model of the "modern girl." See Modern Girl around the World Research Group, *Modern Girl around the World*.

Chapter 1: Conditions of Thinking

1 "Although Andersen, Meyer, & Company Ltd. is an American corporation and the Board of Directors meets in New York, the administrative office of the Company is located in Shanghai." Ferguson, *Andersen, Meyer and Company*, 1. The CEO of

AMCO, Vilhelm Meyer, came from a background in finance banking, but AMCO sought capital everywhere, including Fearon, Daniel and Company, an insurance company linked to General Electric Company, and Mutual Life Insurance Company underwrote AMCO's engineering department.

2 Armand, "Digging Up Lost Billboards."

3 Peng Changxin's "Zhongguo jindai gongye sheji de xianqu—Shenchang yanghang de jianzhu shijian" details the architectural contribution to reinforced-concrete building construction. See Brook and Wakabayashi, *Opium Regimes*.

4 Peng Changxin, "Zhongguo jindai gongye sheji de xianqu."

5 Ferguson, *Andersen, Meyer and Company*, 2.

6 Meyer gathered $350,000 in new capital investment and reorganized his firm into a stock company with Galen L. Stone and Willard D. Straight in order to capitalize on a relationship with a finance company called Pacific Commercial Company of Manila. After AMCO was acquired by this finance company, its capital increased to $1 million and then to $5 million. The Pacific Commercial Company went bankrupt in the recession of 1920–1922 but, with the support of GE, Baldwin Locomotive Works, Saco Lowell, and other manufacturers, AMCO survived, restructured but intact. When Pacific Commercial liquidated, AMCO became an arm of the International General Electric Company. See Ferguson, *Andersen, Meyer and Company*, 4–5.

7 Unless otherwise noted, all information about global electrification can be confirmed with reference to Hausman, Hertner, and Wilkins, *Global Electrification*. For earlier discussions of finance capitalism, see Hou, *Foreign Investment and Economic Development in China*, which notes, "The chief function of foreign banks in China was to finance foreign trade and to handle foreign exchange transactions. As late as the early 1930s over 90% of the total import and export business in Shanghai was still financed by foreign banks" (54).

8 Garke, *Progress of Electrical Enterprise*, cited in Hausman, Hertner, and Wilkins, *Global Electrification*. See Henry, *Assimilating Seoul*, for how this worked in Seoul and Tokyo.

9 Christian Henriot has posted photographs of the electrical stations and a map of the French Concession's electrification, like an AMCO ad, on the website "Virtual Shanghai."

10 Christopher Bo Bramsen's *Open Doors: Vilhelm Meyer and the Establishment of General Electric in China* notes that Meyer became the sole agent for GE in 1906, but it was not until 1920 that the relationship took off and GE/AMCO products began selling well in China. This chronology is legible in the pattern of advertising.

11 Yamamura, "Zaibatsu, Prewar, and Zaibatsu, Postwar."

12 It appears that in English the idea that "market" is a place or spatially demarked area enters the language in the late nineteenth century. It is a modernist term, to put a fine point on this, see *Oxford English Dictionary*, https://www.oed.com/view/Entry/114178?rskey=vmWMSp&result=1&isAdvanced=false#eid, accessed

December 27, 2020. Before then, *market* was transitive: "to market" or "going to the market," but not in the sense of "opening markets" or market*ing*. Theories of marketing may precede "the market": advertising might be the prose of transitive marketing activity.

13 Cheng, "United States Petroleum Trade with China," 210.

14 Hausman, Hertner, and Wilkins, *Global Electrification*. Also see Cox, *Global Cigarette*; and Lenin, "Finance Capital and the Political Oligarchy."

15 Bramsen, *Open Doors*.

16 Garke, *Progress of Electrical Enterprise*, cited in Hausman, Hertner, and Wilkins, *Global Electrification*. Also see Henriot, "Virtual Shanghai." The same advertising and selling techniques appeared in the United States and treaty-port China at around the same time.

17 Etemad and Luciani, *World Energy Production*, cited in Hausman, Hertner, and Wilkins, *Global Electrification*, 19, 28. Japan ranked well from 1905 despite its catastrophic imperial adventures, or perhaps because of them, meaning it was around the same level as France, the United Kingdom, and Italy.

18 Bickers, "Fly on an Elephant's Back."

19 See the Chinese Commercial Advertising Archive I cofounded with Professor Chen Jing, Nanjing University (https://ccaa.nju.edu.cn/html/index.html). With generous support from the Luce Foundation and the Rice University History Department, the website archives "metadates" ads in five cities. See Manovich, "Metadating the Image."

20 Pär Kristoffer Cassel's *Grounds of Judgment: Extraterritoriality and Imperial Power in Nineteenth-Century China and Japan* is a recent example. Works that lay new historiographical emphasis on financialization, trade, and fixed commodities include Bickers and Jackson, *Treaty Ports in Modern China*; Bickers and Howlett, *Britain and China*; and Bickers and Henriot, *New Frontiers*. See also Betta, "Myth and Memory"; Kent, "Problems of Circulation"; and Reinhardt, *Navigating*.

21 Barlow, "Semifeudalism, Semicolonialism."

22 Hausman, Hertner, and Wilkins, *Global Electrification*, 37; my emphasis.

23 Karl, *China's Revolutions in the Modern World*, 90.

24 Cochran, *Chinese Medicine Men*.

25 Zhang Weibao, Luo, and Zhao, "Yousheng zhuanshuai."

26 Robert Gardella, Jane K. Leonard, and Andrea McElderry, eds., "Chinese Business History: Interpretive Trends and Priorities for the Future, special issue of *Chinese Studies in History* 31, nos. 3–4 (1998).

27 Cochran, *Big Business in China*.

28 See Zhang and Zhao, "Nanyang xiongdi de guanli zhibai." Also see Zhang, Luo, and Zhao, "Yousheng zhuanshuai." In recent years, China-based historians are writing business history, but the heritage of the cultural argument remains strong, and what "Chinese" indicates in the context of a multinational LLC has not been clarified.

29 *Tobacco: An Illustrated Weekly* noted in its April 15, 1920, issue that a shipment of $1.5 million worth of U.S. tobacco had left San Francisco for Hong Kong and Shanghai, to be rolled into Chinese Nanyang Bros. cigarettes. See "From the Firing Line."

30 Köll, "Nanyang Brothers Tobacco."

31 Kwan, *Beyond Market and Hierarchy*. On the basis of early manuscripts that Kwan shared with me, I have been able to demonstrate a fallacy in thinking that national products expressed national capital and sold in national markets to strengthen the nation in my earlier publications. I thank him again for his early generosity and congratulate him on the publication of his work in monograph form.

32 Metzler, *Lever of Empire*.

33 Zelin, "Informal Law and the Firm in Early Modern China"; Kirby, "China Unincorporated."

34 Zelin, "Informal Law and the Firm in Early Modern China," 167.

35 Morgan, "Transfer of Taylorist ideas to China." Thanks to Professor Morgan for alerting me to this important essay. Morgan notes a blip of interest in corporate forms and business practices among some Chinese readers and perhaps entrepreneurs when he notes that *Eastern Miscellany* ran many discussions about scientific management, industrial psychology and rationalization of production.

36 See Cochran, *Chinese Medicine Men*, and other work. Cochran understands business practices in the framework of culturalism, as does Gary Hamilton. See Hamilton, *Commerce and Capitalism*. Thanks to Rebecca Karl for flagging the point about Mao strategy.

37 Zuo, *Zhongguo jindai shangbiao jianshi*, 1–63. Also see Bowker, *Copyright*.

38 Lury, *Brands*, 98.

39 "Trade house Optorg—diversifying from its ancient activities in Russia—moved to Hong Kong and Shanghai in 1923 and started there [*sic*] import trade of goods (mainly wool cloth, but also spirits and champagne, pharmaceutics) which it delivered against promissory notes, and BIC Hong Kong became its leverage in Asia; it collected its remittances on Hong Kong, fueled exchange contracts (FRF 982,000 in 1931), and carried a large portfolio of bills drawn on Chinese clients ($82,000 on I. P. Hang Fong in 1931) for goods stored at the name of the bank pending sales." Bonin, "French Banks in Hong Kong," 14.

40 *Trademark Gazette*, December 15, 1928, 269, 270, 275, and 77.

41 Marchand, *Advertising the American Dream*. Also see Modern Girl around the World Research Research Group, *Modern Girl around the World*.

42 According to Ellen Laing's "The British American Tobacco Company Advertising Department and Four of Its Calendar Poster Artists," BAT's advertising department, founded in 1915, employed Shanghai school commercial artists. See also Zhongguo Kexueyuan, *Nanyang xiongdi yancao gongsi shiliao*.

43 Qu Zhengming, "Hong xibao yu yongtai he yancao gongsi."

44 Barlow, "Advertising Ephemera and the Angel of History."

45 Cox, *Global Cigarette*, 161.

46 Cox, *Global Cigarette*, 30.

47 For full details on the New York brand's advertising rhetoric and images, see
    Barlow, "Advertising Ephemera and the Angel of History."

48 Witzel, *History of Management Thought*, 125–26.

49 Hilferding, *Finance Capital*.

50 Hilferding, *Finance Capital*, 22.

51 "The transition from commercial to investment credit is also apparent in inter-
    national markets. In the early stages of development, England (and Dutch policy
    was similar in the early period of capitalism) *extended commercial credit to countries
    which bought English products, while paying for a larger proportion of her own
    imports in cash. The situation is different today: credit is not provided exclusively
    or mainly in the form of commercial credit, but for capital investment, the object of
    which is to gain control of foreign production.*" Hilferding, "The Banks and Industrial
    Credit," ch. 5 in *Finance Capital*; my emphasis.

52 Wagel, *Finance in China*, 260.

53 Wagel, *Finance in China*, 261–62.

54 Wagel, *Finance in China*, 300.

55 Edkins, *Banking and Prices in China*, 19, 26.

56 Ji Zhaojin, *History of Modern Shanghai Banking*.

57 Crow, preface, cited in Liang and Lin, "Historical Value."

58 Hilferding, preface to *Finance Capital*.

59 Lingzhen Wang, *Women's Autobiographical Practice*.

60 Modern Girl around the World Research Group, *Modern Girl around the World*.

61 Benjamin, *Arcades Project*, 463.

62 Benjamin, *Arcades Project*, 465.

63 Benjamin, "Announcement of the Journal *Angelus Novus*," 293.

64 L. Liu, Karl, and Ko, *Birth of Chinese Feminism*.

65 L. Liu, Karl, and Ko, *Birth of Chinese Feminism*, 152.

66 L. Liu, Karl, and Ko, *Birth of Chinese Feminism*, 152

67 Meillassoux, "Decision and Undecidability of the Event," 25.

68 I am drawing on the tradition in Jacques Derrida's thinking that considers origi-
    nality and authority: "There is finally a signature, which is not the signature one
    calculated, which is naturally not the patronymic name, *which is not the set of strat-
    agems elaborated in order to propose something original or inimitable. But, whether one
    like it or not, there is an 'effect of the idiom for the other.'*" Derrida, "Jacques Derrida,
    There Is No 'One' Narcissism (Autobiophotographies)"; my emphasis.

69 L. Liu, Karl, and Ko, *Birth of Chinese Feminism*, 57.

70 L. Liu, Karl, and Ko, *Birth of Chinese Feminism*, 63.

71 L. Liu, Karl, and Ko, *Birth of Chinese Feminism*, 102.

72 L. Liu, Karl, and Ko, *Birth of Chinese Feminism*, 118.

73 Extending Hobbesian and Rousseauian arguments, He-Yin doubtless read the
    Japanese translation about the state of nature (brute force) and the rise of private-
    property regimes. He-Yin's essay "Economic Revolution and Women's Revolution"

argues that after the rise of the slave mode of production, China became a special kind of hell. Livelihood issues led to the prostitution-marriage system, concubinage, female suicide, illicit affairs, and marriage markets where rape, philandering, bitterness, wallowing in sorrow, starvation, and hopelessness became the norm for women of all classes. Lewdness and obscenity result from the fact that *"when a man sees a woman what appears before him is merely a commodity that money can buy."* L. Liu, Karl, and Ko, *Birth of Chinese Feminism*, 96; my emphasis.

74 L. Liu, Karl, and Ko, *Birth of Chinese Feminism*, 103; my emphasis.

75 L. Liu, Karl, and Ko, *Birth of Chinese Feminism*, 106; my emphasis.

76 L. Liu, Karl, and Ko, *Birth of Chinese Feminism*, 107.

77 The polemical, painfully conflicting logics and desires—revenge or love, murder or erotic engagement, love or kill—rested on Wang Zhong's (1745–1794) earlier critique of the chastity cult and He-Yin's understanding of Edward Jenks (1861–1939), Herbert Spencer (1820–1903), Japanese anarchists, and Chinese scholar-theorists Cheng Yichou (1725–1814), Fang Bao (1668–1749), and Gui Youguang (1507–1571). This shows her scholarly capacity and the depth of her citational practices.

78 "A Dual Mishap—Tram Collides with Motor Car," *Shanghai Times*, May 27, 1920. Thanks to Victor K. Seow for sending me this news clipping.

Chapter 2: Foundational Chinese Sociology

1 Howard Chiang's *After Eunuchs: Science, Medicine, and the Transformation of Sex in Modern China* shows that Chinese thinkers absorbed the intellectual impact of the anatomical revolution that began in 1851 with Benjamin Hobson's publication of clinical drawings taken from autopsy dissections of male and female reproductive organs. Gradually, the life science of physiology moved toward the center of the discussion. See Andrews, *Making of Modern Chinese Medicine*, for the political evolution of "Western medicine" and its body.

2 Lorraine Wong explores Qu's similarity to international Marxism and Marxists. See Wong, "Language Matters in Global Communism."

3 Foucault, *Order of Things*.

4 Yang Yabin in *Zhongguo shehuixue shi* aims to "trace the historical trajectory of the Chinese sociology" (2). See also Yan Ming, *Yimen xueke, yige shidai*; Y.-C. Chiang, *Social Engineering and the Social Sciences in China*.

5 Yao, *Shehuixue zai jindai Zhongguo de jincheng*.

6 "When," Sang wrote, "the research is conducted on the transformation of knowledge systems, the ideal situation would be simultaneously providing keys on understanding the tradition, the knowledge-generating process, as well as understanding the present and grasping the future." Sang, "Wanqing minguo de zhishi yu zhidu tixi zhuanxing," 20.

7 Kantianism's importance in Chinese letters has not been adequately addressed although its aesthetics was widely known in this era. Hannah Ginsborg suggests

European and anglophone scholarship ignores Immanuel Kant's aesthetics, perhaps because Kant tied aesthetics to naturalistic teleologies. Ginsborg, "Kant's Aesthetics and Teleology."

8 A *sympode* or *sympodium* is "an axis that develops when growth occurs by means of lateral branches rather than continuing along the principal stem, often having a zigzag or irregular form." Also called *pseudaxis*. See *The Free Dictionary*, s.v. "sympodium," accessed August 18, 2017, http://www.thefreedictionary.com /Sympodium.

9 Doleželová-Velingerová and Wagner, *Chinese Encyclopaedias of New Global Knowledge*, 1–28.

10 Foucault, *Order of Things*.

11 Doleželová-Velingerová and Wagner, *Chinese Encyclopaedias of New Global Knowledge*, 8.

12 This section is indebted to Doleželová-Velingerová and Wagner, *Chinese Encyclopaedias of New Global Knowledge*.

13 Mill, Montesquieu, Comte, and Huxley are foundational figures in the establishment of philosophical sociology. That fact makes Yan an undersung hero of Chinese sociology, for he chose and translated all of them. Yan's grasp of sociology and philosophy was unparalleled among Chinese thinkers in his time. Unlike most social philosophers, he resembled He-Yin Zhen, who used Japanese neologisms in her theorizations because she lived in Japan and read Japanese general theory and Japanese anarchism.

14 Howland, *Personal Liberty and Public Good*, 70.

15 Thanks to Barbara Mittler and Kaja Müller-Wang, who allowed me access to their online version of the *New Erya* while I was in China. HEIDENC, Institute of Chinese Studies, Heidelberg, http://www.zo.uniheidelberg.de/sinologie/digital _resources/heidenc/.

16 Wang Rongbao and Ye, *Xin Erya*; my emphasis.

17 Tang, *Global Space and the Nationalist Discourse of Modernity*.

18 Yan Fu, *Tianyanlun*.

19 Ishikawa Yoshihiro, "Chinese Translations from Japanese of Works on Socialism, 1919–1922," in *History of the Formation of the Chinese Communist Party*, 443–58. The English translation of Ishikawa's article that was published in *Sino-Japanese Studies* (2009) states that Yamakawa Kikue was the translator of Ward's famous essay and that both Li Da and Xia Mianzun translated it from Japanese into Chinese. It is curious that the Chinese translated only Ward's essay and not Edward Carpenter's *The Intermediate Sex*, which Yamakawa also translated and released with the Ward essay. Nick Knight notes that Li used the Sakai Toshihiko translation released in 1921. Knight, *Li Da and Marxist Philosophy in China*, 308.

20 Gong and Liu, "Li Da yu Qu Qiubai de funü guan bijiao."

21 Engels's book arrived in Russian in 1894 and in Japanese in 1922. See Hoston, *Marxism and the Crisis of Development in Prewar Japan*, 44–46. Also see Suzuki, *Becoming Modern Women*, 136.

22 Kang, *Kang Youwei xiansheng yizhu huikan, riben shumuzhi*. Kang Youwei was not a sociologist but knew that Chinese students accessed European philosophy through the Meiji social sciences. Kang started his bibliography with the category of physiology and in doing so recognized the philosophical significance of the anatomical body. Further research might show that Kang had read Ward, though it is not likely. Still, Kang echoes the Wardian argument that physiology is the key to understanding human sexual reproduction and social evolution and outstrips anatomy because physiology is a temporal process linked to the problem of human awareness, our semi-instinctual keenness to make good eugenic choices, and the ability to share or to oppress.

23 Marwa Elshakry, *Reading Darwin in Arabic, 1860–1950* shows how particularly Egypt-based scholars worked the same set of texts as Chinese intellectuals. She finds a different range of interests and different conclusions than I have and this is no doubt because underlying conditions of thought were different.

24 Zhong Shaohua, "Studies on the Characteristics of Late Qing Encyclopaedia Entries."

25 This section is adapted from Barlow, "'History's Coffin Can Never Be Closed.'" The online dictionary *Hudong baike* (Interactive encyclopedia) provides the history of the organization "Society for Social Improvement in Beijing" (see http://www.baike.com/wiki/社会实进会, accessed December 21, 2020), which began in 1913 under the auspices of the YMCA and included social-service and social-survey activities like those described in Yan Ming's book *Yimen xueke, yige shidai*.

26 Yu, *Qu qiubai xueshu sixiang pingzhuan*, 112–13. Qu began Russian-language studies in the old-school way, by translating literature. He chose Leo Tolstoy, Alexander Pushkin, Nicolai Gogol, Maxim Gorky, and Ivan Turgenev before turning his attention to August Bebel, Georgi Plekhanov, and the Russian New Philosophers.

27 Knight, *Marxist Philosophy in China*, 18, 20. See 10n18 for evaluation of Nicolai Bukharin's probable influence and pages 13–28 for the introduction to international Marxism that Qu appears to have read. Knight's thesis on "determinism" is the basis of this section.

28 Knight, *Marxist Philosophy in China*, 33.

29 Knight, *Marxist Philosophy in China*, 32; and Knight, *Marxist Philosophy and Social Theory*, ch. 2.

30 Qu Qiubai, *Qu Qiubai wenji*, 1015–40.

31 Chinese-to-English translation creates phrases that do not appear in English. Read "raped logic" metaphorically and it makes perfect sense.

32 Qu Qiubai, *Qu Qiubai wenji*, 1020.

33 See Feng, "Qu Qiubai zaoqi fanyi huodong shuping." Feng argues that Qu, in his essays, not only has deep sympathy and concern for women in the man-eating Old Society but also investigates the root cause of the oppression of women, arguing that women are spiritually in jail and bound by many shackles, such as feudal ethics, Confucian codes, the family system, social organization, and the notion that the sexes are oppositional.

34 Chen Tiejian, *Qu Qiubai zhuan.*

35 Bebel, *Women and Socialism,* 97–98.

36 This would appear, contextually, to have been August Wilhelm Schlegel (1767–1845), who translated Shakespeare into German and advocated the intellectualization of romantic love.

37 Bebel, *Women and Socialism,* 240.

38 Bebel, *Women and Socialism,* 471.

39 Knight's monograph *Li Da and Marxist Philosophy in China* establishes that Chinese Marxism is a form of Soviet Marxism and not an orientalist deviation. Knight traces arguments in the German, Russian, and Chinese traditions to underscore Mao's internationalism and carefully notes Li's lifelong commitment to sexual difference and social justice but chooses not to pursue this line of analysis. Knight, *Li Da and Marxist Philosophy in China,* 63–64. I focus on Li's 1926 *Modern Sociology* and not his 1937 magnum opus, *Li Da shehuixue dagang.*

40 Ward split from the socialist camp, saying explicitly that he was doing "pure sociology." Ward, *Pure Sociology,* vii. *Pure* meant scientific and not political. He disavowed all social usefulness for his work. The implication is that a scientist (he was originally a botanist) is not swayed by social movements or mores, and the value of pure sociology is its scienticity.

41 Knight, *Marxist Philosophy and Social Theory,* ch. 2.

42 Knight, *Marxist Philosophy and Social Theory,* 155.

43 Li Da, *Shehuixue dagang.* Because his overarching concern is to demonstrate that Chinese Marxism was "orthodox," Knight's conclusions override points that would show the singularity of Li Da. This is particularly true of the women's question, which Knight carefully footnotes but does not pursue exegetically.

44 Li Da, *Xiandai shehuixue,* 16.

45 Li Da, *Xiandai shehuixue,* 32.

46 Li Da, *Xiandai shehuixue,* 21.

47 The status of the debate over the matriarchal stage of Chinese history remains to be analyzed. To my knowledge, no contemporary scholar is working on this problem.

48 See Y.-C. Chiang, *Social Engineering and the Social Sciences in China.*

Chapter 3: Vernacular Sociology

1 On Schaff's contribution to the debate over the role of the future anterior in Marxist philosophy, see Petrilli and Ponzio, "Adam Schaff." The essay analyzes a famous debate over Marxist humanism between Schaff and Althusser, a structuralist Marxist. Schaff took the position that all philosophy is written in the future anterior. The statement "By next year I will have completed this book" is not philosophical but encodes anticipation that hard work today will prove successful. The statement "In five years the Chinese working class in itself and for itself will have seized control over the means of production" is both a philosophical aspiration

and a practical statement. However unlikely to occur, this revolutionary prediction is an expectation many people have lived and died attempting to achieve.

2 Bray, *Technology and Gender.* See also Sommer, *Sex, Law, and Society in Late Imperial China.*

3 Barlow, *Question of Women in Chinese Feminism,* ch. 3.

4 Zarrow, *Educating China.*

5 Yan Fu, *Tianyanlun.*

6 T. Shen, "Evolutionism through Chinese Eyes"; Wang Xiaodan, *Fanyi shihua.*

7 Shiao, "Culture, Commerce, and Connections."

8 T. Shen, "Evolutionism through Chinese Eyes," 23.

9 Fan, "Shehui kexue he benneng de wenti," 2–3.

10 Fan, "Shehui kexue he benneng de wenti," 2–3.

11 Wang Xiaodan, *Fanyi shihuo,* 88–98.

12 "In view of his work as a standardizer it is strange to discover how eclectic and perhaps even disorganized Yan Fu [was]. Yan Fu's neologisms had little influence on the terminology which followed, in contrast to the ideas in his translations, which were enormously influential." Wright, "Yan Fu and the Tasks of the Translator," 242, 245.

13 Reynolds, *East Meets East.*

14 Wang Xiaodan, *Fanyi shihuo,* esp. ch. 2, p. 37.

15 Wang, *Fanyi shihuo,* 49.

16 The translation by Mai Zhonghua was published in 1902 and 1903. The translation by Min Housa was published in 1903 and 1915.

17 See Li, "Guoqing," for his views on Ariga.

18 Howland, *Translating the West,* 51–54.

19 Howland, *Translating the West,* 52, 207n49. The article Howland cites is Ariga's "Shina no kaimei to seiyo no kaimei to no sabestsu," 357–64, 368–75.

20 In 1877 a Japanese translation of Herbert Spencer stabilized the term for "society" as *shakai.* Ariga's 1883 publication of *On Social Evolution* and his part in renaming Tokyo Imperial University's department of sociology as Shakaigaku confirmed that *shakai* would henceforth be what Howland calls "the preferred term for the new abstraction 'society.'" Howland, *Translating the West,* 173.

21 Figal, *Civilization and Monsters,* 52–73. The creativity of Japanese social theorists detracts nothing from Yan's achievement. The gifted natural and social scientist Minakata Kumagusu (1867–1941) found in the relation of social and natural science a source of creative sociological speculation. Minakata, *Minakata Kumagusu nikki.*

22 Ariga, *Shehui jinhua lun,* 1. All cites of Ariga's *Shehui jinhua lun* are from the 1902 edition.

23 Ariga, *Shehui jinhua lun,* 20, 84. Ariga argues that society is organistic and thus just like a living organism *in some respects,* per Herbert Spencer. However, since societies are not literally alive, sociology, although analogous to physiology, differs from it since it plays a regulatory role in national social evolutionary progress. Ariga's

historical sociology (and canonical sociology, generally speaking) proposed that property relations and regulations caused the evolution of human society from rampant primitive social life to the nation.

24 Ariga, *Shehui jinhua lun*, 53–55.

25 Ariga, *Shehui jinhua lun*, 9.

26 Endo, *Jinshi shehuixue*.

27 Endo, *Jinshi shehuixue*, 212.

28 Endo, *Jinshi shehuixue*, 245.

29 Takezawa, "Transcending the Western Paradigm of the Idea of Race," 14–18. Shibue was likely influenced by Karl Gützlaff's *Wanguo dili quantuji*, particularly the "Borneo" part, cited in *Shakaigaku* (Sociology). On Shibue's debt to John Ruskin and William Morris, see Kikuchi, *Japanese Modernisation and Mingei Theory*, 25. Shibue wrote on Poland and political partition, as well as on Otto von Bismarck, which suggests he was either a professional academic translator or a new-style social or political scientist. See Shibue, *Pōrando Suibō Senshi*.

30 Shibue Tomotsu, translated by Jin Minglua, *Shehuixue zhilun* 4, 1903.

31 Ishikawa, "Anti-Manchu Racism and the Rise of Anthropology in Early 20th Century China"; and Simpson, "Sir Daniel Wilson and the Prehistoric Annals of Scotland."

32 See Yan Enchun, *Jiating jinghualun*. A glossary of pop sociological publications is available as an index at the back of Yan's book.

33 Guo, "Benneng."

34 Leon Rocha notes that German intellectual history has multiple terms for instinct. Email to author, November 19, 2009.

35 Guo, "Benneng." Amanda Spink summarizes the history of instinct theory. Spink, *Information Behavior*, 3–5.

36 Gray, "Spalding, His Influence on Research in Developmental Behavior."

37 See Uhls, "Lu Xun–Huxley–Nietzsche"; and Deleuze, *Bergsonism*.

38 Everyone from Georgi Plekhanov to Charles Pierce, Bertrand Russell, Ludwig Wittgenstein, and Henry James—many known to Chinese intellectuals—criticized Bergson.

39 Yan Yucheng, "Fei benneng lun zhi piping."

40 Barlow, *Question of Women in Chinese Feminism*.

41 Yan Jibo, "Faming shi renlei de benneng.

42 L.-K. Sun, *Chinese National Character*, 3.

43 Zhou, "Lian'ai de yiyi yü jiazhi."

44 Yan Wei, "Nüzi tiyü yanjiu."

45 On the social problem of suicide, see Goodman, "New Woman Commits Suicide."

46 Letourneau, "Lihun de jinhua."

47 Lionel Tiger is the Charles Darwin Professor of Anthropology at Rutgers University. Now in his eighties, he has for sixty years been *the* pioneer in neovernacular sociology or social Darwinist popular anglophone ideologies.

48 Gao Junzhe, "Shehuixue de shengwu xuepai."

49 See Dikötter, *Discourse of Race in Modern China*; Dikötter, *Imperfect Conceptions*; and also Stern, "Unraveling the History of Eugenics in Mexico."

50 Chung, "Eugenics in China and Hong Kong." In *The Question of Women in Chinese Feminism*, I argue that scientific racism is a core element of progressive feminism.

51 Sakamoto, "Cult of 'Love and Eugenics' in May Fourth Movement Discourse."

52 Yan Wei, "Nüzi tiyu yanjiu."

53 Pan, "Shengyu xianzhi yu youshengxue."

54 Pan, "Yousheng yu wenhua"; and Sun Benwen, "Zai lun wenhua yu youshengxue."

55 Although not sociologists, the reformer Kang Youwei and his philosopher disciple Tan Sitong (1865–1898) argued that improving sexual relations was the state's responsibility.

Chapter 4: The Social Life of Commercial Ephemera

1 Xu Xiuli, "Saochu wenmang, zuoyu xinmin." Also see Zhonghua pingmin jiaoyu cujinhui, *Shimin qianzi ke*.

2 J. Ernest Black, August 1930, Trinity College Digital Collections, https:// digitalrepository.trincoll.edu/.

3 Lefebvre, *Critique of Everyday Life*, 76, 134, 159.

4 Benjamin, *Arcades Project*, N1a, 6.

5 Lefebvre, *Critique of Everyday Life*, 76, 134, 159.

6 This is my reservation with Anne McClintock's pioneering *Imperial Leather*.

7 See Badiou, "Subject of Art"; and Benjamin, *Arcades Project*, 460–63. I loosen and even invert Badiou's theses on political voluntarism. Also see Black, "Advertising in Shanghai," app. II, which lists the sizes, cost, and estimated distribution of newspapers in Shanghai along with the mechanical requirements for setting ads. Black judged the ad industry too chaotic and corrupt, needing Americanization.

8 Crystal, *Cambridge Encyclopedia of the English Language*; *Webster's Third New International Dictionary of the English Language, Unabridged* (Springfield, MA: Merriam, 1961), s.v. "International Scientific Vocabulary"; and "International Scientific Vocabulary," Merriam-Webster's online, https://www.merriam-webster.com/, accessed December 23, 2020. For a brief history of how ISV works, see https://en .wikipedia.org/wiki/International_scientific_vocabulary. Many scholars disparaged ISV, but it is just another system of calques. See Morton, *Story of Webster's Third*.

9 See Romaine, *Cambridge History of the English Language*; and Durkin, *Borrowed Words*, which both establish the history of modern English and International Scientific Vocabulary to bridge gaps in scientific references during the international scientific revolution, as well as Neo-Latin, which surfaced in English in the 1840s and 1850s.

10 Pound, *The Confucian Odes*. Professor C. J. Chen Jing has collaborated with me on the Luce Foundation–funded Ephemera Project at the Chao Center for Asian

Studies. Her pioneering work interprets technical means for interpreting ephemera and she has thoughtfully created this rendition. https://ccaa.nju.edu.cn/html/index.html, accessed February 22, 2021.

11 Mrazek, *Engineers of Happy Land*; and Alloula, *Colonial Harem*.

12 Muñoz, "Ephemera as Evidence," 10. Muñoz proposes that "ephemera is always about specificity and resisting dominant systems of aesthetic and institutional classification . . . without abstracting them outside of social experience and a larger notion of sociality [since ephemera] is firmly anchored *within* the social." Here I argue that ephemera *establish* the social.

13 Ding Song, *Minguo fengqin baimei tu*; and Ding Song, *Ding Song manhuaji*.

14 Joan Judge gets close to this argument in her *Republican Lens: Gender, Visuality, and Experience in the Early Chinese Periodical Press*. Catherine Yeh noted the association of modern-women images and advanced technology. Catherine Vance Yeh, *Shanghai Love*.

15 Su Shangda, *Guanggaoxue gailun*, also cited in Morgan, "Selling Chinese Dreams." I appreciate Morgan's generosity (private letter, July 22, 2014). See ch. 1 of Su's study for the history of Vee Loo and BAT. Also see *Shanghai difangzhi bangongshi*, ch. 12, "Di shier pian: Guanggao shangye" [Advertising business]. This source notes the 1915 founding of Parme's Italian agency, but there is no business history yet for this agency.

16 Zhu Shuai, "Guanggaoshi yanjiu zai zhongguo."

17 Ling, *China's Progress in Advertising*. Thanks to Ms. Yunzhu Bamboo Zhu, who located materials at the Shanghai Municipal Archive (email, March 13, 2016). Nakayama was first to use the advertising balloon in Tokyo, 1913. See Clark Parker, "The Tokyo Files," October 13, 2015, for a photograph of the event. https://thetokyofiles.com/2015/10/13/balloons-on-the-ginza-float-young-advertisers-1890-1989/.

18 See Barlow and Chen, "Jintan Distribution Networks in Five Treaty Port Commercial Newspapers." Also, Ling's *China's Progress in Advertising* includes a map of Ling's empire. See Crow, *Four Hundred Million Customers*, for the branding of Sun-Maid made in California.

19 Zhu Shuai, a Beijing University historian, has recently made an argument similar to mine. In "Guanggaoshi yanjiu zai zhongguo: Jiyu shixueshi shijiao de yizhong fansi," he mentions that as the first systematic research work on advertising in China, Jiang Yuquan's *Shiyong guanggaoxue*, has nine chapters that include topics such as definition of ads, history of ads, tendencies in modern advertising, and so on. Available materials on C. P. Ling are held in the Shanghai Archive, "China Commercial Advertising Agency" (C. P. Ling, Proprietor, Report on Audit of Accounts for the Period From July 1, 1926, To December 31, 1931). Haskins & Sells" and "China Commercial Advertising Agency, Ltd. Advertising Merchandising Council, Shanghai, China, September 12, 1928" both include material about how the agency worked and how it made profits.

20 Crow, *Four Hundred Million Customers*, 32.

21 Shi Quan, "Guanggao xinlixue gailun."

22 Crow, *Four Hundred Million Customers*, 237–39.

23 Tao Xisheng, "Xijiu shangpin yü xinjiu funü."

24 Scott, *Theory of Advertising*; and Scott, *Psychology of Advertising*. He intended
   to become a missionary educator in China but ended up in Germany, where
   he studied applied psychology with Wilhelm Wundt, who also appealed to
   Japanese intellectuals and came into Chinese via Japanese translation. See
   finding aid, Walter Dill Scott (1969–1955) Papers, 1891–1977, Northwestern University Archives, Evanston, Illinois, accessed March 22, 2021, https://files.library
   .northwestern.edu/findingaids/walter_d_scott.pdf; and Brisco, *Economics of
   Efficiency*.

25 Huang Kewu, "Cong shenbao yiyao guanggao kan minchu Shanghai de yiliao
   wenhua yü shehui shenghuo."

26 Barlow, "Buying In." Placing teeth into a female figure's mouth broke convention.
   Elite and popular female images closed the mouth and did not expose teeth.

27 Allen, *War on Bugs*.

28 *Shenbao*, March 7, 1920; my emphasis.

29 Professor Nanxiu Qian identified this figure for me. Grateful thanks.

30 Sakamoto, "Manga Hyōjyō ni miru syanhai modangāru."

31 Isaka, *Onnagata*; Isaka, "Gender of *Onnagata* as the Imitating Imitated."

32 Isaka, "Gender of Onnagata"; Isaka, *Onnagata*.

33 Barlow, "Advertising Ephemera and the Angel of History."

34 In the 1912 image, a Manchurian-garbed woman holds a bottle of washing powder
   printed with a lovely brand mark called the *sobijin*. The next image, also from 1912,
   shows an equally advanced begowned girl with a hair band, holding an advertising
   fan and staring at the product jars.

35 Yeh, *Shanghai Love*. Also see Yeh, "Shanghai Leisure, Print Entertainment, and the
   Tabloids, *Xiaobao*"; Yeh, "Press and the Rise of Peking Opera Singer as National
   Star"; and McCloud, *Understanding Comics*.

36 McCloud, *Understanding Comics*.

37 Morishita Jintan, *Morishita Jintan 80-nenshi*, 32; and Morishita Jintan, *Sōgō hoken
   yaku Jintan kara sōgō hoken sangyō Jintan e*, 28. Ms. Miho Matsumura, Institute
   for Global Studies at Hitotsubashi University, undertook the research into Jintan
   Corporation's marketing policies with assistance from Patrick O'Dwyer.

38 Morishita Jintan, *Morishita Jintan 80-nenshi*, 56–60. Morishita's Jintan Corporation pioneered newsprint advertising. Morishita created long-running, pleasing
   print media advertising campaigns, to which he added music, billboards, balloons,
   cars, neon signs, and giveaway campaigns.

39 Morishita Jintan, *Sōgō hoken yaku Jintan kara sōgō hoken sangyō Jintan e*, 52.

40 According to Professor Chen Zu'en, Nakayama could not compete with American
   brands in Shanghai because of anti-Japanese patriotic sentiment there. Even so,
   the ccc outstripped European, American, and Chinese cosmetic creams and soap
   companies. See Chen Zu'en, *Shanghai ri qiao shehui shengshuo shi*.

41 Dentsu (in full, the Japan Advertising Limited and Telegraphic Service Company) reconsolidated in 1906 and consolidated once again in 1907, as the company came increasingly to specialize in newsprint advertising. Between 1912 and 1926, "Chinese newspapers were refusing to run advertisements for Japanese products. However, the Shanghai branch of Dentsu, vanguard of Japanese capitalism, was applying pressure to various Chinese newspapers, and from January 1923 . . . these [papers] started carrying Japanese advertising represented by Dentsu." Nakase, "Development of the Advertising Industry."

42 Benjamin, *Arcades Project*, 14, 460–88.

43 Zhao Chen, *Zhongguo jindai guanggao wenhua*, 65–68.

44 Jintan ad, *Dagongbao*, 49.

45 Much has been written on the theme of "degenerance." The funniest is Long, *Zhongguo Jindai Sheying Yishu Meixue Wenxuan*, ch. 3, section "Degenerance in Political Polemics."

46 Moeran, "Newspapers, Advertising and the Japanese Economy." This invaluable document records the chronological political economy of advertising agencies in Osaka and Tokyo from 1880. Yamamoto, *Kōkoku no shakai shi*, 190–94; and Yamamoto and Nishizawa, *Nihon no kōkoku*, 43–47.

47 Nakagawa conducted seminars on advertising theory at Kobe University, later joining the advertising agency Mannensha. He authored collections, books, and other documents, including *Kōkoku to senden* and *Kōkokuron*, and he launched *Kōkoku ronsō* (Essays on advertising), the nation's first advertising research journal. See Yamamoto and Nishizawa, *Nihon no kōkoku*, 314–15.

48 Yamamoto and Nishizawa, *Nihon no kōkoku*, 308. Satō Uhei's press, Satō Shuppanbu, as well as Jitsumu Sōshō Hakkōshō press published many volumes on advertising.

49 Scott, *Psychology of Advertising*, cited by Hiraoka, *Jiyūjizai kōkoku-ho*; Hollingworth, *Kōkoku to hanbai*; and Poffenberger, *Kōkoku shinrigaku*. Scott's book was republished by Sasaki Jūku in 1917 as *Kōkoku shinrigaku*, without crediting Scott. It was republished again by Sasaki Jūku in 1924 as *Sukotto kōkoku shinrigaku*. Scott's *The Psychology of Advertising in Theory and Practice*, a revised version of the 1908 edition supplemented by Scott, was translated into Japanese in 1921, and Matsumiya Saburō produced *Kōkoku shinrigaku* in 1939. See also Yamamoto and Tsuganezawa, *Nihon no kōkoku*, 312–13.

50 Quoted in Yamamoto, *Kōkoku no shakai shi*. See also Hamada, *Jitsuyō kōkoku-hō*. Historian Yamamoto Taketoshi considers this to be the inauguration of literature advocating the social scientific study of advertising among Japanese intellectuals and advertisers.

51 See Eiji, *Genealogy of "Japanese" Self-Images*; and a review of Eiji in Askew, "Melting Pot or Homogeneity?"

52 K. Suzuki, *State and Racialization*.

53 See Barlow, "Buying In," for detailed analysis of the ad's format, formulaic qualities, probable origin, and remarkable success.

54 Bergère, *Golden Age of the Chinese Bourgeoisie* (1990).

55 *Dagongbao* 95, no. 761 (April 17, 1930). On love triangles and their popularity, see Ling Shiao, "Culture, Commerce, and Connections"; and Lung-Kee Sun, *Chinese National Character*.

56 Benjamin, *Arcades Project*, n3, and 1, 462–63. "Only dialectical images are genuinely historical—that is not archaic—images. The image that is read—which is to say, the image in the now of its recognizability—bears to the highest degree the imprint of the perilous critical moment on which all reading is founded."

57 Benjamin, *Arcades Project*, n3, 2.

58 Monnais, *Colonial Life of Pharmaceuticals: Medicines and Modernity in Vietnam*.

59 The only reference to Vagitoran that I can find occurs in *Japanese-English Medical Dictionary* in a long "List of Japanese Drugs."

60 See YS, "Renshenqi zhong funü yingzhi zhi changzhi jiqi weisheng."

61 Robinson, "Nüzi zhi xing de zhishi."

62 Yi, Liu, and Gan, *Lao Shanghai guanggao*; and Song, *Lao yuefenpai*.

63 Norris, *Badiou's "Being and Event,"* 32–33. This paragraph reiterates the points that Peter Hallward makes in *Badiou: A Subject to Truth* (114–15). Badiou asserts that human voluntarism flings itself beyond given ontological conditions and then continues engaging the ambiguous and as yet unproven, until it, too, becomes the known or is left behind.

64 Tsin, "Imagining 'Society' in Early Twentieth-Century China," 213. See also Tsin, *Nation, Governance and Modernity in China: Canton, 1900–1927*.

Chapter 5: Nakedness and Interiority

1 Marx, "Estranged Labor." I gratefully acknowledge Martin J. Powers's contributions to this chapter and Powers and Katherine R. Tsiang's *Companion to Chinese Art*.

2 Print technologies and new media genres in the last half of the nineteenth century have been amply researched. See Mittler, "Between Discourse and Social Reality." The pioneers in this area are Xiaoqing Ye, Andrea Janku, Natascha Vittinghoff, Kai-Wing Chow, and particularly Christopher Reed.

3 Welland, *Experimental Beijing*.

4 Teo, "Modernism and Orientalism."

5 Kuiyi Shen has drawn a line between the commercial arts that emerged in the 1880s and the specific genealogy of formulaic drawn commercial art. See K. Shen, "*Lianhuanhua* and *Manhua*."

6 Lu Cheng, "Meishu geming," 85, cited in M. Huang, "Spectacle of Representation."

7 Tsai, "Having it All," 133.

8 Lai, *Life and Art Photography of Lang Jingshan*.

9 Lai, *Life and Art Photography of Lang Jingshan*, 168.

10 Lang wrote, "When foreigners visited China, they often went to the street corners to photograph those disgraceful scenes [opium smoking, gambling, foot binding,

etc.]. In the course of time this would create a wrong impression: people in the foreign countries would believe that these images show the real Chinese community. Our objective [as art photographers] was to publicize the beautiful views of China and hence correct those mistaken views. At that time we did not really care whether our works would be selected, we just sent our photographs whenever we heard of the news of the exhibitions." Quoted in Lai, *Life and Art Photography of Lang Jingshan*, 171.

11 Lai, *Life and Art Photography of Lang Jingshan*, 212.

12 Lai quotes Lang: "I have furthermore discovered that here, once and for all, photography has approached the technique of Chinese painting. *Have not Chinese artists been making composite pictures all the time?*" Lai, *Life and Art Photography of Lang Jingshan*, 167; my emphasis.

13 Reed, "Hybrid China." Reed hypothesizes what early photographers found significant. In "Transferring the Image: The Acceptance of Photography in China," Frances Terpak and Jeff Cody consider how and why photography was readily taken up in China.

14 Tian, *Chinese Dialectics*, 78.

15 Z. Gao, "Emergence of Modern Psychology in China."

16 Lin, *Peking University*.

17 Quoted in Lai, *Life and Art Photography of Lang Jingshan*, 216; my emphasis. From Liu Bannong, preface, reprinted in Long, *Zhongguo jindai sheying yishu meixue wenxuan*, 208–9. Lang quoted this passage in one form or another in at least four of his essays. Lang also drew on *Six Canons of Xie He* (500–535), arguing that 1,400 years earlier, Chinese painters had discovered the aesthetic structure that he rediscovered in composite darkroom technologies.

18 Lai notes that Lang's *guohua* (brush painting) work is coarse and pedestrian and was often compared to the inferior paintings of Ma Yuan, active in the late twelfth and early thirteenth centuries, and Ma Lin, active in the mid-thirteenth century. Lai, *Life and Art Photography of Lang Jingshan*, 291. Once Lai established his formula, his images became formulaic.

19 Lai, *Life and Art Photography of Lang Jingshan*, 427.

20 Cahill, "Beauty's Face in Later Chinese Painting."

21 Naked eugenics sexy girl dances with sponge board (advertisement), *Funü yuebao* 2, no. 9 (October 10, 1936).

22 Brennan, *History*, 184.

23 Badiou, *Handbook of Inaesthetics*, 2.

24 Badiou, *Handbook of Inaesthetics*, 29. Inaesthetics, this clever term for insisting that we ask art about truth, is part of Badiou's well-known four-part schema of science, politics, art, and love. As a philosopher, Badiou takes the position that "art is a thought in which artworks are the Real (and not the effect). And this thought, or rather the truths that it activates are irreducible to other truths—be they scientific, political, or amorous" (9). Art possesses the two characteristics of immanence and singularity as well. To operate its own truth procedure, art is

"rigorously coextensive with the truths that it generates" and therefore singular, in the sense that "these truths are given nowhere else than in art" (29).

25 Lair, *Advertising Progress*.

26 See Barlow, "What Is Wanting?"; and Sullivan, *Art and Artists of Twentieth-Century China*.

27 Sarris, "Notes on the Auteur Theory."

28 My example is the ad campaign for Cutex hand-care products, analyzed in Barlow, "Buying In." Also see Hodsdon, "Mystique of Mise-en-Scène Revisited."

29 Rocha, "Quentin Pan 潘光旦 in *The China Critic*."

30 Spivak, "Echo," 32; my emphasis

31 Brennan, *Interpretation of the Flesh*, 161–63. Particular thanks to Timothy Murray, who engaged me on my use of Brennan's work, informing me that Brennan had written her major work at Cornell, and to Arnika Fuhrmann, who invited me to present about this book in the first instance.

32 Both Gad C. Issy's *The Philosophy of the View of Life in Modern Chinese Thought* and Laurence Schneider's *Biology and Revolution in Twentieth-Century China* modified Daniel Kwok's 1965 classic *Scientism in Chinese Thought, 1900–1950*.

33 There are three feminist studies of this history: Ko, *Teachers of the Inner Chambers*; Widmer, "Xiaoqing's Literary Legacy and the Place of the Woman Writer in Late Imperial China"; and J. Zhang, *Psychoanalysis in China*, particularly ch. 5. I am grateful, as always, for the late Jingyuan Zhang's astute, learned, and pathbreaking work.

34 Pan, "Feng Xiaoqing kao," 24.

35 Pan, "Feng Xiaoqing kao," 25.

36 Ellen Widmer lists two more from the 1930s: Pan, "Xiaoqing kaozheng bulu"; and Pan, "Shu Feng Xiaoqing quanji hou." The 1927 version is longer because a Xiaoqing scholar, Yu Xiangyuan, had given Pan more historical evidence. See Widmer, "Xiaoqing's Literary Legacy." For a more recent discussion of women painters who referenced Xiaoqing to express themselves, also see Wang Yuanfei, "Emaciated Soul."

37 Adapted from Elam, *Feminism and Deconstruction*. Diane Elam argues that woman was itself a "ms en abyme." In feminist representation, that would mean that "women" is always going to be an unstable signifier for an indefinable linguistic attempt to be "woman." While I learned a lot from Elam, I suggest that in commodity-woman commercial ephemera, the relation being struck is not textual but graphic and, the mirroring of two unlike qualities—commodity and female—is an infinite regress in which they define one another. Every ad of a commodity woman appreciating herself in a mirror sets up this mise en abyme.

38 J. Zhang, *Psychoanalysis in China*, 135.

39 Brennan, *Interpretation of the Flesh*, 167–68; my emphasis.

40 J. Zhang, *Psychoanalysis in China*, 135.

41 See Laing, *Selling Happiness*.

42 See Ye Weili, *Seeking Modernity in China's Name*, for a helpful capsule biography of Pan, who was also educated at Columbia University and like C. P. Ling was a Boxer Indemnity scholar.

43 See Tani Barlow, "Commercial Advertising Art in 1840s–1940s China," 457, 469.

44 Joan Judge has reproduced a number of these images in her *Republican Lens: Gender, Visuality, and Experience in the Early Chinese Periodical Press.*

45 Thanks to Judith Zeitlin for providing the image and to Christine Tan for calling my attention to it in the first case.

46 For a summary analysis of women in Chinese painting, see Cahill, "Beauty's Face in Later Chinese Painting."

47 T. Lu, *Persons, Roles, and Minds*, ch. 1.

48 Text translation is from Haun Saussey, who believes the reference is to a popular Cantonese opera score. Others are currently studying the text and have other interpretations. I am grateful for Saussey's translation, which is better than mine. Permission to cite granted by Haun Saussey, letter to author, April 8, 2010.

49 Athanasius Kircher's *China Monumentis* (1667) includes an image of a young female literatus but she too looks away from the artist and the viewer.

50 Badiou, *Being and Event*, 24:

"Let's fix the terminology: I term *situation* [as] any presented multiplicity. Granted the effectiveness of the presentation, a situation is the place of taking-place, whatever the terms of the multiplicity in question. Every situation admits its own particular operator of the count-as-one. This is the most general definition of a structure; it is what prescribes, for a presented multiple, the regime of its count-as-one.

When anything is counted as one in a situation, all this means is that it belongs to the situation in the mode particular to the effects of the situation's structure.

In Badiou's approach to the event, set theory is integral. Because he is arguing that ontology is mathematical, his concepts—the logic of the situation, the eventual site, the name, the retrospectively denominated event as such—are all figured in relation to superfluity or void. Simply put, a rupture of conventional drawings of female mimesis (women who draw themselves), that is, the inclusion of a commodity, changes everything. The commodity's presentation may have occurred in the seductive violence of corporate imperialism, but here we see an art beholden to a new situation in which an artist refers to canonical female mimesis *but rethinks it as a new situation.*

51 Sophisticated rhetoric and a robust game culture of erotic play among courtesans and clients are well documented from the seventeenth century on. See Lowry, "Duplicating the Strength of Feeling."

52 The obvious example for such an argument would be the classic sexual morality tale by Lanling Xiaoxiao Sheng, *Jinpingmei.*

53 Pan incorrectly cites U.S. psychoanalyst Trigant Burrow's 1917 essay, "The Genesis and Meaning of 'Homosexuality' and Its Relation to the Problem of Introverted Mental States."

54 Xu Junjie, *Zhongguo guanggao shi*, 122, 140; Barlow, "'What Is a Poem?'"

55 Formulated in Helmling, "Constellation and Critique."

56 In Asian studies this concept is familiar from the work of Naoki Sakai's "co-configuration," a transference relation in which one's "own" relation is thinkable only because language always includes the desire to see one's self as a foreigner would see one, object-like. Sakai, *Translation and Subjectivity*, 59–60.

57 Tan, *Exposition of Benevolence*, 85.

58 Spivak, "Echo," 20; my emphasis.

59 Bensaïd, "Alain Badiou and the Miracle of the Event," 95–96.

60 Mann, "'Fuxue.'" Scholars publishing regularly in the Leiden-based specialist journal *Nan Nü*, founded in 1997, and in monographs in many languages have revealed cloistered, wealthy, and literate women's lives and have interpreted writing by male literati about their relationships with female kin.

61 Bray, *Technology and Gender*.

62 Barlow, *Question of Women in Chinese Feminism*, ch. 3.

63 Leutner and Spakowski, *Women in China*. Also see Judge, *Republican Lens*.

64 Young, "Policing the Modern Woman," 132–33.

65 Zito and Barlow, *Body, Subject, and Power in China*, 18.

66 S. Zhang, "Shaping the New Woman," 405.

67 P. Huang, *Code, Custom, and Legal Practice in China*.

68 Gilmartin, *Engendering the Chinese Revolution*.

69 Barlow, "Politics and Protocols of Funü."

Chapter 6: Wang Guangmei's *Qipao*

1 According to Tang Shaojie's research, Kuai Dafu put Wang Guangmei on trial with the cooperation of the Central Committee and the Beijing People's Liberation Army garrison. See Tang Shaojie, *Yi ye zhi qiu*, 51–53. See also MacFarquhar and Schoenhals, *Mao's Last Revolution*, 523n35. Elizabeth Perry's eloquent description, "The 1960s: Wang Guangmei and Peach Garden Experience," implies that Wang Guangmei reluctantly carried out Liu Shaoqi's orders but had no personal agenda. Also see a more recent Tang essay regarding the sequence of the trial. Tang Shaojie, "Qinghua daxue 'wenhua da geming de shou kuangbiao qu."

2 Barlow, "Semifeudalism, Semicolonialism." Those who argue that Wang was a proxy for Liu Shaoqi are correct.

3 Hortense Spillers and Chris Connery, eds., "The Sixties and the World Event," special issue of *boundary 2* 36, no. 1 (2009).

4 Barlow, "Politics and Protocols of Funü"; and Russo, "'Probable Defeat.'"

5 Drucker, *Graphesis*, 15–16. Assuming that Johanna Druker's argument, the struggle session—and its accoutrements of the dunce cap for "hatting" class enemies, the body cangue (a wooden penal yoke), costumes, and accusatory posters—graphically and performatively created meaning.

6 Spakowski, "Socialist Feminism in Post-socialist China."

7 Zhou Yuan, *Xinbian hongweibing ziliao*, vol. 8.

8　Zhou Yuan, *Xinbian hongweibing ziliao*, vol. 8.

9　See, for instance, the long-running series of articles in April 1967, "Liuxiu waizhuan." See Qinghua daxue jinggangshan bingtuan/baoshihua zhandou zu, *Liuxiu waizhuan*. In other words, the newspaper's primary target was always Liu.

10　Aminda Smith makes the point regarding the stakes of struggle fully and with great sophistication in her "Maoist Epistemology."

11　Hinton, *Hundred Day War*, 101–5. Also see Tang Shaojie, *Yi ye zhi*, qiu 13–15n3, for a confirmation that Hinton's viewpoint reflected Great Proletarian Cultural Revolution perspectives.

12　J. Chen, *Mao's China and the Cold War*, 242–43.

13　This section draws inspiration from Russo, "'Probable Defeat.'"

14　Barlow, "Advertising Ephemera and the Angel of History." See Liu Tao, "Zao Liu Shaoqi de fan, genzhe Mao zhuxi gan yibeizi geming"; Ye Lin, "Wang Guangmei shi Liu Shaoqi pai de guizishou"; and Qinghua daxue jinggangshan bao bianjibu, "Dou Wang Guangmei te kan." Heightening the dramatic situation, stepdaughter Liu Tao repudiated her father and Wang in the December 31, 1966, issue of *Jinggangshan News* with an accompanying critique of Wang provided by Ye Lin, a former leader of the Qinghua University work team. Liu Tao, "Zao Liu Shaoqi de fan, genzhe Mao zhuxi gan yibeizi geming."

15　"Qinghuayuan sanshen Wang Guangmei: Qiangpo chuanqi Yinni fuzhuang xixiao numa jinqing wuru" (page unknown; the University of Washington copy is a clipped and mounted version of the newspaper article and does not include pagination); and "Trials of Wang Kuang-mei." The transcript appeared in Chinese in early May 1968 in the Taiwanese journal *Xingdao* and in English a week earlier in the U.S. consulate's Hong Kong listening post's briefing document, *Current Background*. I am grateful to Michael Meng, librarian for Chinese studies, East Asia Library, Yale University, for his help in locating the Chinese text and guiding me through the morass of Cultural Revolution materials. It is difficult to say how much noncombatants knew. Certainly, contemporaries appeared to enjoy reading the great character posters, and they copied them into revolutionary notebooks.

16　Chao, *Wenhua da geming cidian*, 54.

17　This tone resonates with interviews she gave a year before her death in October 2006. See "Mei ri fu gao."

18　"Trials of Wang Kuang-mei," 3.

19　Hongdaihui Beijing gongnongbing tiyuan Mao Zedong sixiang bingtuan xuanchuanzu, *Liushi fufu milan de shenghuo chou'e de linghun*; and Qinghua daxue jinggangshan bingtuan, *Sikai Wangguangmei de huapi*. I gratefully acknowledge the kindness of Nancy Hearst, Harvard University, Fairbank Center librarian, and Michael Meng in securing copies of these rare documents.

20　Hongdaihui Beijing gongnongbing tiyuan Mao Zedong sixiang bingtuan xuanchuanzu, *Liushi fufu milan de shenghuo chou'e de linghun*, 1–5.

21　For an excellent account of these events, see Roosa, *Pretext for Mass Murder*. I am grateful to Laurie Sears for her background lectures and recommendation of this book.

22 Hongdaihui Beijing gongnongbing tiyuan Mao Zedong sixiang bingtuan xuan-chuan, *Liushi fufu milan de shenghuo chou'e de linghun*, 3.

23 The acronym NASAKOM is based on the Indonesian words for "nationalism," "religion," and "Communism."

24 "Trials of Wang Kuang-mei," 7.

25 Huang Zheng, *Zhibi: Wang Guangmei fangtanlu.*

26 Huang Zheng, *Zhibi: Wang Guangmei fangtanlu*, 308.

27 Included in Huang's transcripts are individual chapters on Wang's diplomatic missions with Liu to Pakistan in 1966, missions to Burma, and photographs of Wang wearing the Hong Kong tailored qipao that Kuai's group had used to indict her.

28 Shao, *Zhou Enlai and the Foundations of Chinese Foreign Policy*, 212–37.

29 The accusation that Wang and Liu had a separate policy imperative is easily disproved. The Indonesian Communist Party and Sukarno's unity government were part of the People's Republic of China's overall pursuit of the "people's war" strategy to decolonize Asia and the nonaligned African countries. This is further suggested by Subandrio's trips to consult Mao Zedong, China's explicit support of Sukarno's push against British neo-imperialism, Aidit's and other Indonesian Communist Party officials' visits to China, and the Mao-style land-revolution proposals that Aidit advocated in mid-1965, which led to panic among Indonesia's military oligarchs. Also, Sukarno gave a speech on August 17, 1965, supporting a Maoist-style arming of people's militias, and on returning from Beijing that same day, Aidit called for arming workers and peasants. Liu Shaoqi's policy was no different from the general position of the CCP (foreign policy is made by the party, not the state) on people's wars in Asia.

30 Bensaïd, "Alain Badiou and the Miracle of the Event," 99.

31 Badiou, *Saint Paul.*

32 I wrote this section under the influence of a joint project, Reconsidering Communist Feminism, in two workshops. The first occurred at Rice University's Chao Center for Asian Studies on March 23, 2012, and the second at Bowdoin College on September 28–30, 2012. The participants were Maria Bucur-Deckard, Suzy Kim, Kristin Ghodsee, and Anna Krylova. An important book on redeeming socialist feminism is Dong, *Xinbie yujing yu shuxie de zhengzhi.* Suzy Kim's edited issue of *positions: asia critique* on "Cold War Feminisms in East Asia," 28, no. 3 (2020) is the fruit of those discussions.

33 Jiang Qing, *Collected Works*, 35–39.

34 Jiang Qing, *Collected Works*, 1–2.

35 Jiang Qing, *Collected Works*, 45.

36 Jiang Qing, *Collected Works*, 40.

37 Jiang Qing, *Collected Works*, 43.

38 Jiang Qing, *Collected Works*, 46.

39 Jiang Qing, *Collected Works*, 152–69.

40 Xiaomei Chen, *Reading the Right Text*, 1–63.

41 Qinghua daxue jinggangshan bingtuan, *Sikai Wangguangmei de huapi.*

42 Qinghua daxue jinggangshan bingtuan, *Sikai Wangguangmei de huapi,* 11.

43 Iconographically and ideologically, Jiang Qing would pioneer an alternative performance. See Chao, *Wenhua da geming cidian,* 63. This entry concerns Jiang Qing's proposal in 1974 to mandate a standard skirt in a simple, proletarian style, so that all women could use the same model.

44 This is the feminine performance that so concerned the Red Guard and Kuai that they forced her to put on the Indonesia-trip garment for a photograph even though during the mass struggle session she appeared in a garment that covered her dress, festooned with the famous necklace of gold Ping-Pong balls.

45 On the origins of the qipao, see Finnane, *Changing Clothes in China,* ch. 6, "Qipao China," 139–76.

46 Gilmartin, *Engendering the Chinese Revolution.* I am paraphrasing Hallward, *Badiou,* 120. Badiou's words are: "It is only through this discovery that there irrupts a gap between what is counted as one in a situation and the intrinsic one that the element is. Retroactively, we will have to declare that this something which appears, eventually, as needing to be counted, did indeed belong to the situation." Badiou, *Abrégé de métapolitique,* 83. In this regard, a moving instance of this problem, the natural rights of the subaltern woman, is Ding Ling's late polemic, "Du Wanxiang."

47 In other words, Wang did not qualify as a woman under this construction.

48 Hallward, *Badiou,* 122.

49 *Dazibao xuan* [Selected big-character posters], no. 6 (?) [cover missing] (July 1966).

50 See Ip, "Fashioning Appearances"; Tina Chen, "Proletarian White and Working Bodies in Mao's China"; and Roberts, "Positive Women Characters in the Model Revolutionary Works of the Chinese Cultural Revolution."

51 Echols, *Daring to Be Bad.*

Conclusion

1 See H. Peng, *Dandyism and Transcultural Modernity;* Tsu, *Failure, Nationalism, and Literature.* See Bevan, *Modern Miscellany,* for the history of Miss Ing Tang.

2 Quoted in Auerbach, "Imagine No Metaphors"; my emphasis. For a discussion of the mutilated woman revolutionary corpse and the mutilated Japanese woman corpse, see Barlow, "How Chinese Are You?"

3 Elman, "Failures of Contemporary Chinese Intellectual History."

4 Louis Althusser and Étienne Balibar, *Reading Capital,* 316: "Freud used this term to describe (among other things) the re-presentation of the dream-thoughts in images privileged by their condensation of a number of thoughts in a single image (condensation/Verdichtung), or by the transference of psychic energy from a particularly potent thought to apparently trivial images (displacement/Verschiebung-Verstellung). Althusser uses the same term to describe the effects of

the contradictions in each practice (q.v.) constituting the social formation (q.v.) on the social formation as a whole, and hence back on each practice and each contradiction, *defining the pattern of dominance and subordination, antagonism and non-antagonism of the contradictions in the structure in dominance* (q.v.) at any given historical moment. More precisely, the overdetermination"; my emphasis.

5 Tsu, *Failure, Nationalism, and Literature*, 6. For discussions of the significance of the huabao, or pictorials, see Henriot and Yeh, *Visualising China*.

6 See Yang Kai, "Mao Zedong yu Zhao Wuzhen shijian," for more detailed information about the suicide and how Mao understood and analyzed it.

7 Hallward, *Badiou*. I am paraphrasing this exposition of "the event" showing how this worked under the historical conditions concerning me here.

8 I am grateful to Andrew Liu for sharing his unpublished work on the figure Y.D. with me. See Liu, "Woman Question and the Agrarian Question."

9 Zupančič, "Fifth Condition."

10 Badiou, *Handbook of Inaesthetics*, 14.

11 Badiou, *Infinite Thought*, 169–93. Badiou has clarified what he means by "our times" in *Logics of Worlds*.

12 Badiou, "Question of Being Today," 43.

13 Badiou, "Question of Being Today," 43.

14 Badiou, *Century*, 72.

15 Badiou, *Century*, 72–73.

16 Badiou, *Century*, 1.

17 Badiou, *Century*, 13.

18 Badiou, *Conditions*, 68.

19 Badiou, *Century*, 49.

20 Barlow, "'What Is a Poem?'"

21 Žižek, Slavoj, "Psychoanalysis in Post-Marxism," 245.

22 Žižek, Slavoj, "Psychoanalysis in Post-Marxism," 257.

23 Antagonism, in Ernesto Laclau and Chantal Mouffe's sense, is "a relation wherein the limits of everyday objectivity are *shown*—in the sense in which Wittgenstein used to say that what cannot be *said* can be shown. [Since] the social only exists as a partial effort for constructing society . . . antagonism, as a witness of the impossibility of a final suture, is the 'experience' of the limit of the social. Strictly speaking, antagonisms are not *internal* but *external* to society; or rather, they constitute the limits of society, the latter's impossibility of fully constituting itself." Laclau and Mouffe, *Hegemony and Socialist Strategy*, 125. For a discussion of Žižek's theories of women, see the conclusion to Barlow, *Question of Women*.

24 Nancy, *Inoperative Community*, 24, 28.

25 Badiou, *Century*, 108.

26 Remaining in the "immanent method established at the very start of this series" of characterizations of the twentieth century, Badiou continues to resolve all immanency of femininity or women as subjects into love: "Women climb onto the stage of love just as the masses had climbed upon that of History," or time, "[André]

Breton's formula for the devastated women," fatigued from throwing herself constantly into the abyss or participating in waves of civil rights claims for a subject that historically has only a body and never a subjectivity. Badiou, *Century*, 145.

27 Badiou, *Century*, 3.
28 Toscano, addendum, 201.
29 This is an indirect reference to Benjamin, "On the Theory of Knowledge," 460.

Bibliography

Allen, Will. *The War on Bugs*. White River, VT: Chelsea Green, 2008.

Alloula, Malek. *The Colonial Harem*. Minneapolis: University of Minnesota Press, 1986.

Althusser, Louis, and Étienne Balibar. *Reading Capital*. Translated by Ben Brewster. New York: New Left Books, 1970.

Andrews, Bridie. *The Making of Modern Chinese Medicine, 1850–1960*. Honolulu: University of Hawai'i Press, 2015.

Ariga Nagao. *Shehui jinhua lun* [On social evolution]. Translated by Mai Zhonghua. Shanghai: Guangzhi shuju, 1902.

Ariga Nagao. *Shehui jinhua lun* [On social evolution]. Translated by Mai Zhonghua. n.p., 1903.

Ariga Nagao. *Shehui jinhua lun* [On social evolution]. Translated by Sa Tuan [Min Housa]. Shanghai: Shangwu chubanshe, 1903, 1915, 1925, 1927.

Ariga Nagao. "Shina no kaimei to seiyō no kaimei to no sabetsu" [The difference between Western open-mindedness and China's open-mindedness]. In Douglas Howland, *Translating the West: Language and Political Reason in Nineteenth-Century Japan*. Honolulu: University of Hawai'i Press, 2002.

Armand, Cécile. "Digging Up Lost Billboards: A Photographic Archaeology of Outdoor Advertising in Early Twentieth-Century Shanghai." *Chinese Historical Review* 25, no. 5 (2018): 118–42.

Askew, David. "Melting Pot or Homogeneity? An Examination of Modern Theories of the Japanese Ethnicity." *Electronic Journal of Contemporary Japanese Studies* 2, no. 1 (2002).

Auerbach, Anthony. "Imagine No Metaphors: The Dialectical Image of Walter Benjamin." *Image[&]Narrative: Online Magazine of the Visual Narrative*, September 2007. http://www.imageandnarrative.be/inarchive/thinking_pictures/auerbach.htm.

Badiou, Alain. *Abrégé de métapolitique*. Edited by Jason Barker. Sciences humaines Philosophie L'Ordre philosophique. Paris: Seuil, 1998.

Badiou, Alain. "Affirmative Dialectics: From Logic to Anthropology." *Journal of Badiou Studies* 2, no. 1 (2013): 1–13.

Badiou, Alain. *Being and Event*. Translated by Oliver Feltham. New York: Continuum, 2005.

Badiou, Alain. *The Century*. New York: Polity, 2005.

Badiou, Alain. *Conditions*. New York: Continuum, 2008.

Badiou, Alain. *Handbook of Inaesthetics*. Translated by Alberto Toscano. Stanford, CA: Stanford University Press, 2005.

Badiou, Alain. *Infinite Thought*. New York: Bloomsbury Academic, 2014.

Badiou, Alain. *Logics of Worlds: Being and Event II*. Translated by Alberto Toscano. New York: Continuum, 2009.

Badiou, Alain. "The Question of Being Today." In *Theoretical Writings*, edited by Ray Brassier and translated by Alberto Toscano, 39–48. London: Continuum, 2004.

Badiou, Alain. *Saint Paul: The Foundation of Universalism*. Stanford, CA: Stanford University Press, 2003.

Badiou, Alain. "La scène du deux" [The scene of the two]. In *Éloge de l'amour* [In praise of love], edited by Alain Badiou, Panagiotis Karakatsanis, and Alexandros Theodoridis, 177–90. Paris: Flammarion, 2011.

Badiou, Alain. "The Subject of Art." *The Symptom*, September 26, 2016. http://www .lacan.com/symptom6_articles/badiou.html.

Barlow, Tani. "Advertising Ephemera and the Angel of History." *positions: asia critique* 20, no. 1 (Winter 2012): 111–58.

Barlow, Tani. "Buying In: Advertising and the Sexy Modern Girl Icon in Shanghai in the 1920s and 1930s." In *The Modern Girl around the World: Consumption, Modernity, and Globalization*, edited by the Modern Girl around the World Research Group, 288–316. Durham, NC: Duke University Press, 2008.

Barlow, Tani. "Commercial Advertising Art in 1840s–1940s China." In *A Companion to Chinese Art*, edited by Martin J. Powers and Katherine R. Tsiang, 431–55. Chichester, UK: Wiley Blackwell, 2016.

Barlow, Tani. "Event, Abyss, Excess: The Event of Women in Chinese Commercial Advertisement, 1910s–1930s." *differences: a journal of feminist cultural studies* 24, no. 2 (2013): 51–92.

Barlow, Tani. "Gender." In *The Making of the Human Sciences in China: Historical and Conceptual Foundations*, edited by Howard Chiang, 243–64. Leiden: Brill, 2020.

Barlow, Tani. "History and Border." *Journal of Women's History* 18, no. 2 (2006): 8–32.

Barlow, Tani. "'History's Coffin Can Never Be Closed': Qu Qiubai Translates Social Science." *boundary 2* 43, no. 3 (2016): 253–86.

Barlow, Tani. "How Chinese Are You? Or It Could Have Been Me." *positions: asia critique* 23, no. 1 (2015): 121–29.

Barlow, Tani. "Politics and Protocols of Funü: (Un)Making the National Woman." In *Engendering China: Women, Culture, and the State*, edited by Christina K. Gilmartin, Gail Hershatter, Lisa Rofel, and Tyrene White, 339–59. Cambridge, MA: Harvard University Press, 1994.

Barlow, Tani. *The Question of Women in Chinese Feminism*. Durham, NC: Duke University Press, 2004.

Barlow, Tani. Review of *The Birth of Chinese Feminism: Essential Texts in Transnational Theory*, edited by Lydia H. Liu, Rebecca E. Karl, and Dorothy Ko. Modern Chinese Literature and Culture Resource Center, October 2013. https://u.osu .edu/mclc/book-reviews/chinese-feminism-barlow/.

Barlow, Tani. "Semifeudalism, Semicolonialism." In *Afterlives of Chinese Communism*, edited by Ivan Franceschini, Nicholas Loubere, and Christian Sorace, 237–43. Canberra: ANU Press; London: Verso, 2019.

Barlow, Tani. "Wanting Some: Natural Science, Social Science and Consumerism." In *Women in China: The Republican Period in Historical Perspective*, edited by Mechthild Leutner and Nikola Spakowski, 312–50. Berlin: LIT, 2005.

Barlow, Tani. "'What Is a Poem?': The Event of Women and the Modern Girl as Problems in Global or World History." In *Immanuel Wallerstein and the Problem of the World: System, Scale, Culture*, edited by David Palumbo-Liu, Bruce Robbins, and Nirvana Tanoukhi, 155–83. Durham, NC: Duke University Press, 2011.

Barlow, Tani. "What Is Wanting." *positions: east asia cultures critique* 9, no. 1 (2001): 267–75.

Barlow, Tani, and C. J. Chen. "Jintan Distribution Networks in Five Treaty Port Commercial Newspapers." Unpublished manuscript, 2014.

Bebel, August. *Women and Socialism*. Translated by Meta L. Stern (Hebe). New York: Socialist Literature, 1910.

Benjamin, Walter. "Announcement of the Journal *Angelus Novus*." In *Walter Benjamin: Selected Writings*, vol. 1, *1913–1926*, edited by Marcus Bullock and Michael W. Jennings, 292–97. Cambridge, MA: Harvard University Press, 2004.

Benjamin, Walter. *The Arcades Project*. Translated by Howard Eiland and Kevin McLaughlin. Cambridge, MA: Belknap Press of Harvard University Press, 1999.

Benjamin, Walter. *Illuminations*. Translated by Harry Zohn. Edited and with an introduction by Hannah Arendt. New York: Schocken Books, 1968.

Benjamin, Walter. "On the Theory of Knowledge." In Benjamin, *Illuminations*, 255–64.

Bensaïd, Daniel. "Alain Badiou and the Miracle of the Event." In *Think Again: Alain Badiou and the Future of Philosophy*, edited by Peter Hallward, 94–105. New York: Continuum, 2004.

Bergère, Marie-Claire. *The Golden Age of the Chinese Bourgeoisie, 1911–1937*. Cambridge: Cambridge University Press, 1990.

Betta, Chiara. "Myth and Memory: Chinese Portrayals of Silas Aaron Hardoon, Luo Jialing and the Aili Garden between 1924 and 1995." In *From Kaifeng . . . to Shanghai: Jews in China*, edited by Roman Malek, 375–400. London: Routledge, 2017.

Bevan, Paul. *A Modern Miscellany: Shanghai Cartoon Artists, Shao Xunmei's Circle and the Travels of Jack Chen, 1926–1938*. Leiden: Brill 2015.

Bickers, Robert. "Fly on an Elephant's Back: The Rise and Fall of Suidi, a Forgotten Treaty Port." *Robert Bickers: History, Empire, China, and Things Found on the Way* (blog), June 15, 2016. https://robertbickers.net/2016/06/15/fly-on-an -elephants-back-the-rise-and-fall-of-suidi-a-forgotten-treaty-port/.

Bickers, Robert, and Christian Henriot, eds. *New Frontiers: Imperialism's New Communities in East Asia, 1842–1953*. Manchester: Manchester University Press, 2000.

Bickers, Robert, and Jonathan J. Howlett, eds. *Britain and China, 1840–1970: Empire, Finance, and War*. London: Routledge, 2015.

Bickers, Robert, and Isabella Jackson, eds. *Treaty Ports in Modern China: Law, Land, and Power*. London: Routledge, 2016.

Black, J. Ernest. August 1930. Trinity College Digital Collections. https://digitalrepository.trincoll.edu/.

Boleslavsky, Richard. *Acting: The First Six Lessons*. New York: Theatre Arts, 1933.

Bonin, Hubert. "French Banks in Hong Kong (1860s–1950s): Challengers to British Banks?" *Cahiers du GREThA*, 2007. https://ideas.repec.org/p/grt/wpegrt/2007-09.html.

Bove, Arianna. "A Critical Ontology of the Present (Foucault and the Task of Our Times)." https://www.generation-online.org/other/writing.htm.

Bowker, Richard Rogers. *Copyright: Its History and Its Law*. Boston: Houghton Mifflin, 1912. Accessed April 7, 2021. https://www.gutenberg.org/files/39502/39502-h/39502-h.htm.

Bramsen, Christopher Bo. *Open Doors: Vilhelm Meyer and the Establishment of General Electric in China*. Richmond, UK: Curzon, 2001.

Bray, Francesca. *Technology and Gender: Fabrics of Power in Late Imperial China*. Berkeley: University of California Press, 1997.

Brennan, Teresa. *History after Lacan*. London: Routledge, 1993.

Brennan, Teresa. *The Interpretation of the Flesh: Freud and Femininity*. London: Routledge, 1992.

Briggs, Elissa, and Gary M. Wessel. "In the Beginning . . . Animal Fertilization and Sea Urchin Development." *Developmental Biology* 300 (2006): 15–26.

Brisco, Norris Arthur. *Economics of Efficiency*. London: Macmillan, 1914.

Brook, Timothy, and Bob Tadashi Wakabayashi, eds. *Opium Regimes: China, Britain, and Japan, 1839–1952*. Berkeley: University of California Press, 2000.

Brown, Frederick. *The Statistical Year-Book of the World Power Conference, 1933/34*. London: Central Office, World Power Conference, 1936.

Burrow, Trigant. "The Genesis and Meaning of 'Homosexuality' and Its Relation to the Problem of Introverted Mental States." *Psychoanalytic Review* 4 (1917): 272–84.

Cahill, James. "The Beauty's Face in Later Chinese Painting." Lecture, Chicago, April 23, 1998. http://jamescahill.info/the-writings-of-james-cahill/women-in-chinese-paintings/120-beautys-face-in-later-chinese-painting.

Cao Xueqin. *Hongloumeng* [The dream of the red chamber]. N.p., ca. 1750s.

Carpenter, Edward. *The Intermediate Sex*. 1908. Reprint, Frankfurt am Main: Outlook, 2018.

Cassel, Pär Kristoffer. *Grounds of Judgment: Extraterritoriality and Imperial Power in Nineteenth-Century China and Japan*. Oxford: Oxford University Press, 2012.

Chakrabarty, Dipesh. *Provincializing Europe: Postcolonial Thought and Historical Difference*. Princeton, NJ: Princeton University Press, 2000.

Chao Feng. *Wenhua da geming cidian* [Dictionary of the Cultural Revolution]. Hong Kong: Gang long chubanshe, 1993.

Chen Dingmou. "Putong xinli, yi benneng" (Common psychology, translating instinct).

Chen, Jian. *Mao's China and the Cold War.* Chapel Hill: University of North Carolina Press, 2001.

Chen Tiejian. *Qu Qiubai zhuan* [Biography of Qu Qiubai]. Beijing: Shehui kexue Press, 1980.

Chen, Tina Mai. "Proletarian White and Working Bodies in Mao's China." *positions: east asia cultures critique* 11, no. 2 (2003): 361–93.

Chen, Xiaomei, ed. (2003). "Introduction." *Reading the Right Text: An Anthology of Contemporary Chinese Drama*, 1–63. Honolulu: University of Hawai'i Press.

Chen Zu'en. *Shanghai ri qiao shehui shengshuo shi* [A social history of Japanese expatriates in Shanghai]. Shanghai: Shanghai cishu chubanshe, 2009.

Cheng, Chu-yuan. "The United States Petroleum Trade with China, 1867–1949." In *America's China Trade in Historical Perspective: The Chinese and American Performance*, edited by Ernest R. May and John King Fairbank, 205–33. Cambridge, MA: Harvard University Press, 1986.

Chiang, Howard. *After Eunuchs: Science, Medicine, and the Transformation of Sex in Modern China.* New York: Columbia University Press, 2020.

Chiang, Howard, ed. *The Making of the Human Sciences in China: Historical and Conceptual Foundations.* Leiden: Brill, 2019.

Chiang, Yung-Chen. *Social Engineering and the Social Sciences in China, 1919–1949.* Cambridge: Cambridge University Press, 2001.

Chung, Yuehtsen Juliette. "Eugenics in China and Hong Kong: Nationalism and Colonialism, 1890s–1940s." In *The Oxford Handbook of the History of Eugenics*, edited by Alison Bashford and Philippa Levine, 258–73 New York: Oxford University Press, 2010.

Cobb, Matthew. "An Amazing 10 Years: The Discovery of Egg and Sperm in the 17th Century." *Reproduction in Domestic Animals* 47, no. S4 (2012): 2–6. https://onlinelibrary.wiley.com/doi/pdf/10.1111/j.1439-0531.2012.02105.x.

Cochran, Sherman. *Big Business in China: Sino-Foreign Rivalry in the Cigarette Industry, 1890–1930.* Cambridge, MA: Harvard University Press, 1980.

Cochran, Sherman. *Chinese Medicine Men: Consumer Culture in China and Southeast Asia.* Cambridge, MA: Harvard University Press, 2006.

Cooper, Frederick. *Colonialism in Question: Theory, Knowledge, History.* Berkeley: University of California Press, 2005.

Coward, K., C. P. Ponting, H.-Y. Chang, O. Hibbitt, P. Savolainen, K. T. Jones, and J. Parrington. "Phospholipase Cζ, the Trigger of Egg Activation in Mammals, Is Present in a Non-Mammalian Species." *Reproduction* 130, no. 2 (2005): 157–63. https://rep.bioscientifica.com/search?f_o=author&q_o=K+Coward.

Cox, Howard. *The Global Cigarette: Origins and Evolution of British American Tobacco, 1880–1945.* Oxford: Oxford University Press, 2000.

Crow, Carl. *Four Hundred Million Customers.* New York: Harper, 1937.

Crow, Carl. Preface to *Newspaper Directory of China (Including Hong Kong).* Shanghai: Crow, 1935.

Crystal, David. *The Cambridge Encyclopedia of the English Language.* New York: Cambridge University Press, 1995.

Day, Alex. "Interpreting the Cultural Revolution Politically." *Inter-Asia Cultural Studies* 7, no. 4 (December 2006): 705–12.

Deleuze, Gilles. *Bergsonism*. Translated by Hugh Tomlinson and Barbara Habberjam. New York: Zone Books, 1988.

Derrida, Jacques. "Jacques Derrida, There Is No 'One' Narcissism (Autobiophotographies)." Hydra, March 22, 1986. University of California, Irvine. http://hydra .humanities.uci.edu/derrida/narc.html. Previously published as "Entretien avec Jacques Derrida," *Digraphe* 42 (December 1987).

Dikötter, Frank. *The Discourse of Race in Modern China*. Stanford, CA: Stanford University Press, 1992.

Dikötter, Frank. *Imperfect Conceptions: Medical Knowledge, Birth Defects, and Eugenics in China*. New York: Columbia University Press, 1998.

Ding Ling. "Du Wanxiang" [Du Wanxiang]. In *I Myself Am a Woman: Selected Writings of Ding Ling*, edited by Tani E. Barlow with Gary Bjorge, 329–55. Boston: Beacon, 1989.

Ding Song. *Ding Song manhuaji* [Collected cartoons of Ding Song]. Edited by Guojia tushuguan. Shanghai: Zhongguo wenlian chubanshe, 2004.

Ding Song. *Minguo fengqin baimei tu* [Lovely republican-era images of 100 beauties]. Shanghai: Zhongguo wenlian chubanshe, 2004.

Ding Song. *Shanghai shizhuang tuyong* [Shanghai fashion images]. Taibei: Guangwen shuju, 1968.

Doleželová-Velingerová, Milena, and Rudolf G. Wagner, eds. *Chinese Encyclopaedias of New Global Knowledge (1870–1930): Changing Ways of Thought*. Heidelberg: Springer, 2014.

Dong, Limin. *Xinbie yujing yu shuxie de zhengzhi* [Gender, context, and the politics of writing]. Beijing: Renmin wenxue chubanshe, 2012.

Drucker, Johanna. *Graphesis: Visual Forms of Knowledge Production*. Cambridge, MA: Harvard University Press, 2014.

Drucker, Johanna. "Graphesis: Visual Knowledge Production and Representation." *Poetess Archive Journal* 2, no. 1 (2010). https://journals.tdl.org/paj/index.php/paj /article/view/4.

Duara, Prasenjit. *Rescuing History from the Nation: Questioning Narratives of Modern China*. Chicago: University of Chicago Press, 1997.

Durkin, Philip. *Borrowed Words: A History of Loanwords in English*. Oxford: Oxford University Press, 2014.

Echols, Alice. *Daring to Be Bad: Radical Feminism in America, 1967–1975*. Minneapolis: University of Minnesota Press, 1989.

Edkins, J. D. *Banking and Prices in China*. Shanghai: Kelly and Walsh, 1905.

Eiji, Oguma. *The Genealogy of "Japanese" Self-Images*. Translated by David Askew. Melbourne: Trans Pacific Press, 2002.

Elam, Diane. *Feminism and Deconstruction: Ms. en Abyme*. New York: Routledge, 1993.

Elman, Benjamin A. "The Failures of Contemporary Chinese Intellectual History." *Eighteenth-Century Studies* 43, no. 3 (2010): 371–91.

Elshakry, Marwa. *Reading Darwin in Arabic, 1860–1950.* Chicago: University of Chicago Press, 2013.

Endo Ryukichi. *Jinshi shehuixue* [Modern sociology]. Translated by Tan Shougong. Shanghai: Taidong tushu yin, 1920.

Engels, Friedrich. *Dialectics of Nature.* London: Wellred, 2012.

Engels, Friedrich. *The Origin of the Family, Private Property and the State, in the Light of the Researches of Lewis H. Morgan.* London: Lawrence and Wishart, 1977.

Etemad, Bouda, and Jean Luciani. *World Energy Production, 1800–1985.* Geneva: Publications du Centre d'histoire économique internationale de l'Université de Genève, 1991.

Fan Jichang. "Shehui kexue he benneng de wenti" [Social science and the instinct problem]. *Shehui kexue jikan,* 1924, 2–3.

Feng Wenjie. "Qu Qiubai zaoqi fanyi huodong shuping" [Comment on Qu Qiubai's earliest translations]. *Jiangsu gongye shuyuan xuebao* 10, no. 2 (June 2009): 6–25.

Ferguson, Charles J., ed. *Anderson, Meyer and Company Limited of China: Its History; Its Organization Today, Historical and Descriptive Sketches Contributed by Some of the Manufacturers It Represents, March 31, 1906 to March 31, 1931.* Chinese section translated and prepared by Li Guangzhao. Shanghai: Kelly and Walsh, 1931.

Figal, Gerald. *Civilization and Monsters: Spirits of Modernity in Meiji Japan.* Durham, NC: Duke University Press, 1999.

Finnane, Antonia. *Changing Clothes in China: Fashion, History, Nation.* New York: Columbia University Press. 2007

Foucault, Michel. *Discipline and Punish: The Birth of the Prison.* New York: Pantheon, 1978.

Foucault, Michel. *Foucault Live: Collected Interviews, 1961–1984.* Edited by Sylvère Lotringer. Translated by Lysa Hochroth and John Johnston. New York: Semiotext(e), 1996.

Foucault, Michel. *The Order of Things.* New York: Pantheon Books, 1970.

"From the Firing Line: Personal and Trade Jottings." *Tobacco: An Illustrated Weekly,* April 15, 1920, 32.

Furth, Charlotte. *A Flourishing Yin: Gender in China's Medical History, 960–1665.* Berkeley: University of California Press, 1999.

Gao Junzhe. "Shehuixue de shengwu xuepai" [The biological school of sociology]. *Shehui xuejie,* no. 4 (1930): 87–139.

Gao, Zhipeng. "The Emergence of Modern Psychology in China, 1876–1922." *Annual Review of Critical Psychology* (2013): 293–307.

Garke, Emile. *The Progress of Electrical Enterprise: Reprints of Articles from the Engineering Supplement of the Times on the British Electrical Industries.* London: Electrical Press, 1907.

Ghosh, Arunab. *Making It Count: Statistics and Statecraft in the Early People's Republic of China.* Princeton, NJ: Princeton University Press, 2020.

Gilmartin, Christina Kelley. *Engendering the Chinese Revolution: Radical Women, Communist Politics and Mass Movements in the 1920s.* Berkeley: University of California Press, 1995.

Ginsborg, Hannah. "Kant's Aesthetics and Teleology." In *The Stanford Encyclopedia of Philosophy*, edited by Edward N. Zalta. Stanford, CA: Stanford University, 1997–. Article first published July 2, 2005; revised February 13, 2013. https://plato.stanford.edu/archives/fall2014/entries/kant-aesthetics/.

Gong Yanhong and Liu Shipeng. "Li Da yu Qu Qiubai de funüguan bijiao" [A comparative study of Li Da's and Qu Qiubai's opinions on women]. *Dangdai jiaoyü lilun yi shixian* 4, no. 9 (2012). Accessed January 21, 2021. https://wenku.baidu.com/view/3bcdf81c55270722192ef7d1?pu=.

Goodman, Bryna. "The New Woman Commits Suicide: The Press, Cultural Memory, and the New Republic." *Journal of Asian Studies* 64, no. 1 (February 2005): 67–101.

Gorki, Maxim. *The Mother.* 1906. Mumbai: Jaico Publishing House, 2011.

Gray, Philip Howard. "Spalding, His Influence on Research in Developmental Behavior." *Journal of the History of the Behavioral Sciences* 3, no. 2 (April 1967): 168–79.

Guo Renyuan. "Benneng" [Instinct]. *Fudan zazhi* [Fudan magazine], (1918): 317–33.

Gützlaff, Karl. *Wanguo dili quantuji* [Illustrated geography of the myriad countries]. N.p. 1843.

Hallward, Peter. *Badiou: A Subject to Truth.* Minneapolis: University of Minnesota Press, 2003.

Hamada Shirō. *Jitsuyō kōkoku-hō* [Practical techniques of advertising]. Tokyo: Hakubunkan, 1902.

Hamilton, Gary G. *Commerce and Capitalism in Chinese Societies.* London: Routledge, 2006.

Hausman, William J., Peter Hertner, and Mira Wilkins. *Global Electrification: Multinational Enterprise and International Finance in the History of Light and Power, 1878–2007.* Cambridge: Cambridge University Press, 2008.

Hayden, Wendy. *Evolutionary Rhetoric: Sex, Science, and Free Love in Nineteenth-Century Feminism.* Carbondale: Southern Illinois University Press, 2013.

Helmling, Steven. "Constellation and Critique: Adorno's Constellation, Benjamin's Dialectical Image." *Postmodern Culture* 14, no. 1 (September 2003). doi:10.1353/pmc.2003.0036.

Henriot, Christian. "Virtual Shanghai." Accessed March 23, 2021. https://www.virtualshanghai.net/.

Henriot, Christian, and Wen-hsin Yeh, eds. *Visualising China, 1845–1965: Moving and Still Images in Historical Narratives.* Leiden: Brill, 2013.

Henry, Todd. *Assimilating Seoul: Japanese Rule and the Politics of Public Space in Colonial Korea, 1910–1945.* Berkeley: University of California Press, 2016.

Hilferding, Rudolf. *Finance Capital: A Study of the Latest Phase of Capitalist Development.* Edited by Tom Bottomore. London: Routledge and Kegan Paul, 1981.

Hinton, William. *Hundred Day War: The Cultural Revolution at Tsinghua University.* New York: Monthly Review Press, 1972.

Hiraoka, Keiichi. *Jiyū jizai kōkokuhō* [Effortless advertising techniques]. Tokyo: Nanbokusha, 1914.

Hodge, Russ. *Human Genetics: Race, Population, and Disease.* Brainerd, MN: Hermitage, 2010.

Hodsdon, Barrett. "The Mystique of Mise-en-Scène Revisited." *Australian Journal of Media and Culture* 5, no. 2 (1990): 1–12.

Hollingworth, Harry. *Modan gāru to shokuminchiteki kindai: Higashi Ajia ni okeru teikoku, shihon, jendā* [Advertising and selling the Advertising Men's League of New York City]. Translated by Sasaki Jūku. Tokyo: Satō Shuppanbu, 1914.

Hongdaihui Beijing gongnongbing tiyuan Mao Zedong sixiang bingtuan xuanchuanzu. *Liushi fufu milan de shenghuo chou'e de linghun* [The Lius' decadent life and despicable souls]. N.p.

Hoston, Germain. *Marxism and the Crisis of Development in Prewar Japan*. Princeton, NJ: Princeton University Press, 1987.

Hou, Chi-ming. *Foreign Investment and Economic Development in China, 1840–1937*. Cambridge, MA: Harvard University Press, 1965.

Howland, Douglas. *Personal Liberty and Public Good: The Introduction of John Stuart Mill to Japan and China*. Toronto: University of Toronto Press, 2005.

Howland, Douglas. *Translating the West: Language and Political Reason in Nineteenth-Century Japan*. Honolulu: University of Hawai'i Press, 2002.

Huang Kewu. "Cong shenbao yiyao guanggao kan minchu Shanghai de yiliao wenhua yv shehui shenghuo, 1912–1926" [Looking at early republican Shanghai medical tonic ads and social life in Shenbao advertising images]. *Zhongyang yanjiu yuan Jindai shi yanjiu suo jikan* 17 (December 1988): 141–94.

Huang, Martha E. "The Spectacle of Representation: Calendar Girls, the Gaze and the Atelier." *Transtext(e)s Transcultures: Journal of Global Cultural Studies* 2 (2007): 84–131. https://journals.openedition.org/transtexts/87?lang=en.

Huang, Philip C. C. *Code, Custom, and Legal Practice in China: The Qing and the Republic Compared*. Stanford, CA: Stanford University Press, 2002.

Huang Zheng. *Wang Guangmei fangtanlu* [Interviews with Wang Guangmei]. Beijing: Zhongyang wenxian chubanshe, 2006.

Huxley, Thomas Henry. *Evolution and Ethics*. London: Macmillan, 1893.

Ibsen, Henrik. *A Doll's House*. N.p., 1879.

Ip, Hung-Yok. "Fashioning Appearances: Feminine Beauty in Chinese Communist Revolutionary Culture." *Modern China* 29, no. 33 (July 2003): 329–61.

Isaka, Maki. "The Gender of *Onnagata* as the Imitating Imitated: Its Historicity, Performativity, and Involvement in the Circulation of Femininity." *positions: east asia cultures critique* 10, no. 2 (Fall 2002): 245–84.

Isaka, Maki. *Onnagata: A Labyrinth of Gendering in Kabuki Theater*. Seattle: University of Washington Press, 2016.

Ishikawa, Yoshihiro. "Anti-Manchu Racism and the Rise of Anthropology in Early 20th Century China." *Sino-Japanese Studies* 15 (April 2003): 7–26. http://chinajapan.org/articles/15/15ishikawa7-26.pdf.

Ishikawa, Yoshihiro. "Chinese Translations from Japanese of Works on Socialism, 1919–1922." *Sino-Japanese Studies* 19 (2009): 14–35. http://chinajapan.org/articles/index.php/sjs/article/viewFile/2/14.

Ishikawa, Yoshihiro. *History of the Formation of the Chinese Communist Party*. Translated by Joshua A. Fogel. Tokyo: Iwanami Shoten, 2001.

Issy, Gad C. *The Philosophy of the View of Life in Modern Chinese Thought*. Wiesbaden: Harrassowitz, 2013.

Ito Ruri, Sakamoto Hiroko, and Tani Barlow, eds. *Modan garu to shokuminchi taki kindai higashijia ni okeru teikoku shihon jenda* [The modern girl, colonial modernity, and East Asia]. Tokyo: Iwanami shoten, 2010.

James, William. *Principles of Psychology*. New York: Henry Holt, 1890.

Japanese-English Medical Dictionary. Allied Translator Interpreter on Pacific Axis Publication 9, February 7, 1945. https://collections.nlm.nih.gov/ocr/nlm:nlmuid -2641o08oR-bk.

Jenks, Edward. *History of Politics*. London: Dent, 1900.

Ji, Zhaojin. *A History of Modern Shanghai Banking: The Rise and Decline of China's Finance Capitalism*. London: Routledge, 2016.

Jiang Qing. *Jiang Qing wen lu* [Jiang Qing records]. N.p. 2011.

Jiang Yuquan. *Shiyong guanggaoxue* [Practical advertising]. N.p. 1926.

Judge, Joan. *Republican Lens: Gender, Visuality, and Experience in the Early Chinese Periodical Press*. Berkeley: University of California Press, 2015.

Kang Youwei. *Riben shumuzhi* [Bibliography of Japanese books]. In *Kang Youwei quanji 3* [Collected works of Kang Youwei, vol. 3], 585–86. Beijing: China Renmin University Press, 2007.

Karl, Rebecca. *China's Revolutions in the Modern World: A Brief Interpretive History*. New York: Verso, 2020.

Ke Shi. "Funü zai jinhua zhong de renwu" [The responsibility of women in evolution]. *Funü zazhi* 8, no. 9 (1922): 27–35.

Kent, Stacie. "Problems of Circulation in the Treaty Ports." In *Treaty Ports in Modern China: Land, Law, and Power*, edited by Robert Bickers and Isabella Jackson, 78–100. London: Routledge, 2016.

Kikuchi, Yūko. *Japanese Modernisation and Mingei Theory: Cultural Nationalism and Orientalism*. New York: RoutledgeCurzon, 2004.

Kim, Myung Mi. "Anna O Addendum." In *The Bounty*, 97–100. Minneapolis: Chax, 1996.

Kirby, William. "China Unincorporated: Company Law and Business Enterprise in Twentieth Century China." *Journal of Asian Studies* 54, no. 1 (1995): 43–63.

Kircher, Athanasius. *China Monumentis*. 1667.

Knight, Nick. *Li Da and Marxist Philosophy in China*. Boulder, CO: Westview, 1996.

Knight, Nick. *Marxist Philosophy and Social Theory: The Origins of Li Da's Thought*. Boulder, CO: Westview, 1996.

Knight, Nick. *Marxist Philosophy in China: From Qu Qiubai to Mao Zedong, 1923–1945*. Dordrecht: Springer, 2005.

Ko, Dorothy. *Teachers of the Inner Chambers*. Stanford, CA: Stanford University Press, 1994.

Köll, Elisabeth. "Nanyang Brothers Tobacco." *Encyclopedia.com*. Updated December 23, 2020. https://www.encyclopedia.com/history/news-wires-white-papers -and-books/nanyang-brothers-tobacco.

Kwan, Man Bun. *Beyond Market and Hierarchy: Patriotic Capitalism and the Jiuda Salt Refinery, 1914–1953*. New York: Palgrave Macmillan, 2014.

Kwok, Danny Wynn Ye. *Scientism in Chinese Thought, 1900–1950*. New Haven, CT: Yale University Press, 1965.

Laclau, Ernesto, and Chantal Mouffe. *Hegemony and Socialist Strategy: Towards a Radical Democratic Politics*. London: Verso, 1985.

Lai, Edwin Kin-keung. *The Life and Art Photography of Lang Jingshan (1892–1995)*. Hong Kong: Hong Kong University Press, 2000.

Laing, Ellen. "The British American Tobacco Company Advertising Department and Four of Its Calendar Poster Artists." Paper presented at the Symposium on Urban Cultural Institutions in Early Twentieth Century China, March 26, 2002.

Laing, Ellen. *Selling Happiness: Calendar Posters and Visual Culture in Early Twentieth-Century Shanghai*. Honolulu: University of Hawai'i Press, 2004.

Lair, Pamela Walker. *Advertising Progress: American Business and the Rise of Consumer Marketing*. Baltimore: Johns Hopkins University Press, 2001.

Lam, Tong. *A Passion for Facts: Social Surveys and the Construction of the Chinese Nation-State, 1900–1949*. Berkeley: University of California Press, 2011.

Lanling Xiaoxiao Sheng [pseud.]. *Jinpingmei*. In *The Plum in the Golden Vase*, edited and translated by David Tod Roy. 5 vols. Princeton, N.J.: Princeton University Press, 1993–2013.

Lefebvre, Henri. *Critique of Everyday Life*. London: Verso, 1991.

Lenin, Vladimir Ilyich. "Finance Capital and the Political Oligarchy." In *Imperialism, the Highest Stage of Capitalism: A Popular Outline*, ch. 3. 1916. Marxists Internet Archive. https://www.marxists.org/archive/lenin/works/1916/imp-hsc/ch03 .htm.

Letourneau, Charles Jean Marie. "Lihun de jinhua" [The evolution of divorce]. Translated by Wei Xin. *Funü zazhi* 8, no. 4 (1922): 106–14.

Leutner, Mechthild, and Nicola Spakowski, eds. *Women in China: The Republican Period in Historical Perspective*. Somerset, NJ: Transaction, 2005.

Li Da. *Xiandai shehuixue* [Modern sociology]. Wuhan: Wuhan daxue chubanshe, 1926.

Li Da. *Li Da shehuixue dagang* [Outline of Li Da's sociology]. Shanghai: Shanghai chubanshe, 1937.

Li Da. "Nüzi jiefanglun" [On the liberation of women]. *Jiefang yu gazao* [Emancipation and reform], 1, no. 31 (October 1919). In *Wusi shiqi funü wenti wenxuan* [Selected articles of the women's problem in May Fourth era], edited by the All-China Women's Federation, 35–48. Beijing: Zhongguo funü chubanshe, 1981.

Liang Ai-xiang and Lin Jin-hui. "The Historical Value of *Newspaper Directory of China*." *Journal of Literature and Art Studies* 10, no. 2 (2020): 169–75.

Lin, Xiaoqing Diana. *Peking University: Chinese Scholarship and Intellectuals, 1898–1937*. Albany: State University of New York Press, 2005.

Ling, C. P. *China's Progress in Advertising*. Shanghai: Chinese Commercial Advertising Agency, 1936.

Liu, Andrew. "The Woman Question and the Agrarian Question." Unpublished paper, 2016.

Liu Bannong. Preface to *Beiping Guangshe Nianjian* [Annual of Guangshe, Beiping] 2 (1928).

Liu, Lydia H., Rebecca E. Karl, and Dorothy Ko, eds. *The Birth of Chinese Feminism: Essential Texts in Transnational Theory.* New York: Columbia University Press, 2013.

Liu Tao. "Zao Liu Shaoqi de fan, genzhe Mao zhuxi gan yibeizi geming" [Rebel against Liu Shaoqi, follow Chairman Mao for a lifelong revolution]. In *Xinbian hongweibing ziliao* [A new collection of Red Guard publications], edited by Zhou Yuan, vol. 8. Oakton, VA: Center for Chinese Research Materials, 1999.

Long Xizu, ed. *Zhongguo jindai sheying yishu meixue wenxuan* [Selected essays on photography, art, and aesthetics in modern China]. Tianjin: Tianjin wenhua chubanshe, 1988.

Lowry, Kathryn. "Duplicating the Strength of Feeling: The Circulation of Qingshu [Love Letters] in the Late Ming." In *Writing and Materiality in China: Essays in Honor of Patrick Hanan*, edited by Judith Zeitlin and Lydia Liu, 239–72. Cambridge, MA: Harvard University Press, 2003.

Lu Cheng. "Meishu geming" [A revolution in the arts]. *Xin Qingnian* 6, no. 1 (January 1919): 85.

Lu, Tina. *Persons, Roles, and Minds: Identity in Peony Pavilion and Peach Blossom Fan.* Stanford, CA: Stanford University Press, 2001.

Lury, Celia. *Brands: The Logos of the Global Economy.* London: Routledge, 2004.

MacFarquhar, Roderick, and Michael Schoenhals. *Mao's Last Revolution.* Cambridge, MA: Harvard University Press, 2006.

Mann, Susan. "'Fuxue' (Women's Learning) by Zhang Xuecheng (1738–1801): China's First History of Women's Culture." *Late Imperial China* 13, no. 1 (June 1992): 40–62.

Manovich, Lev. "Metadating the Image," https://v2.nl/archive/articles/metadating -the-image/view. Accessed December 20, 2020.

Marchand, Roland. *Advertising the American Dream.* Berkeley: University of California Press, 1985.

Marx, Karl. "Estranged Labor." In *Economic and Philosophical Manuscripts of 1844.* 1844. Marxists Internet Archive. https://www.marxists.org/archive/marx/works /1844/manuscripts/labour.htm.

Matsumiya Saburō. *Kōkoku shinrigaku* [The psychology of advertising]. Tokyo: Chikura, 1939.

McClintock, Anne. *Imperial Leather: Race, Gender, and Sexuality in the Colonial Contest.* New York: Routledge, 1995.

McCloud, Scott. *Understanding Comics: The Invisible Art.* Northampton, MA: Tundra, 1993.

McDougall, William. *An Introduction to Social Psychology.* London: Methuen, 1908.

Meillassoux, Quentin. "Decision and Undecidability of the Event in Being and Event, I and II." Translated by Alyosha Edlebi. *Parrhesia* 19 (2014): 22–35.

"Meiri fugao: Liu Shaoqi yishuang Wang Guangmei qu shi" [Everyday obituary: Liu Shaoqi's widow Wang Guangmei passes away]. October 13, 2006. Accessed July 23, 2007. http://lifestory.Blogbus.com/s1063585/.

Metzler, Mark. *Lever of Empire: The International Gold Standard and the Crisis of Liberalism in Prewar Japan.* Berkeley: University of California Press, 2006.

Mill, John Stuart. *On Liberty.* London: Parker, 1859.

Minakata Kumagusu. *Minakata Kumagusu nikki* (Minakata Kumagusu's diary). Tokyo: Yasaka shobō, 1987–89.

Mittler, Barbara. "Between Discourse and Social Reality: The Early Chinese Press in Recent Publication" (review essay). Modern Chinese Literature and Culture Resource Center, February 2007. http://u.osu.edu/mclc/book-reviews/chinese-press/.

The Modern Girl around the World Research Group. *The Modern Girl around the World: Consumption, Modernity, and Globalization.* Durham, NC: Duke University Press, 2008.

Moeran, Brian. "Newspapers, Advertising and the Japanese Economy: Early Development." 2001. Accessed December 29, 2020. https://research.cbs.dk/en/publications/newspapers-advertising-and-the-japanese-economy-early-development.

Monnais, Laurence. *Colonial Life of Pharmaceuticals: Medicines and Modernity in Vietnam* Cambridge: Cambridge University Press, 2019.

Montesquieu, Baron de. *The Spirit of the Laws.* Translated by Thomas Nugent, revised by J. V. Prichard. New York: Appleton, 1900.

Morgan, C. Lloyd. *Habit and Instinct.* London: Arnold, 1896.

Morgan, Stephen L. "Selling Chinese Dreams." Paper presented at the joint meeting of the Business History Conference and European Business History Association, Milan, Italy, June 11–13, 2009.

Morgan, Stephen L. "Transfer of Taylorist Ideas to China, 1910–1930s." *Journal of Management History* 12, no. 4 (2006): 408–24.

Morishita Jintan. *Morishita Jintan 80-nenshi* [Morishita Jintan: Eighty years of history]. Tokyo: Morishita Jintan, 1974.

Morishita Jintan 100-Year Commemorative Journal Editorial Committee, ed. *Sōgō hoken yaku Jintan kara sōgō hoken sangyō Jintan e: Morishita Jintan 100-shūnen kinenshi* [Jintan, from comprehensive pharmaceutical care to comprehensive health care industry: Commemorating 100 years of Morishita Jintan]. Osaka: Jintan, 1995.

Morton, Herbert C. *The Story of Webster's Third: Philip Gove's Controversial Dictionary and Its Critics.* Cambridge: Cambridge University Press, 1994.

Mrazek, Rudolph. *Engineers of Happy Land: Technology and Nationalism in a Colony.* Princeton, NJ: Princeton University Press, 2002.

Muñoz, José Esteban. "Ephemera as Evidence: Introductory Notes to Queer Acts." *Women and Performance: A Journal of Feminist Theory* 8, no. 2 (2009): 5–16.

Murray, Hugh. *An Encyclopaedia of Geography*. London: Longman Rees, Orme, Brown, Green, and Longman, 1834.

Nakagawa, Shizuka. *Kōkokuron* [Advertising theory]. Tokyo: Chikura Shobō, 1930.

Nakagawa, Shizuka. *Kōkoku to senden* [Advertising and marketing]. Tokyo: Hōbunkan, 1924.

Nakase, Toshikazu. "The Development of the Advertising Industry in Japan." *Japan Business History Review* 1, no. 3 (1966): 28–55.

Nancy, Jean-Luc. *The Inoperative Community*. Minneapolis: University of Minnesota Press, 1991.

Norris, Christopher. *Badiou's "Being and Event": A Reader's Guide*. London: Continuum, 2009.

Ostrovsky, Aleksandr. *The Storm*. Translated by Constance Garnett. Boston: Luce, 1907.

Pan Guangdan. "Feng Xiaoqing kao" [Research on Feng Xiaoqing]. *Funü zazhi* 10, no. 11 (1924): 16–25.

Pan Guangdan. "Shengyu xianzhi yu youshengxue" [Birth control and eugenics]. *Funü zazhi* 11, no. 10 (1925): 1560–69.

Pan Guangdan. "Shu Feng Xiaoqing quanji hou" [After writing on Xiaoqing's collected works]. *Renjianshi* 29 (1935): 19–22; 30 (1935): 19–21.

Pan Guangdan. "Xiaoqing kaozheng bulu" [Supplementary evidential scholarship on Xiaoqing]. *Renjianshi* 1, nos. 2–3 (1934): 18–21, 11–15.

Pan Guangdan. "Yousheng yu wenhua: Yu Sun Benwen xiansheng shangque de wenzi" [Eugenics and culture: On Mr. Sun Benwen's discussion]. *Shehui xuekan* 1, no. 2 (1929): 1–19.

Pan Guangdan *Xiaoqing zhi fenxi* [An analysis of Xiaoqing]. Shanghai: Xinyue shudian, 1927.

Pan Guangdan, *Feng Xiaoqing: Yijian yinglian zhi yanjiu* [Feng Xiaoqing: A study in narcissism]. Shanghai: Xinyue shudian, 1929.

Parker, Clark. "The Tokyo Files." October 13, 2015. https://thetokyofiles.com/2015/10/13/balloons-on-the-ginza-float-young-advertisers-1890-1989/.

Patton, Paul. "The World Seen from Within: Deleuze and the Philosophy of Events." *Theory and Event* 1, no. 1 (1997). https://muse.jhu.edu/article/32443.

Peng Changxin. "Zhongguo jindai gongye sheji de xianqu—Shenchang yanghang de jianzhu Shijian" [The pioneer of industrial design in modern China: Anderson, Meyers and Co. Ltd. and its architectural practice]. *Zhongguo jindai jianzhu yanjiu*, 2017, pp. 59–66.

Peng, Hsiao-yan. *Dandyism and Transcultural Modernity: The Dandy, the Flaneur, and the Translator in 1930s Shanghai, Tokyo, and Paris*. London: Routledge, 2010.

Perry, Elizabeth J. "The 1960s: Wang Guangmei and Peach Garden Experience." In *The Chinese Communist Party: A Century in Ten Lives*, edited by Timothy Cheek, Klaus Mühlhahn, and Hans van de Ven. Cambridge: Cambridge University Press, 2021.

Petrilli, Susan, and Augusto Ponzio. "Adam Schaff: From Semantics to Political Semiotics." Paper presented at World Congress of IASS/AIS, University of Hel-

sinki, June 11–17, 2007. https://marxismocritico.files.wordpress.com/2013/05/2
  -_hommageadamschaff.pdf.

Philips, D. F. *Elements of Psychology.* New York: Henry Holt, 1893

Poffenberger, Albert T. *Kōkoku shinrigaku* [Psychology in advertising]. Translated by
  Shimoji Kenji. Tokyo: Kōkōsha Press, 1933.

Pound, Ezra, trans. *The Confucian Odes: The Classic Anthology Defined by Confucius.*
  Cambridge, MA: Harvard University Press, 1954.

Powers, Martin J., and Katherine R. Tsiang, eds. *Companion to Chinese Art.* Oxford,
  UK: Wiley-Blackwell, 2015.

Qian, Nanxiu. *Politics, Poetics, and Gender in Late Qing China: Xue Shaohui and the Era
  of Reform.* Stanford, CA: Stanford University Press, 2015.

Qinghua daxue jinggangshan bao bianjibu. *Dou Wang Guangmei te kan* [Special edition on the struggles against Wang Guangmei]. N.p.

Qinghua daxue jinggangshan bingtuan. *Sikai Wangguangmei de huapi* [Rip off Wang
  Guangmei's evil disguise]. N.p.

Qinghua daxue jinggangshan bingtuan/baoshihua zhandou zu. *Liuxiu waizhuan*
  [Unrecorded history of revisionist Liu Shaoqi]. N.p.

"Qinghuayuan sanshen Wang Guangmei: Qiangpo chuanqi Yinni fuzhuang xixiao
  numa jinqing wuru" [Three trials of Wang Guangmei in Qinghua University:
  Please laugh at, scold, and insult her as you like as she is forced to wear the Indonesian apparel]. In Qinghua daxue jinggangshan bingtuan, *Sikai Wangguangmei
  de huapi.* N.p.

Qu Qiubai. *Qu qiubai wenji* [Collected works of Qu Qiubai]. Beijing: Renmin chubanshe, 1987.

Qu Qiubai. "Shehui yundong de yixingzhe" [Sacrificed to social movements]. *Xin
  shehui* 8, no. 2 (November 1, 1919–May 1, 1920).

Qu Qiubai. "Xiaoxiao yige wenti—fun funü jiefang de wenti" [A teensy question:
  Women's liberation]. *Xin shehui* 8 (1920).

Qu Zhengming. "'Hong xibao' yu yongtai he yancao gongsi" [Red tin package and
  Yongtaihe Tobacco Company]. August 25, 2014. http://www.etmoc.com/culture
  /Looklist?Id=10280.

Rancière, Jacques. *Althusser's Lesson.* New York: Continuum, 2011.

Rancière, Jacques. *The Names of History: On the Poetics of Knowledge.* Translated by
  Hassan Melehy. Minneapolis: University of Minnesota Press, 1994.

Reed, Chris. "Hybrid China: Early Chinese Industrial Photography." *Summaries of
  Scholarly Symposia* 1, no. 1 (2010). http://quod.lib.umich.edu/t/tap/7977573
  .0001.114?trgt=div1_01;view=fulltext.

Rees, Abraham. *Cyclopaedia; or, Universal Dictionary of Arts, Sciences, and Literature.*
  London: Longman, Hurst, Rees, Orme, and Brown, 1819.

Reinhardt, Anne. *Navigating Semi-Colonialism: Shipping, Sovereignty, and Nation-
  Building in China, 1860–1937.* Cambridge, MA: Harvard University East Asia
  Center, 2018.

Reynolds, Douglas R. *East Meets East: Chinese Discover the Modern World in Japan,
  1854–1898; A Window on the Intellectual and Social Transformation of Modern*

Japan. With Carol T. Reynolds. Ann Arbor, MI: Association for Asian Studies, 2014.

Ribot, Th. *The Psychology of the Emotions*. London: Scott, 1897.

Roberts, Rosemary. "Positive Women Characters in the Model Revolutionary Works of the Chinese Cultural Revolution: An Argument against the Theory of the Erasure of Gender and Sexuality." *Asian Studies Review* 28 (December 2004): 407–22.

Robinson, William J. "Nüzi zhi xing de zhishi" [Sex knowledge of woman]. Translated by Wei Xin. [Excerpt from *Woman: Her Sex and Love Life*]. Shanghai: Shangwu yinshuguan, 1923.

Rocha, Leon Antonio. "Quentin Pan 潘光旦 in *The China Critic*." *China Heritage Quarterly*, nos. 30–31 (2012). http://www.chinaheritagequarterly.org/features.php?searchterm=030_rocha.inc&issue=030.

Romaine, Suzanne, ed. *The Cambridge History of the English Language*. Vol. 4, *1776–1997*. Cambridge: Cambridge University Press, 1999.

Roosa, John. *Pretext for Mass Murder: The September 30th Movement and Suharto's Coup d'Etat in Indonesia*. Madison: University of Wisconsin Press, 2006.

Russo, Alessandro. "'The Probable Defeat': Preliminary Notes on the Chinese Cultural Revolution." *positions: east asia cultures critique* 6, no. 1 (Spring 1998): 179–202.

Sakai, Naoki. *Translation and Subjectivity*. Minneapolis: University of Minnesota Press, 1997.

Sakamoto, Hiroko. "The Cult of 'Love and Eugenics' in May Fourth Movement Discourse." Translated by Rebecca Jennison. *positions: east asia cultures critique* 12, no. 2 (2004): 329–76.

Sakamoto Hiroko. "Manga Hyōjyō ni miru syanhai modangāru" [Shanghai modern girl from the representation of comics]. In *Modan garu to shokuminchi taki kindai higashijia ni okeru teikoku shihon jenda* [The modern girl, colonial modernity, and East Asia], edited by Ito Ruri, Sakamoto Hiroko, and Tani Barlow, 117–50. Tokyo: Iwanami shoten, 2010.

Sang Bing. "Wanqing minguo de zhishi yu zhidu tixi zhuanxing" [Transformation of the knowledge system in the late Qing and republican era]. Shanghai: Shanghai guji chubanshe, n.d.

Sanger, J. W. *Advertising Methods in Japan, China, and the Philippines*. Washington, DC: US Department of Commerce, 1921.

Sarris, Andrew. "Notes on the Auteur Theory in 1962." *The Film Artist*. https://dramaandfilm.qwriting.qc.cuny.edu/files/2011/06/Sarris-Notes-on-the-Auteur-Theory.pdf.

Sasaki Jūku. *Kōkoku shinrigaku* [The psychology of advertising]. Tokyo: Satōshuppanbu, 1917.

Sasaki Jūku. *Sukotto kōkoku shinrigaku* [Scott's psychology of advertising]. Tokyo: Shōtenkaisha, 1927.

Schneider, Laurence. *Biology and Revolution in Twentieth-Century China*. Lanham, MD: Rowman and Littlefield, 2003.

Scott, Walter Dill. *The Psychology of Advertising: A Simple Exposition of the Principles of Psychology in Their Relation to Successful Advertising*. Boston: Small, Maynard, 1908.

Scott, Walter Dill. *The Theory of Advertising: A Simple Exposition of the Principles of Psychology in Their Relation to Successful Advertising*. Boston: Small, Maynard, 1903.

Shao, Kuo-kang. *Zhou Enlai and the Foundations of Chinese Foreign Policy*. New York: Macmillan, 1996.

Shen, Kuiyi. "*Lianhuanhua* and *Manhua*—Picture Books and Comics in Old Shanghai." In *Illustrating Asia: Comics, Humor Magazines, and Picture Books*, edited by John A. Lent, 100–120. Honolulu: University of Hawai'i Press, 2001.

Shen, Tsing-song Vincent. "Evolutionism through Chinese Eyes: Yan Fu, Ma Junwu, and Their Translations of Darwinian Evolutionism." *ASIANetwork Exchange* 22, no. 1 (Fall 2014): 49–60.

Shi Quan. "Guanggao xinlixue gailun" [An outline of advertising psychology]. *Dongfang zazhi* 21, no. 21 (November 1924): 81–95.

Shiao, Ling. "Culture, Commerce, and Connections: The Inner Dynamics of New Cultural Publishing in the Post–May 4th Period." In *From Woodblock to the Internet*, edited by Cynthia Brokow and Christopher Reed, 2013–248. Leiden: Brill, 2010.

Shibue Tomotsu. *Pōrando suibō senshi* [The war history of Poland: Its decline and fall] Tokyo: Hakubunkan, 1895.

Shibue Tomotsu, translated by Jin Minglua, *Shehuixue zhilun* 4, 1903.

Simpson, W. Douglas. "Sir Daniel Wilson and the Prehistoric Annals of Scotland: A Centenary of Study." *Proceedings of the Society of Antiquaries of Scotland* 96 (1963): 1–8.

Smith, Adam. *The Wealth of Nations*. London: W. Strahan and T. Cadell, 1776.

Smith, Aminda. "Maoist Epistemology." Paper presented at Rice University, January 25, 2021.

Sommer, Matthew H. *Sex, Law, and Society in Late Imperial China*. Stanford, CA: Stanford University Press, 1997.

Song Jialin, ed. *Lao yuefenpai* [Old calendars]. Shanghai: Shanghai huabao chubanshe, 1997.

Spakowski, Nicola. "Socialist Feminism in Post-Socialist China." *positions: asia critique* 26, no. 4 (November 2018): 561–92.

Spalding, Douglas Alexander. "On Instinct." *Nature* 6 (1872): 485–86.

Spencer, Herbert. *The Principles of Psychology*. London: Longman, Brown, Green and Longmans, 1855.

Spencer, Herbert. *Study of Sociology*. London: Henry S. King, 1873.

Spink, Amanda. *Information Behavior: An Evolutionary Instinct*. Leicestershire, UK: Springer, 2010.

Spivak, Gayatri Chakravorty. "Echo." *New Literary History* 24, no. 1 (1993): 17–43.

Stern, Alexandra. "Unraveling the History of Eugenics in Mexico." Institute for the Study of Academic Racism, August 1, 1998. http://ferrispages.org/ISAR/archives2/sources/mexico.htm.

Su Shangda. *Guanggaoxue gailun* [Outline of advertising study]. Shanghai: Shangwu yinshuguan, 1931.

Sullivan, Michael. *Art and Artists of Twentieth-Century China*. Berkeley: University of California Press, 1997.

Sun Benwen. "Zai lun wenhua yu youshengxue: Pan Guangdan xiansheng shangque de wenzi" [Again on culture and eugenics: Mr. Pan Guangdan's discussion]. *Shehui xuekan* 1, no. 2 (1929): 1–45.

Sun, Lung-Kee. [Longji Sun, Warren Sun]. *The Chinese National Character: From Nationhood to Individuality*. Armonk, NY: Sharpe, 2002.

Suzuki, Kazuko. *The State and Racialization: The Case of Koreans in Japan*. San Diego: University of California, San Diego, Center for Comparative Immigration Studies, 2003.

Suzuki, Michiko. *Becoming Modern Women: Love and Female Identity in Prewar Japanese Literature and Culture*. Stanford, CA: Stanford University Press, 2010

Takezawa, Yasuko. "Transcending the Western Paradigm of the Idea of Race." *Japanese Journal of American Studies*, no. 16 (2005): 1–30.

Tan Sitong. *An Exposition of Benevolence: The "Ren xue" of Tan Sitong*. Translated by Chan Sin-wai. Hong Kong: Hong Kong University Press, 1984.

Tang Shaojie. "Qinghua daxue wenhua da geming de shou kuangbiao qu 1967-4-10 Qinghua daxue (bidou Wang Guangmei da hui shuping)" [A wild song of Tsinghua University's "Cultural Revolution" (comments on the criticism of Wang Guangmei at Tsinghua University on April 10, 1967)]. *Cultural Revolution Museum Newsletter* 104, China Digest Supplement No. 172 (zk1904d). Accessed January 29, 2021. http://museums.cnd.org/CR/ZK19/cr1004.gb.html.

Tang Shaojie. *Yi ye zhi qiu: Qinghua daxue 1968 nian "Bai ri da wudou"* [The falling of one leaf heralds the autumn: The "Hundred Days of Great Violence" at Tsinghua University in 1968]. Hong Kong: Hong Kong Chinese University Press, 2003.

Tang, Xiaobing. *Global Space and the Nationalist Discourse of Modernity: The Historical Thinking of Liang Qichao*. Stanford, CA: Stanford University Press, 1996.

Tao Xisheng. "Xijiu shangpin yu xinjiu funü" [New and old commodities, new and old women]. *Funü zazhi* 17, no. 2 (February 1, 1931).

Taylor, Frederick Winslow. *The Principles of Scientific Management*. New York: Harper, 1919.

Teo, Phyllis. "Modernism and Orientalism: The Ambiguous Nudes of Chinese Artist Pan Yuliang." *New Zealand Journal of Asian Studies* 12, no. 2 (December 2010): 65–80.

Terpak, Frances, and Jeff Cody. "Transferring the Image: The Acceptance of Photography in China." Paper presented at The Role of Photography in Changing China's Image, 1860–1945, Northwestern University, Evanston, Illinois, April 24–25, 2009.

Terrill, Ross. *Madame Mao, the White-Boned Demon: A Biography of Madame Mao Zedong*. With a new postscript. New York: Simon and Schuster, 1992.

Thompson, J. Arthur, and Patrick Geddes. *The Evolution of Sex*. New York: Humboldt, 1889.

Tian, Chenshan. *Chinese Dialectics: From Yijing to Marxism*. Lanham, MD: Lexington Books, 2005.

Tipper, Harry. *The Principles of Advertising: A Text Book*. New York: Ronald, 1920.

Tipper, Harry, and George French. *Advertising Campaigns*. New York: Van Nostrand, 1925.

Toscano, Alberto. Addendum, *The Century*, by Alain Badiou, 179–201. Malden, MA: Polity, 2007.

"The Trials of Wang Kuang-mei." *Current Background*, no. 848 (February 27, 1968): 1–42.

Tsai, Weipin. "Having It All: Patriotism and Gracious Living in Shenbao's Tobacco Advertisements, 1919 to 1937." In *Creating Chinese Modernity: Knowledge and Everyday Life, 1900–1940*, edited by Peter G. Zarrow, 117–46. New York: Lang, 2006.

Tsin, Michael. "Imagining 'Society' in Early Twentieth-Century China." In *Imagining the People: Chinese Intellectuals and the Concept of Citizenship, 1890–1920*, edited by Joshua A. Fogel and Peter G. Zarrow, 212–31. Armonk, NY: Sharpe, 1997.

Tsin, Michael. *Nation, Governance, and Modernity in China: Canton, 1900–1927*. Stanford, CA: Stanford University Press, 1999.

Tsu, Jing. *Failure, Nationalism, and Literature: The Making of Modern Chinese Identity, 1895–1937*. Stanford, CA: Stanford University Press, 2005.

Uhls, Christian. "Lu Xun–Huxley–Nietzsche: A Footnote to a Familiar Subject." In *Whither Japanese Philosophy*, edited by John C. Maraldo, Thomas P. Kasulis, Michael F. Marra, Christian Uhl, Viren Murthy, Eddy Dufourmont, Takeshi Kimoto, and Takahiro Nakajima, 141–68. Tokyo: University of Tokyo Center for Philosophy, 2009.

Wagel, Srinivas Ram. *Finance in China*. Shanghai: North China Daily News and Herald, 1914.

Wang, Lingzhen. *Women's Autobiographical Practice in Twentieth Century China*. Stanford: Stanford University Press, 2004.

Wang Rongbao and Ye Lan. *Xin erya* [New Erya dictionary]. Shanghai: Minquan chubanshe, 1903.

Wang Xiaodan. *Fanyi shihua* [Short history of translation]. Beijing: Shehui kexue wenxian chubanshe, 2000.

Wang Yuanfei. "The Emaciated Soul: Four Women's Self-Inscriptions on Their Portraits in Late Imperial China." *Nan Nü* 22 (2020): 36–69.

Ward, Lester. "Evolution in the Vegetable Kingdom." *American Naturalist* 19 (July–August 1885): 537–644, 745–53.

Ward, Lester. *Nüxing zhongxin shuo* [On the centrality of females]. A translation of "Gynaeccentric Theory" from Lester Ward's, *Pure Sociology*. Translated by Toshihiko Sakai and Li Da. Shanghai: Shangwu yinshuguan, 1933.

Ward, Lester. *Outlines of Sociology*. New York: Macmillan, 1898.

Ward, Lester. *Pure Sociology*. London: Macmillan, 1903.

Wei Xin. "Shengming zhi wuzhi de jichu" [The material basis of life]. *Funü zazhi* 8, no. 3 (1922): 78–83.

Welland, Sasha. *Experimental Beijing: Gender and Globalization in Chinese Contemporary Art*. Durham, NC: Duke University Press, 2018.

White, Hayden V. *Metahistory: The Historical Imagination in Nineteenth-Century Europe*. Baltimore, MD: Johns Hopkins University Press, 1987.

Widmer, Ellen. *The Beauty and the Book: Women and Fiction in Nineteenth-Century China*. Cambridge, MA: Harvard University Press, 2006.

Widmer, Ellen. "Xiaoqing's Literary Legacy and the Place of the Woman Writer in Late Imperial China." *Late Imperial China* 13, no. 1 (1992): 111–55.

Witzel, Morgen. *A History of Management Thought*. New York: Routledge, 2012.

Wong, Lorraine. "Language Matters in Global Communism: V. N. Volosinov, Antonio Gramsci, and Qu Qiubai." Unpublished paper, 2017.

Wright, David. "Yan Fu and the Tasks of the Translator." In *New Terms for New Ideas: Western Knowledge and Lexical Change in Late Imperial China*, edited by Michael Lackner, Iwo Amelung, and Joachim Kurtz, 235–56. Leiden: Brill, 2001.

Xu Baiyi, Ding Hao, and Jin Xuechen. *Lao Shanghai guanggao* [Advertising of old Shanghai]. Shanghai: Xinhua shudian, 1995.

Xu Junjie. *Zhongguo guanggao shi* [History of advertising in China]. Beijing: Zhongguo quanmei daxue chubanshe, 2005.

Xu Xiuli. "Saochu wenmang, zuoyu xinmin" [Eliminating illiteracy, cultivating new citizens]. Chinese Academy of Social Science, Modern History Section, 2005. http://jds.cass.cn/Item1613aspx.2005.

Yamamoto Taketoshi. *Kōkoku no shakai shi* [A social history of advertising]. Tokyo: Hosei dagaku shuppan kyoku, 1984.

Yamamoto Taketoshi and Nishizawa Tamotsu. *Nihon no kōkoku* [Japan advertising]. Tokyo: Nihon keizai shingunsha, 1986.

Yamamura, Kozo. "Zaibatsu, Prewar, and Zaibatsu, Postwar." *Journal of Asian Studies* 23, no. 4 (1964): 539–54.

Yan Enchun. *Jiating jinhualun* [On family evolution]. Shanghai: Commercial Press, 1917.

Yan Fu. *Tianyan lun: Wujingtianze* [On evolution: Struggle for survival and natural selection]. Edited and translated into colloquial Chinese by Feng Junhao. Zhengzhou: Zhongzhou guji chubanshe, 2000.

Yan Jibo. "Faming shi renlei de benneng" [Invention is the instinct of humanity]. *Mindong zazhi* 4, no. 1 (1922).

Yan Jicheng. "Fei bennenglun zhi piping [A critique of anti-instinctual theory]. *Mindong zazhi* 4, no. 1 (1922).

Yan Ming. *Yimen xueke, yige shidai: Shehuixue zai Zhongguo* [One discipline, one era: Sociology in China]. Beijing: Qinghua daxue chubanshe, 2004.

Yan Wei. "Nüzi tiyu yanjiu" [A study on female physical education]. *Funü zazhi* 9, no. 7 (1923): 6–12.

Yan Jibo, "Faming shi renlei de benneng" [Discovery is a human instinct]. *Mindong zazhi* 4, no. 1 (1922).

Yang Kai. "Mao Zedong yu Zhao Wuzhen shijian" [Mao Zedong and the Zhao Wuzhen incident]. Accessed January 21, 2021. https://www.bilibili.com/read /cv446900/.

Yang Kelin, ed. *Wenhua dageming bowuguan* [Museum of the Cultural Revolution]. Hong Kong: Dongfang chubanshe youxian gongsi, Tiandi tushu youxian gongsi, 1995.

Yang Yabin. *Zhongguo shehuixue shi* [History of Chinese sociology]. Jinan: Shandong renmin chubanshe, 1987.

Yao Chun'an. *Shehuixue zai jindai Zhongguo de jincheng, 1895–1919* [The progression of sociology in modern China]. Shanghai: Sanlian shudian, 2006.

Ye Lin. "Wang Guangmei shi Liu Shaoqi pai de guizishou" [Wang Guangmei is the executioner dispatched by Liu Shaoqi]. In *Xinbian hongweibing ziliao* [A new collection of Red Guard publications], vol. 8, edited by Zhou Yuan. Oakton, VA: Center for Chinese Research Materials, 1999.

Ye Weili. *Seeking Modernity in China's Name: Chinese Students in the United States.* Stanford, CA: Stanford University Press, 2002.

Yeh, Catherine Vance. "The Press and the Rise of Peking Opera Singer as National Star: The Case of Theater Illustrated (1912–17)." *East Asian History* 28 (2004): 53–86.

Yeh, Catherine Vance. "Shanghai Leisure, Print Entertainment, and the Tabloids, *Xiaobao*." In *Joining the Global Public: Word, Image, and City in Early Chinese Newspapers, 1870–1910*, edited by Rudolf Wagner, 201–34. Albany: State University of New York Press, 2005.

Yeh, Catherine Vance. *Shanghai Love: Courtesans, Intellectuals, and Entertainment Culture, 1850–1910.* Seattle: University of Washington Press, 2006.

Yeh, Wen-hsin, ed. *Becoming Chinese: Passages to Modernity and Beyond.* Berkeley: University of California Press, 2000.

Yi Bin, Liu Youming, and Gan Zhenhu, eds. *Lao Shanghai guanggao* [Advertisements in Old Shanghai]. Shanghai: Shanghai huabao chubanshe, 1995.

Young, Louise. "Policing the Modern Woman in Republican China." *Modern China* 26, no. 2 (April 2000): 115–47.

YS [pseud.]. "Renshenqi zhong funü yingzhi zhi changzhi jiqi weisheng" [Hygienic commonsense that all women ought to know during pregnancy]. *Funü zazhi* 8, no. 8 (1922): 9–11.

Yu Yuhua. *Qu Qiubai xueshu sixiang pingzhuan* [Critical biography of Qiubai's thought]. Beijing: Beijing tushuguan chubanshe, 1999.

Zarrow, Peter G., ed. *Creating Chinese Modernity: Knowledge and Everyday Life, 1900–1940.* New York: Lang, 2006.

Zarrow, Peter G. *Educating China: Knowledge, Society and Textbooks in a Modernizing World, 1902–1937.* New York: Cambridge University Press, 2015.

Zelin, Madeleine. "The Firm in Early Modern China." *Journal of Economic Behavior and Organization* 71, no. 3 (2009): 623–37.

Zelin, Madeline. "Informal Law and the Firm in Early Modern China." Paper presented at the First IERC Conference: The Economic Performance of Civilizations: Roles of Culture, Religion, and the Law, University of South Wales, March 31, 2019.

Zhang, Jingyuan. *Psychoanalysis in China: Literary Transformations, 1919–1949.* Ithaca, NY: East Asia Program, Cornell University, 1992.

Zhang, Shaoqian. "Shaping the New Woman: The Dilemma of Shen in China's Republican Period." *Dao* 17, no. 3 (September 2018): 401–20.

Zhang Weibao, Luo Zhiqiang, and Zhao Shanxuan. "Yousheng zhuanshuai: Nanyang xiongdi yancao gongsi qiye ge'an fenxi (1925–36)." In Zhang Weibao, *Jingji yu zhengzhi zhijian—Zhongguo jingjishi zhuanti yanjiu* [Between economy and politics: special topics in Chinese economic history]. Xiamen: Xiamen University Press, 1999.

Zhang Wei, Paul, and Zhao Shanxuan. "Nanyang xiongdi de guanli shibai" [Bad management defeated Nanyang Brothers Tobacco Co. Ltd.]. China Economic History. Accessed January 21, 2021. http://www.aihuau.com/a/9101032201/29356 .html.

Zhao Chen. *Zhongguo jindai guanggao wenhua* [Chinese modern advertising culture]. Changchun: Jilin keji chubanshe, 2000.

Zhong Shaohua. "Studies on the Characteristics of Late Qing Encyclopedia Entries." In Doleželová-Velingerová and Wagner, *Chinese Encyclopaedias of New Global Knowledge.*

Zhongguo Kexueyuan, ed. *Nanyang xiongdi yancao gongsi shiliao* [Materials on the Nanyang Brothers Tobacco Company]. Shanghai: Jingji Yanjiusuo, 1958.

Zhonghua pingmin jiaoyu cujinhui, ed. *Shimin qianzi ke* [The urban citizen's one thousand Chinese character primer]. Shanghai: Zhonghua pingmin jiayu zujinhui zonghui, 1929.

Zhou Jianren. "Lian'ai de yiyi yu jaizhi" [The meaning and value of love]. *Funü zazhi* 8, no. 2 (1922): 2–6.

Zhou Yuan, ed., *Xinbian Hongweibing ziliao, 1* [A new collection of Red Guard publications, volume 1]. Vol. 1. Oakton, VA: Center for Chinese Research Materials, 1999).

Zhu, Ping. *Gender and Subjectivities in Early Twentieth-Century Chinese Literature and Culture.* New York: Palgrave, 2015.

Zhu Shuai. "Guanggaoshi yanjiu zai zhongguo: Jiyu shixueshi shijiao de yizhong fansi" [The study of advertising in China: A reflection based on the history of historiography]. Yuanchuang li wendang. Accessed July 19, 2019. https://max.book118 .com/html/2014/0516/8288959.shtm.

Zito, Angela, and Tani Barlow, eds. *Body, Subject, and Power in China.* Chicago: University of Chicago Press, 1993.

Žižek, Slavoj. "Psychoanalysis in Post-Marxism: The Case of Alain Badiou." *South Atlantic Quarterly* 97, no. 2 (Spring 1998): 235–61.

Zuo Xuchu. *Zhongguo jindai shangbiao jianshi* [The concise history of modern Chinese trademarks]. Shanghai: Xue lin chu ban she, 2003.

Zupančič, Alenka. "The Fifth Condition." In *Think Again: Alain Badiou and the Future of Philosophy*, edited by Peter Hallward, 191–201. New York: Continuum, 2004.

Zupančič, Alenka. *The Shortest Shadow: Nietzsche's Philosophy of the Two*. Cambridge, MA: MIT Press 2003.

Index

Dolezelova-Velingerova, Milena, 76
A Doll's House (Ibsen), 211
Dongfang zazhi (magazine), 174
Dong Limin, 193
Drucker, Johanna, 13, 233n23, 252n5
Duan Qiriu, 39
Durkheim, Émile, 111

Eastern Miscellany, 150, 236n35
Echols, Alice, 218
"Economic Revolution and Women's Revolu-
    tion" (He-Yin), 237n73
Economics of Efficiency (Brisco), 148
Edkins, J. D., 58, 69
Elam, Diane, 250n37
electrification, 23, 28, 31–37, 51*fi.48*. *See also*
    General Electric (GE)
Elements of Psychology (Philips), 114
Ellis, Havelock, 81–82, 89
Ellwood, Charles A., 72, 83, 93–94, 120–21
Elman, Benjamin A., 222, 225
Elshakry, Marwa, 240n23
Enčmen, Emmanuel Semënovic, 92
An Encyclopaedia of Geography (Murray), 75
Endo Ryukichi, 110–12
Engels, Friedrich, 79–81, 86–87, 92, 96, 239n21
ephemera: Chinese markets and commercial,
    15–19, 22, 36–38, 45, 55–58, 62, 69, 223; the
    event of women and commercial, 13, 210–11,
    222–24, 227–29, 250n37; nakedness and
    interiority and commercial, 163, 168–69,
    172, 181, 189; the social life of commercial,
    16, 102, 123–61, 245n12, 250n37. *See also*
    commodities
Etemad, Bouda, 33
eugenic theory: interiority and, 17, 190; and
    sexual selection, 16, 38, 77, 101, 110–22,
    240n22; women and advertising and, 38, 146,
    156–59, 165–66
events, 6–12, 135, 159, 182, 223, 251n50. *See also*
    women
evolution: advertising and stories about,
    34, 50, 123, 143, 150, 154; and the event of
    women, 4–6, 63, 160, 210, 225–27; and female
    consciousness, 162, 173, 183; and physiology,
    16, 63, 210, 240n22; and sociology, 15–16, 71,
    74–83, 87–99, 154, 242n23; and vernacular
    sociology, 101–22
On Evolution (Yan), 104–5
Evolution and Ethics (Huxley), 74, 104
"Evolution in the Vegetable Kingdom" (Ward),
    75

"The Evolution of Divorce" (Wei), 117
The Evolution of Sex (Thompson), 118

Family Regulation (Zhu), 54
"Faming shi renlei de benneng" (Yan), 114–15
Fang Bao, 238n77
Fan Jichang, 104
Fanon, Frantz, 229
Fei Ying, 167*fs.3*
feminism. *See also* women: and communism,
    193, 211–13, 218–19; and the event of women,
    12–16, 55, 62–65, 228; and modern women,
    172, 186, 189; and sociology, 83, 112–13
Feng Xiaoqing, 170–73, 176, 240n33
Feng Xiaoqing (Pan), 172
Feng Zikai, 163
feudalism, 16, 69, 172, 184, 213
"The Fifth Condition" (Zupančič), 232n20
finance capital, 11, 23–25, 29–31, 34–36, 39, 45,
    55–61, 67, 234n7. *See also* capitalism
Finance in China (Wagel), 57
Five Continents pharmaceuticals, 165–67, 174,
    178
FLIT, 137–39, 174
Ford Motor Company, 128, 138–40, 150
Foucault, Michel, 8, 12, 100, 232n16
French, George, 134
Freud, Sigmund, 77, 81, 162, 170–72, 180, 226,
    232n16, 255n4
Funü shibao (journal), 185
Funü zazhi (journal), 23, 116–17, 138, 158, 171
Fu Sinian, 84

Gamble, Sidney D., 73, 98
Gang of Four, 1, 204
Gao Junzhe, 119
Gao Xian, 115–16
Gardella, Robert, 39
Garke, Emile, 25
GE. *See* General Electric (GE)
Geddes, Patrick, 118
gender. *See* sexual difference; sexuality; women
General Electric (GE). *See also* electrification:
    about, 233n1, 234n10; advertisements, 19–20,
    23, 31–38, 51*fi.48*, 62, 69, 150, 172; and trade in
    China, 25, 28–34, 38, 56, 61, 234n6
Geng Jizhi, 83
Gerth, Karl, 39
Giddings, Franklin Henry, 71, 83
Gilmartin, Christina Kelley, 187
Ginsborg, Hannah, 238n7
Gish, Lillian, 220–22

The Global Cigarette (Cox), 50
gold standard, 42, 57–58
Gong Yan, 81
"Goodbye to Women's Literature" (Qu), 86
Gorki, Maxim, 212
Gove, Philip Babcock, 125
"The Grabbing Hand" (image), 196–99
La Grande Odalisque (Ingres), 163
graphics and images: about, 13–14, 233n23,
    248n56, 249n24; and advertising and sociol-
    ogy, 102–3, 107–8, 112–13; and advertising and
    the Chinese market, 17–37, 40–54, 60–62,
    68–69; and commercial ephemera, 123–60,
    246n26; communism and femininity and,
    191–93, 196–202, 206, 210–12; and the event of
    women, 13–14, 160, 210–12, 220–24, 227–30;
    and high art, 162, 168–74, 182, 223; and low
    art, 162, 168, 182; and nakedness and interior-
    ity, 162–83, 248n10, 249n18, 250n37, 251n50
Great Proletarian Cultural Revolution. *See*
    Cultural Revolution
Groose, Karl, 113–14
Gui Youguang, 238n77
Gu Meijun, 222
Guo Moruo, 104
Guo Renyuan, 113–15

Habit and Instinct (Morgan), 114
Haekel, Ernst, 81
Hallward, Peter, 248n63
Hamada Shirō, 149
Hardini, 199, 203f, 208
Harkness, Margaret, 86
Hausman, William J., 29–31, 36–38
Hayes, Edward C., 73
He Guimei, 193
Hegel, Georg Wilhelm Friedrich, 81
Henriot, Christian, 234n9
Hertner, Peter, 29–31, 36–38
Hertwig, Oskar, 2
He-Yin Zhen. *See also* anarchism: about the
    philosophy of, 16, 22, 55, 119, 151, 180, 237n73,
    238n77, 239n13; and conditions for thinking
    about women, 61–74, 98, 116, 160–62, 172,
    184, 225
high art, 162, 168–74, 182, 223
Hilferding, Rudolf, 13, 22, 29, 55–62, 69–71
History of Politics (Jenks), 104
Hobson, Benjamin, 238n1
Hollingworth, Harry L., 149
Hongloumeng (Cao), 175

Hooke, Robert, 185
Hopkins, Claude C., 169
Howland, Douglas, 77, 242n20
Howlett, Jonathan, 35
Huang Chujiu, 42, 127
Huang Zheng, 207, 254n27
Hu Boxiang, 164
Huxley, Thomas Henry, 74, 77–79, 104–5,
    239n13

Ibsen, Henrik, 211–13
images. *See* graphics and images
imperialism. *See also* corporate imperialism: and
    the event of women, 4, 14, 229; Japanese, 36,
    67, 97, 103, 106, 109, 127, 144–45, 235n17; US,
    207, 215; and vernacular sociology, 103–5, 109
individual will, 80, 94, 101–2, 109–12, 116–20, 135,
    157, 160, 213
Indonesia, 201, 206–9
Indonesian Communist Party, 200, 205, 208,
    254n29
industrial development, 19–22, 25–34
Ingres, Jean Auguste Dominique, 163
Ing Tang, 220–22
Inoue Tetsujiro, 107
Ip, Hung-Yok, 218
instinct, 16–17, 59, 87, 93–95, 99–104, 109–10,
    113–22, 183
interiority and nakedness, 17, 162–90
The Intermediate Sex (Carpenter), 239n19
"Invention is the instinct of humanity" (Yan),
    114–15
Isaka, Maki 142
Iseka Jijurō, 148–49
Ishikawa Yoshihiro, 239n19
Issy, Gad C., 233n26

James, William, 114
Japan: and advertising, 137, 140–45, 148; and im-
    perialism, 36, 67, 97, 103, 106, 109, 127, 144–45,
    149, 235n17; and social science, 76–82, 91–92,
    102–3, 106–9; and trade in China, 23, 36–42,
    45–46, 60, 67
Jenks, Edward, 104, 238n77
Jevons, William Stanley, 104
Ji Zhaojin, 58
Jiang Qing, 1–3, 16–17, 69, 192–93, 199–204,
    208–15, 222, 224, 255n43
Jian Yujie, 39
Jian Zhaonan, 39
Jinggangshan News, 196–98, 253n14

Marxism (continued)
160, 183, 224, 228; and interiority, 162, 171;
and sociology and sexuality, 15–16, 71–72,
79–80, 85–86, 90–92, 97–99, 105–6, 115,
119–22
"Marx, Engels and the Literary Realism" (Qu),
86
"The Material Basis of Life" (Wei), 117
materialism: dialectical, 80, 85, 91; historical,
8, 61, 83, 93–94, 115, 125, 181; and sociology,
90–96, 111, 115, 122, 167
materiality: and commodities, 56, 62, 133, 167;
communism and femininity and, 210–12; and
the event of women, 11–14
matriarchy, 15–16, 87, 96, 99, 121
Maupertuis, Pierre Louis, 2
May Fourth Movement, 15, 101–3, 107, 110, 115–17,
122, 151, 162, 183
Ma Yuan, 249n18
McClennan, John Ferguson, 96
McDougall, William, 114
McElderry, Andrea, 39
Meiji Restoration, 76, 106
Mei Lanfang, 141–43, 146f4.21
Meillassoux, Quentin, 64
Mendel, Gregor, 2
Metzler, Mark, 42
Meyer, Vilhelm, 23–25, 56, 69–71, 100, 233n1,
234n6, 234n10
Miescher, Johannes Friedrich, 231n5
Mill, John Stuart, 74, 77–81, 88, 104, 239n13
mimesis: and nakedness and interiority, 177, 182,
251n50; and sociology, 15–16, 72, 80, 83–86,
96; and vernacular sociology, 100, 106, 121
Minakata Kumagusu, 242n21
Minduo (journal), 115
Min'guo ribao (publication), 175
Mitin, Mark Borisovich, 85, 92
Mitsunga Hoshiro, 144, 148
modernity: and advertising and trade in China,
22, 29, 34–39, 43–55, 59–62, 234n12; and art,
162–65, 168, 223; and commercial ephemera,
124–26, 133–35, 138–46, 149–62, 202; and communism and femininity, 193, 209–17; and the
event of women, 7–11, 63, 69, 143, 172, 209–17,
220–30, 232n17; and nakedness and interiority, 17, 162–65, 168–72, 182–90; and sociology,
5, 16, 71, 74–76, 79, 87; and vernacular sociology, 101–10, 113, 117–19
Modern Sociology (Endo), 110–11
Modern Sociology (Li), 90–95

monogamy, 101, 113, 187
Montesquieu, 74, 104, 239n13
Morgan, C. Lloyd, 114
Morgan, Lewis Henry, 87, 96
Morgan, Stephen L., 236n35
Morishita Hiroshi, 127, 144, 148, 246n38
Morishita Jintan Company, 127, 141, 144–45
Morse, Edward S., 149
The Mother (Gorki), 212
Mouffe, Chantal, 256n23
"Mu dan ting hai hun ji" (Tang), 179f
Muñoz, José Esteban, 245n12
Murray, Hugh, 75
Mu Xiangyue, 42, 55

Nakagawa Shizuka, 127, 148, 247n47
Nakajima Masao, 148
Nakamura Masano. See Nakamura Keiu
Nakamura Keiu, 77
Nakayama Taichi, 59, 127, 141–44, 148, 246n40
Nakayama Taiyōdō, 59, 127, 134, 141–44, 246n40
nakedness and interiority, 17, 162–90
Nancy, Jacques, 228
Nanjing Treaty, 23
Nanyang Brothers Tobacco Company (NBT),
34, 39–42, 236n29
narcissism, 17, 171–73, 177–83, 210–12
NASAKOM, 206–8, 254n23
nationalism, 38–40, 223–24, 228
Nationalist Party, 44, 73, 84, 174, 187–88
Nationalist Revolution of 1911, 36, 58, 73
natural law, 66, 88–89, 92–94
natural rights: and advertising and capitalism,
50, 61, 140, 160; and communism and women,
187, 196, 209, 213, 217, 225–26; and the event of
women, 3, 6, 9, 14, 225–26; and He-Yin Zhen,
62–66; and sociology, 71–72, 116, 121–22
natural science, 4, 7, 16, 75–106, 111, 116–21, 185
natural selection, 15, 79, 105, 115, 118
New Citizens News, 123
New Culture Movement, 82, 101, 104, 107, 151
New Erya (Wang, Ye), 77–79, 83, 110
new intellectuals, 103–6
new women, 185–87, 220
New Women (Ruan), 212
New York cigarettes, 153–57
New Youth (journal), 40, 84, 115
Nietzsche, Friedrich, 115
Ni Gaofeng, 127
Norris, Christopher, 159
"Nüzi jiefanglun" (Li), 89

Tang, Ying, (Yin Tang) 220–22

Tang Shaojie, 252n1

Tang Xianzu, 179fs.10

Tan Sitong, 63, 182, 244n55

Tao Menghua, 98

Tarde, Gabriel, 71, 81–83

Taylor, Frederick Winslow, 42, 55

Taylorism, 38, 55, 131, 144

Tazoe Tetsuji, 66

technology transfer, 33, 233n26

"A Teensy Question" (Qu), 86

Thompson, J. Arthur, 118

Three Lectures on Chinese Philosophy (Li), 115

Tianyan lun (Yan), 104–5

Tiger, Lionel, 243n47

Tipper, Harry, 127, 134, 149

Titian, 163

Tiver, Lionel, 118

Toscano, Alberto, 229

Toyama Shoichi, 107

Trademark Gazette, 44, 47

treaty-ports. *See also* corporate imperialism: and commercial ephemera, 124, 134, 160–61; and interiority, 172, 180; and trade in China, 15, 19–20, 23–25, 29, 34–36, 44–45, 48, 56–60, 67–68

Trotsky, Leon, 85

Tsu, Jing 224

Tsuboi Shōgorō, 149

Union of Soviet Socialist Republics (USSR), 199–201, 215

United States, 23, 200, 209

van Leeuwenhoek, Antonie, 185

Veblen, Thorstein, 81

Vee Loo Advertising Company, 127, 132

Venus of Urbino (Titian), 163

vernacular sociology. *See* sociology

villages. *See* rural areas

voluntarism: and the event of women, 6–7, 64, 68, 210, 217, 220–21, 225; political, 2, 193; and social science, 80–82, 118; theories about, 100, 115, 248n63

Wagel, Srinivas Ram, 57–58, 69–71

Wagner, Rudolf G., 76

Wang Guangmei, 1–3, 17, 191–211, 214–19, 224, 231n1, 252nn1–2, 253n14, 254n27, 254n29, 255n44, 255n47

Wang Guangmei fangtanlu (Huang), 207

Wang Hongwen, 204

Wang Huiwu, 187

Wang Lingzhen, 193

Wang Magu, 150

Wang Rongbao, 77–79, 89

Wang Wanrong, 127

Wang Xiaodan, 103, 106

Wang Zhong, 238n77

Ward, Lester Frank, 13, 75, 81–83, 88–91, 96, 111, 118, 239n19, 240n22, 241n40

The Wealth of Nations (Smith), 74

Wei Xin, 117, 158

Wen-hsin Yeh, 15

Wen Yiduo, 169–70, 173–74, 180–81

White, Hayden, 8

White Terror, 195, 222

Wilkins, Mira, 29–31, 36–38

Wing Tai Vo (wTV), 50–52, 56

Wittgenstein, Ludwig, 256n23

women. *See also* feminism; sexual difference: Badiou and, 9–12, 226–30, 232n17, 232n20, 256n26; and commercial ephemera, 16, 123–25, 129–61, 250n37; and communism and femininity, 1–2, 17, 187–219, 230, 255n47, 255nn43–44; the event of, 2–17, 62–70, 184–90, 220–30, 232n17, 232n20; nakedness and interiority and, 17, 162–90, 251n50; new, 185–87, 220; and reproductive labor, 2–3, 15, 90–91, 119–22, 162; and sociology, 15–16, 71–72, 78–83, 86–92, 96–99, 240n33; and trade and advertising in China, 14–15, 19–20, 23–24, 34–41, 45–50, 54, 60–62, 67–69, 246n26; and vernacular sociology, 16, 101–3, 110–13, 116–22; violence against, 188, 220–21, 237n73

Women and Socialism (Bebel), 81, 87–89

"Women at the Center of the Proletarian Movement" (Qu), 86

Women in a Pavilion and Children Playing by a Lotus Pond (painting), 175

World Energy Production, 1800–1985 (Etemad, Luciani), 33

wTV, 50–52, 56

Wu Juenong, 225

Wundt, Wilhelm, 71, 81, 164, 246n24

Xia Mianzun, 239n19

Xiandai shehuixue (Li), 62, 90–95

Xiang Jingyu, 187

"Xiaoqing in Literature and Sexual Psychology" (Pan), 171

Xin Erya (Wang, Ye). *See New Erya* (Wang, Ye)

Xinhai Revolution of 1911, 36, 58, 73

Xinqingnian (journal), 84

Xin shehui (journal), 83–84

www.ingramcontent.com/pod-product-compliance
Lightning Source LLC
Chambersburg PA
CBHW071732270326
41928CB00013B/2652